Ben + Jeanie,
Bon chance
We will miss you
Robert & Connie

Ben & Jeannie —
We have enjoyed knowing you and have you as colleagues the past several years. Best of luck in New Hampshire.

Steve & Carol

Ben + Jeannie ~
Glad we got to overlap for a few years (again!) - all the best to you guys
Cornelia, Mike + Amelia

Ben and Jeannie — and Evan!
All the best in your new adventure -
you'll be missed in IC!
Ken and Jane (and Anna and Peter!)

FAMILY REUNION

Family Reunion

ESSAYS ON IOWA

EDITED BY *Thomas J. Morain*

IOWA STATE UNIVERSITY PRESS / AMES

TOM MORAIN was born and raised in Jefferson, Iowa. He graduated from Graceland College and then earned a doctorate in American Civilization at the University of Iowa. Morain, who has taught Iowa history at Iowa State University and directed History and Community Relations at Living History Farms, is currently Administrator of the State Historical Society of Iowa. In 1988, Morain's study of his hometown, *Prairie Grass Roots,* was awarded the Benjamin Shambaugh Award from the State Historical Society as the best book of the year. He is a co-author of *Iowa Past to Present,* a history textbook for elementary students.

"The Burning Cross" from *Out of This World* by Mary Swander (copyright © 1995 by Mary Swander) is used by permission of Viking Penguin, a division of Penguin Books USA Inc. "Surveying the Political Landscape" by David Yepsen is published here by permission of the *Des Moines Register.*

♾ Printed on acid-free paper in the United States of America

First edition, 1995
Second printing, 1995

Library of Congress Cataloging-in-Publication Data

Family reunion: essays on Iowa/edited by Thomas J. Morain.—1st ed.
p. cm.
ISBN 0-8138-2186-X (acid-free paper)
1. Iowa. I. Morain, Thomas J.
F625.F36 1995
977.7—dc20 95-23551

CONTENTS

THE ESSAYS

CONTENTS

THIS BOOK IS PUBLISHED THROUGH THE COOPERATION OF

Iowa State University Press

AND

Living History Farms

FAMILY REUNION

INTRODUCTION: THINKING LOCALLY

Tom Morain

NO REGION CAN SURVIVE parasitically on an imported culture. It must interpret itself to itself and to others. It must enhance itself with story and song, must paint and carve its own portrait for the world to see. It takes the creative urge of the single individual, unsatisfied with being the passive spectator of another culture, to effect this interpretation.

— JOSEPH WALL
Iowa: A Bicentennial History

YOU ARE EXACTLY RIGHT, Dr. Wall, and this collection of essays is precisely that: an attempt to interpret Iowa to Iowans. If outsiders want to read them, that's OK, but keep in mind what happens at family reunions. We gather to renew family ties and to catch up on what's happening in the lives of people who are important to us, not to be on display to the outside world. I think of this book as snapshots at such a relaxed family get-together. This is not the formal portrait that hangs on the wall or sits on the piano. These are the candid scenes of brothers and sisters and cousins sitting on the lawn or working in the kitchen, where the best conversation occurs.

This book is not an attempt to summarize what Iowans are, to give the reader all the pieces of a puzzle that, assembled, presents a portrait of the Iowa population. Instead, by sharing their own perspectives and experiences, these authors help us to see our own experiences in a new light. I remember a slide lecture on Iowa City architecture that my wife and I attended when we were students there. The speaker pointed out details of buildings that we had never noticed although we walked past many of them daily—fancy brickwork, window treatments, recessed doors. For days, we were in danger of being run over in the middle of the street as we stared at the second stories of store fronts, rather than looking where we were going. But thanks to that lecture, we became aware of Iowa City in a new way and began making our own observations.

Like that lecture, these essays remind me of Ralph Waldo Emerson's valuable insight on teaching: "Truly speaking, it is not instruction but provocation that I can receive from another soul." I hope these essays provoke you. I hope when you finish each one you have many more questions about what it means to live in Iowa than you did when you started. I hope the next time you see your favorite fellow Iowan you begin the conversation, "You know, I'd never thought about it before, but ... "

To think about ourselves as Iowans, we must think locally, and that is sometimes hard to do. We live in an international age, and things that happen all over the world affect us. But time is a cruel master. We may need to know more today than we did even ten years ago, but there is no more time in the day for news reports, and the front page of the newspaper has no more square inches. With satellites and fiber optics, the same newscast goes not just to millions but tens of millions of people. Stories compete fiercely with each other for attention, and only what is important to the mass audience has a claim to feature billing or a front-page headline.

But what is important to all of us is rarely what is most important to any of us. When WOI radio clicks on at 6:00 in the morning and I lie in bed thinking about the day ahead, the news broadcast may be talking about a shake-up in the Japanese cabinet, the congressional debate on a crime bill, and the race for mayor in Washington, D.C., but I'm beginning to sort out family schedules for the day, appointments at work, people I'll meet, and what the prospects are for breakfast. I'm aware of national issues, but I live locally.

This is a collection of essays by Iowans, some former but most current, about living locally in Iowa. It is a topic that we rarely see in print. Except for the local newspaper, most of what we read is about Somewhere Else—that vast world beyond our city limits or state borders where Important People live and where Important Things happen. We seldom get the opportunity to read a thoughtful analysis about the landscape of the ordinary and familiar.

How strange it feels every four years when reporters flock to Iowa to find out who we are going to support in the presidential caucuses. Important People are interested in what we are thinking. The networks compete to describe us to the outside world, to capture the essence of the "Iowa viewpoint" that will explain why we are leaning toward one candidate or the other. Small details of our local world take on a new dimension when someone from Somewhere Else takes them seriously. Many stories described Iowans' friendly and courteous manners. According to one reporter, Iowans are "terminally civil." Iowans, the story stated, cannot distinguish between murder and being rude on an elevator. Each is simply something that is not done. My wife recalls a day we went horseback riding, and when I jerked the wrong rein, I automatically apologized to the horse. How strange to hear the ordinary patterns of our lives, things we take for granted, examined and analyzed.

There are other reasons why such serious writings about Iowans don't appear more often. An obvious one is economics. Publishers calculate potential buyers, and there is greater buying potential in a feature on New York City than New Sharon or North English. Most high school American history textbooks have a lot of Texas history in them because the state department of education in Texas selects one history book for all high schools, and that means a bonanza for one lucky publisher. Publishers find it worth the gamble to include an extra page or two about the Alamo and Sam Houston and cattle drives in hopes that their textbook will be more appealing to the Texas selection committee. Iowa's entry into the Union usually gets a sentence to illustrate how Congress paired slave and free states (our partner was Florida) to maintain the sectional balance in the Senate. (The index of my son's high school American history textbook has an "extra" entry about Iowa, besides statehood. Iowa, it notes, along with Michigan, Illinois, Nebraska, and Kansas, got a land-grant college out of the Morrill Act.)

But the factors are not all external to us. Besides time and economics, one of the major reasons we don't read much about Iowa is because we don't write much about it. In both big and little ways, we let others set the agenda for what we are willing to accept as important or worth discussing, and others don't see much in Iowa that's important to them.

The authority to certify an act as significant determines who calls the steps of modern culture. And in America, the power to certify lies with those who dominate the national media located on the East and West coasts. The Midwest follows trends that originate elsewhere, as we have done for the past two hundred years. When Woody Allen wears tennis shoes and white socks with his tuxedo, it's news, but don't try it in Davenport. No one in Davenport has the authority to certify what's tacky and what's a fashion statement.

In my high school days, surfing was a national fad, and we all learned the words to the Beach Boys' "Surfin' USA" and wore "Hang Ten" T-shirts. There we were, in Jefferson, Iowa, and Grundy Center and Atlantic and Sibley and Holstein, singing surf songs. I don't know how high the Nishnabotna has to rise to get a good surf on it, but it didn't happen in the mid-sixties. When skiing became popular among the Rich and Famous, "Ski Iowa" posters appeared with pictures of skiers in overalls crashing through hay stacks. In terms of these national trends, Iowa was a joke. We recognized it and laughed along with everyone else, but in retrospect, it seems a little silly.

Iowans have grown accustomed to the fact that we get most fads, fashions, music, movies, and other accouterments of popular culture secondhand, often a bit ragged at the sleeve and rarely a good fit. Although we occasionally look foolish, we can live with that. However, there is a darker side to this pattern that should disturb us. When we allow Somewhere Else to set the agenda, we discount the familiar. One consequence is that we begin to assume at some level of consciousness that what happens here is probably not very important. When I was growing up in Jefferson, my father edited the two weekly newspapers and stored all the bound volumes of back issues in the basement of our home. So we grew up with one hundred years of Jefferson history within easy reach. We could pull down the 1908 *Bee* and laugh at the prices and fashions or find the birth announcement of some old codger and marvel that he was ever a baby. Between my freshman and sophomore years in college, I spent a wonderful summer again poring over those dusty old volumes, writing copy for the *Bee*'s 1966 centennial edition. Yet, for four years as an American history undergraduate and for four more years as a graduate student, never once did I use any of the information from my local newspaper in a research assignment. I wrote papers on other parts of the country—on New Deal policies, on foreign policy issues, and Important People who lived Somewhere Else—but it simply never occurred to me that local history, *my* local history, might contain enough substance to make an examination of it worthwhile.

Many still find it hard to consider local topics as fit subjects for serious analysis. Even when the subject is Iowa history itself, we teach our children the names of famous Iowans, such as John Wayne, Herbert Hoover, and Mamie Eisenhower, who were born here, moved away, and became famous. I suppose we are just trying to start our kids out right, with a healthy respect for their Iowa roots. We want them to believe in themselves and to know that they are just as good as anybody and that if they move away from Iowa when they grow up, they too can lead significant lives and do something important and become famous. But where is the list of Iowans we hold up as role models and community leaders who achieved distinction and made their contributions right here?

Another consequence of allowing Somewhere Else to set

the agenda is that we become passive spectators on topics that have major consequences for the nation and the planet. When I first read in the paper that there was going to be an Iowa Peace Institute, I snickered. Who would ever come to Iowa to discuss something as important as world peace? That is what Important People talk about at conferences in Washington and New York and London and Rome, not Des Moines and Grinnell. World peace seems a bit presumptuous for Iowans. We can do things to make our communities a better place, build a park or pick up litter along the highway, but world peace is a trifle out of our league.

But I don't snicker anymore. For one thing, I'm impressed with the institute's program and accomplishments. For another, I have come to appreciate an impish observation by the English conductor and composer Gustav Holst. "If it's worth doing," Holst declared, "it's worth doing poorly," by which he meant that *everyone* should get a chance to grapple with the masterpieces, to play Shakespeare or to sing Bach, regardless of what it sounds like. Don't limit yourself only to what you already do well. Stretch a little. The attempt is good for us because we grow in the process. We need the challenge and the struggle of sinking our teeth into tough stuff and not worrying about how anyone will judge the results.

In *Letters from the Country,* Carol Bly urges small towns to confer their own "Nobel prizes" on the men and women they feel have made the greatest contributions to the human family. What a great idea! Of course not everyone would agree on the selections. And in the ensuing arguments we would explore with the people who are important to us all sorts of issues, such as the relationship between public and private morality and the factors that distinguish great books from mere best-sellers. Would anyone beyond the city limits pay attention to the results? Who cares?

A third and most serious danger of disregarding the local is that we begin to lose our conviction that our lives have any meaning or significance in the deeper order of things. I think Thornton Wilder is expressing this concern in his play about local America, *Our Town*, when he ends the first act with this dialogue between two small-town residents.

REBECCA: The minister wrote Jane a letter and on the envelope the address was like this: It said: Jane Crofut; The Crofut Farm; Grover's Corners; Sutton County; New Hampshire; United States of America.
GEORGE: What's funny about that?
REBECCA: But listen, it's not finished: The United States of America; Continent of North America; Western Hemisphere; the Earth; the Solar System; the Universe; the Mind of God—that's what it said on the envelope.
GEORGE: What do you know!
REBECCA: And the postman brought it just the same.

Wilder is making the point that there *is* a direct connection between something as familiar and unremarkable as our hometowns and something as infinitely vast and unfathomable as the Mind of God. Like George and Rebecca, we're amazed to discover it, and when it's pointed out, we're fascinated to see our lives in terms of cosmic significance.

Iowa has not been without its recent interpreters. In the early 1970s, Laurence Lafore, a history professor at the University of Iowa, wrote an essay for *Harper's* titled "In the Sticks" in which he compared Iowa favorably with his Eastern origins. Doug Bauer's *Prairie City, Iowa: Three Seasons at Home* put his hometown under the microscope. Jane Smiley won a Pulitzer Prize for *A Thousand Acres*, a novel that recasts the plot of King Lear on a farm in northern Iowa during the Farm Crisis of the 1980s. Before *The Bridges of Madison County* gave Robert Waller lifetime tenure on the best-seller list, Iowans had been touched by his loving and intimate descriptions of the Iowa he knew in essays such as "Road Cat" that appeared periodically in the *Des Moines Register*. Several authors in this collection are already known for their Iowa portraits.

This book continues that tradition, of Iowans drawing on their own experiences and trying to sort out how the land, people, and events have interacted to make us who we are. Putting together the table of contents was about two parts calculation and one part serendipity. I didn't begin the project with a complete list of authors. The list grew slowly. I started with the names of a few whose writings I admired. I contacted some others who are in occupations that keep them in touch with the current pulse of the state. Some names were suggested by friends as they learned about the project. Some authors I knew; some I didn't. I sent out invitations cautiously, a few at a time, and was dumbstruck each time an author said "yes."

Why did they agree to write an essay? It certainly wasn't for the money. I found it less humiliating to ask each author to donate his or her essay than to divide the anticipated net profits by the number of contributing authors and to tell each one that his or her distilled wisdom was worth around $62.35. Instead, the first royalties will go to Living History Farms, a truly not-for-profit enterprise in both spirit and practice.

In essence, this is a "Will Write for Food" bunch of authors. Instead of cash, we promised the group a supper at Living History Farms to meet their fellow contributors and to share the joys and sorrows of their essays. Although all the authors knew who else was on the list, none had access to another's essay while his or her own work was in progress. Their ideas are their own. In some cases I suggested a topic or approach but made it clear that they were free to write what they wanted. I did emphasize, however, that these should not be research papers, and it is the personal voice that comes through as they write about their own experiences and perspectives.

The occasion of the collection is Iowa's sesquicentennial, our 150th birthday party. It's a time for looking back and a time for looking ahead, but it's also a time for looking at now. My hope is that these essays do provoke us, that they open up new ways of looking at this portion of the world we know and live in, and that they give us as Iowans a new and deeper appreciation of who we are—right here.

THE ESSAYS

MICHAEL CAREY is an East Coast transplant, a graduate of the Writers' Workshop at the University of Iowa where he fell in love with an Iowa farm girl and married her. When Kelly's dad needed someone to run the farm for a season and Michael and Kelly weren't having any luck finding teaching jobs, the Careys moved onto the southwest Iowa farm near Farragut, and Michael, who had never driven a tractor in his life, suddenly became an Iowa farmer. But he never quit writing. The land, his neighbors, his machinery, the crops, the weather—these became the subjects of poems that began appearing in literary magazines in America and the British Isles such as *The North American Review, Poet & Critic, The Poetry Ireland Review* (Dublin), and *The Honest Ulsterman* (Belfast). He has published three poetry collections, two plays, and a teaching manual on writing poetry. Most winters he travels the Midwest as a visiting poet-in-residence teaching school children to write and appreciate poetry. In the summer, he serves on the faculty of the U of I's Summer Writing Festival. In his spare time from farming, traveling, and writing, Michael is editor-in-chief for Loess Hills Press, which he co-founded, a subsidiary of Mid-Prairie Press.

When Living History Farms hosted a Midwest museum conference in 1994 and needed a keynote speaker, we lined up Michael, who presented the following essay. To an audience stoically prepared to endure the keynote, Michael's anecdotes about Iowa versus Montana, dancing *Swan Lake* with overalls at half-mast, and a neighbor's comments about his bottom were, yea, verily, release to the captives.

TRANSLATIONS

Michael Carey

I HAVE LIVED IN IOWA now longer than I have lived anywhere else. Four and a half years in New York City, thirteen and a half across the river in New Jersey, four at college in Pennsylvania, and now a solid seventeen years in Iowa. By rights you would think that that would have translated me into an "Iowan." I have been farming for the last thirteen seasons, listening to this soil speak to me, letting it change me, even writing about it to the world; still, I suppose that might not be enough. I remember back in Ireland when my wife and I went to Thoor Ballylee, the twelfth-century Norman tower that served as the summer home of my favorite poet, William Butler Yeats. The gift shop on the premises had books of poetry by prominent Irish writers, one of which I happened to know and study under when I was a graduate student at the University of Iowa. I said to the woman behind the counter, "Richard Murphy! He was one of my instructors in school!" She did not seem impressed. She tortured her face into a disdainful expression.

"Murphy!" she said, "He's not really Irish, you know."

"Not really Irish!" I exclaimed. "How much more Irish can you get than Murphy?"

"Well," she said matter-of-factly, "his family has only been here for *three hundred years!*"

I expected that sort of attitude when I moved here and was ready for it, but it never materialized. I have always felt more at home in Iowa than I ever did in New York or New Jersey. Here, whatever I do seems to matter, people notice and care. In the New York area I felt like one more cog in a wheel that could lose a few (or a few million) and never notice. I have come to the conclusion that love is the dividing line. If you love the place and it loves you, then you're a native. The accident of your birth is irrelevant. If you were born here but love never took root, then maybe you'll find your heart someplace else. For me New Jersey is a good place to be *from,* but Iowa is a good place to *be.*

Maybe one of the reasons I have an attraction to America's heartland is that my mother was from here. Not Iowa exactly, but she knew the smell of fresh-cut hay. She was born and raised in South Bend, Indiana, and talked glowingly of the summers she would work on her uncle's farm. I think she planted a seed in my young poetic soul. When she died, somehow the Midwest became as much my home as anywhere. People here talked like her and were sane like her and warm and loving. Maybe you just find what you are looking for, and I found her beautiful face etched into this landscape. Still, in high school, I would not have been voted most likely to become a farmer. If someone were to have told me then that one day I would move to Iowa and become a farmer, that would have sounded as impractically romantic as saying, "Michael, I can see that someday you will find it in yourself to run away to the sea and become a pirate!" I still remember the look on my father's face when I told him that I was going to move to either Iowa or Montana and study to become a poet. (Iowa City was, and still is, the home of the most famous writing school in the world and Missoula was where Richard Hugo taught, a poet I very much admired and wanted to study under.) You would have thought the world had ended. My father didn't think that this was a "wise career choice."

"OK, Mike," he said in a stern Brooklyn accent. "Whatever you say, but you've got to promise one thing."

"What's that?"

"You've got to promise me that when you're done with this poetry bullshit you'll go to law school."

"Sure thing," I said dutifully (and I still mean to keep my promise; it's just that I don't plan on being done with this "poetry bullshit" for quite a while).

"Get me a map of Iowa," he barked, "I wanna see this place." He studied the map in silence for a few minutes and then he made his verdict. "You can't go."

"Why not?"

"You can't go to Iowa because there isn't a curve in the whole damned state! The whole place is cut up into straight lines! It will be too monotonous. You'll be driving up and down, up and down all day long. You'll go crazy. You can't go there. Forget it. Iowa City? Ha! Probably thinks it's the cultural Mecca of the Midwest. I bet it's so square, that the hippies there got crew cuts. Get me a map of Montana." I got him a map of Montana. He studied it. "Holy go to hell!" he said. "You better go to Iowa."

"Why?" I asked, "what's wrong with Montana?"

"Mike," he exclaimed in true awe, "there're *glaciers* in Montana. The place has got goddamned glaciers! How do you expect to get any poetry written sittin' on a glacier?"

In spite of his desperate attempts to scare some sense into me, I explained gently but firmly to him that I *was* going to one or the other. It's hard to explain to people that this odd and emotionally laden discussion determined which graduate school I was to attend. The reason I moved to Iowa was because it had no glaciers. A few years back when the state was asking for suggestions for a new license plate slogan, one I offered in all sincerity was "Iowa, The Non-glacier State," but no one took me seriously.

The other I offered had to do with my early vision of Iowa. Coming from New Jersey, all I knew about the state was that it had the most fertile farmland in the world, the most prestigious writing school in the world, and the best wrestling in the universe. In 1972 I tried out for the Junior Olympics. That was the year Dan Gable won the gold medal in Munich. Even in New Jersey he was a legend. He was, and to my knowledge still is, the only wrestler in the history of the Olympics to make it through all his matches without a point being scored against him. He was in my weight class and he was my idol. He was the idol of every young American wrestler. I had this idea of Iowa as an unbelievably green place populated by millions of stocky farm boy poetic wrestlers. I thought something about the corn the people ate out here must make boys' bodies hard and their hearts soft and open. The second license plate suggestion I sent to Des Moines was "Iowa, Bountiful Land of Wrestling Poets." It was met with a similar silence.

My vision of Iowa has changed since I moved here. I have changed—as a person and as a poet in large part because of my relationship to the land. The personalities of my father and father-in-law were different for the same reason. My father always had something to say, he always said it, and he had a great penchant for playing the devil's advocate no matter how he really felt on the topic at hand. In New York you couldn't hear the land. There was too much static in the way. The land was down there, somewhere, below the subway, but what people were doing on top of it seemed so much more important. Life was loud and exciting but it had no center, so you had to always reach out to be noticed; you had to seem like the center yourself: be a character, use words in a strange way to catch someone's attention. *Attention* is the operative word I think. Back home no one paid attention. One had to be excited to realize one was even alive. To be quiet was to be depressed or unintellectual or dead. Life was life only if it was complicated and talked about. This made dating, for me, a particularly painful experience.

Every summer, I remember coming home from college and being high as a kite because of some new philosopher or historian I was reading. The whole world would seem transformed for about two weeks. Then the burden of driving a truck around the city with gang members who kept loaded guns and rifles in the cab would begin to get to me. Life would get very complicated very fast, and I was always glad when vacation was over and I could quit my job, leave the city, and be alone at a quiet place with words. Terror and joy always seemed to be next door neighbors; the best and the worst in human nature were always right there in front of me, and I couldn't live in either one of them for long. I always seemed to be living in reaction to something rather than out of my own impulses.

Unlike my father, my father-in-law is soft-spoken, patient, even-tempered, and when he talks he usually says what he means. I have found that Iowa's space has changed everything. Here, "man" is no longer the center of the universe. When I became a farmer I also became a dot on the horizon. Suddenly, I found it easier to believe. There is physical space here, emotional space, and space that is purely spiritual. Iowa's quiet has allowed me to hear who I am and begin to follow such music. My wife was afraid to move back to her hometown area for fear of having to be who she was in high school, of falling, maybe, into some rut she had long ago grown out of. To her delight, she learned her fears were unfounded. Living in the country as we do, with about one or two families per square mile, the life we lead is our own. People rarely just drop in on us and we rarely just drop in on anyone else. There is too much effort involved. When I go out to my backyard, it is just my backyard, it is not contiguous to Fred's and Tony's and the Dombrowski's. As a result, the heaven or hell we live is the one we've created. If you've got a good marriage and loving family, there's not a lot to get in the way and disturb it. On the other hand if you don't, there's not much of a way out without leaving.

One evening when I was first learning how to farm, I had just come in from the fields and had begun to unbutton my dirty overalls when I switched on the TV and discovered that Public Television was presenting *Swan Lake*. At the time, my wife Kelly and I were preparing to play Ed and Essie in *You Can't Take It with You* at the local community theater. Essie was supposed to be a bad ballerina, and Kelly in that role was supposed to do a terrible dying swan. The only trouble was that she had never seen *Swan Lake* and didn't know how the dance really went or how to alter it just enough to make it look bad but recognizable. The swan had already begun dying. "Kelly!" I called. "Come quickly! It's the dying swan!" In the middle of getting dressed, she ran downstairs to see what all the hollering was about, but she was too late. "How did it go?" she demanded. "Show me." Reluctantly, I began to circle around the room flapping my arms slowly and sadly and she followed keeping her face in front of mine, mirroring my every movement. In the process my overalls came completely unhinged. We didn't care. This was the answer to a big problem. It was then I noticed, out of the corner of my eye, Ray, a cousin's hired man. He was at the front door with his hand frozen in mid-knock, backing slowly and silently away from us two half-naked swans in the middle of what must have seemed to him some elaborate mating ritual. What gets me most about the whole incident was that I continued to work with that man on a daily basis for a year afterward and he never mentioned that he had called or what he saw. He never inquired about it. We were a newly married couple and Lord knows what we might have been up to. Still, it was our life and he decided to give us our space.

The distance from our house in New Jersey to my father's office in downtown New York was not much more than the five miles from our farm in the country by Farragut to my in-laws home in Shenandoah. For my father to drive to work it may have taken him an hour or two or, once in a while, three. There would be thousands of decisions he would have to make before he ever got there. Which shortcut to take if the roads got jammed. When to stop. When to go. He would pass by thirty or forty towns on his way—a few million people. What he was thinking about when he left would never be what he was thinking about on his return. If he were holding on to a beautiful idea when he left that made him feel happy, it would be blasted out of him the first time he slammed on the brakes to avoid a seemingly suicidal child running out between the cars.

When I drive to town now, whoever I was when I left is whoever I am when I get there. I complete the thought I started out with, unhurried. I hold on to the feeling. There is nothing but space around me. A space, it is true, full of subtle messages, but messages that do not intrude. That is why most farmers are quiet. They know that Nature speaks to those who listen, and those who listen when she speaks hardly speak at all. Space is why Iowans rarely touch each other when they talk, like Easterners do. When I first came, I was looked at very suspiciously when I did that, especially if the person I was talking to was a woman. People around here are used to space: around their houses, around their words, around their person. At home in my family, we couldn't be sure if anyone was listening if we didn't grab them. We sat close to one another and talked in each other's faces. I will always remember the first Christmas my wife-to-be came home to meet the Carey family. Kelly said very little. She just kept nodding her head and listening, nodding her head and listening with this mysterious smile on her face. My aunts and uncles were completely baffled. No one could figure her out. It was a compliment around the house I grew up in to interrupt someone while they were talking. That showed the speaker that you were so excited by what she was saying that you just couldn't hold yourself back. The whole family talked fast, closely, and in a loud, excited fashion. Christmas dinner must have sounded like mayhem to Kelly. Everyone was trying to be polite, so she never got a chance to speak and didn't know enough to butt her way into the conversation.

To my family this meant either that she was mentally deficient and couldn't hold her own in conversation or that she had something up her sleeve. "She must have an angle," they thought. "She is obviously being disingenuous. We aren't all *that* pleasant. Why is she smiling all the time? Everyone knows life is hell. It just isn't right for a sane person to smile for that long." Finally her sincerity and intelligence came through and my aunt called me over and whispered to me in confidence, "Michael, your girlfriend, she's just ... why she's just ... *nice* isn't she?" I could tell from the way she said "nice" that she wasn't used to using that word as a compliment.

Christmas dinner with a neighboring Iowa farmer is a completely different experience. The first time I helped a neighbor bring in his crop, I was shocked at how we didn't talk all day. I knew the man to be intelligent and articulate, but he said very little while he was working. I had to learn that he was listening to his equipment and to the land and silently nodding much like my wife did that Christmas to my family. Talking too much would be a waste of energy, even impossible across a windy field. It might actually get in the way of an important message. When we ate dinner with his parents, things were relaxed but quiet, a few words here or there found their way across the table. I kept trying to fill in the silences with nervous conversation, but they didn't need to be filled in, everyone else seemed to be communicating just fine without them. After we left, my friend told me that he had an uncle who liked to talk a lot, and his father would shake his head whenever he'd mention his name, "Uncle Bernie," he'd say, "is a terrible talker," as if the words "terrible" and "talker" were somehow synonymous. I'm sure I made a wonderful impression. The first time I backed his truck up to the hopper to load corn into the bin, his father insisted on signaling to me with his hands. He didn't say "Whoa!" or "Stop!" Just a slight flick of the wrist, and you had better be watching when he did it. The same was true in dumping the truck. Thumbs up meant raise the box. I don't know what meant stop. I kept waiting for him to yell "Enough!" but the word never came. It was a full truck and I just about buried the elderly gentleman in grain. He stared at me in disbelief as I jumped out of the cab to inspect the mess I had made. I didn't want to be rude but I had to attempt a defense,

"You said raise it," I bumbled.

"And *you* did," was his cryptic reply. Those three words had as much impact as a whole lecture from my father.

Not only are the silences meaningful out here, but normal English words take on different meanings. There is no longer any difference between what I say and what I am doing. I really do have to "make hay while the sun shines." My chickens really have "flown the coop." More than once, I have said to my wife, "this sure is a hard row to hoe" and meant it. When I dig my roots now I really learn about my wife's ancestors and I really get my hands dirty. Sometimes I find I have discarded the old familiar words of childhood for the new and harsher ones of the prairie. When I was growing up we had a "davenport."

Now I own a "couch." We drank "soda" not "pop," and we licked "lollipops" not "suckers." I still am not used to polite children saying the word "sucker." We blew our small noses in "tissue" not "Kleenex" and threw the used wads into "waste paper baskets" not "the garbage." When my mother went to the grocery store, the items she purchased were put into "bags" not "sacks." The bags were then placed in "carriages" not "carts." The first time Kelly bought groceries at the Shop Rite in New Jersey and the attendant asked, "Shall I get you a carriage, ma'am?" she said she felt as if she would suddenly turn into Cinderella and be taken to a ball.

However, in Iowa, the word, for me, that has changed the most in meaning is the word "bottom." Where I come from the word "bottom" refers to the part of the body that one usually sits on. Until I moved to Iowa I had never heard it used in reference to land. One Saturday afternoon I pulled up to the tube shoots at the teller's window at our local bank. My wife and I were thinking about how little we had to live on and wondering how on earth we were going to make it another season. At that point in our lives a trip to the bank was a great source of tension. When the van in the row next to us started to pull away, I knew it would soon be our turn. Before I could get my hand out the window, however, the van stopped, backed up, and its passenger side window slid down. It was Wayne, kind Wayne, sincere and sober. He was a friend of my wife's father and he knew that I took over the family farm under adverse conditions and was under stress, so he always tried to say something encouraging.

"Michael," he called out in his always serious voice, "I just wanted to tell you that your bottom has never looked better."

"Thank you," I said. "Thank you very much. I appreciate that."

Then he rolled up his window and drove away. My wife raised her eyebrows and looked quizzically at me across the front seat of the pickup. For a moment I was stunned. I couldn't think what to say. Then we both fell to laughing.

One way or the other, I find that the longer I live here, the more time I spend translating: my old self into a new one, messages from one idiom to another, from silence into words and from words into silence. As a farmer I am always taking air, water, sunlight, and soil and translating them into food. Food I must translate into money, the language of bankers and farm board meetings. Money I attempt to change into our lives. As a poet I attempt to act like the priest that I, as a child, always wanted to be but never got around to becoming. What is the Bible but an old poem written thousands of years ago using words and images that were meaningful to a certain people in a given point in time? As Robert Frost said, "Poetry is that which is lost in translation." It is the priest's job to take that old poem and to "translate" it successfully, to make the old images resonate again with meaning. I attempt to take the same divine resonance and fashion my own poem from it, one for my people, using images from my place and my point in time. I try to take our "ordinary" Iowa lives and twist them in such a way that anyone can see the "extra-ordinary" in them. As an artist I keep trying to crack the temporal so the divine shines through. It does anyway, for everyone, but so few see it.

What I want to do here on my farm in Farragut is to take words that can mean such different things to different people and to use them in a way that anyone, anywhere will experience the awe that I saw in my father's face when he first realized that Montana had glaciers and that his son might one day find himself sitting on one. It's not a glacier I'm sitting on now, but something just as amazing and primal—dirt, pure beautiful soil, what we all come from, where we all go, that which holds us up on our passage through life. In spite of my father's worried wish, I am sure now that I will spend the rest of my life on this land, rough and windy though it is, attempting to express, in a communal Iowa form the Word I could hardly hear before, the one true Word that our tender arrangement of flesh and bone miraculously embodies, but that no lips could ever mouth and remain living.

IMAGINE THAT YOU ARE a personnel director of a big company reviewing job applications and you come upon this one halfway down the stack: "Mary Swander, born Carroll County, Iowa. Desk clerk at Blue Top Motel, worked in a Pediatric Intensive Care Unit, taught at Lake Forest College, practiced hypnotherapy and therapeutic massage for Winnipeg Ballet on tour, castrated pigs for veterinarian. A graduate of the U of I Writers' Workshop and author of three books of poetry, one nonfiction collection of oral histories of Midwestern gardeners, and two plays, and a coeditor of a collection of essays on Iowa's Loess Hills. Currently associate professor of English at Iowa State." Unusual?

Mary Swander was born in the same county where her Irish great-grandparents homesteaded and shared their cabin with native Americans. Her role model, she claims, was her grandmother, who ran two farms and walked the beans until she was eighty with a corn knife that she also used to decapitate chickens. Her writing was influenced by Flannery O'Connor, who grew up Catholic, graduated from the Iowa Writers' Workshop, and then raised peacocks and a one-eyed black swan. Swander is also a Catholic graduate of the Writers' Workshop, but she chose a different path: she raises sheep and a one-eyed pygmy goat on her farm in Kalona when she is not living in Ames and teaching at Iowa State University.

THE BURNING CROSS

Mary Swander

I'M ON MY KNEES praying along with the rest of the Beachy Amish congregation in Kalona, Iowa, facing backwards toward the rear of the church, my lips mumbling the Our Father, my folded hands resting on the pew seat. Beside me, my neighbor Esther Chupp bows her head, her eyes closed. Throughout this service, I've taken my cue from Esther, squeezing into the seat beside her with all the other women who take their position on the left side of the church, sharing her hymnal, my fingers supporting one side of the book, hers the other, my alto stabbing at the notes I sight read, her soprano sliding up and down in familiarity. But having been raised a Catholic, I've never gotten the hang of head bowing and eye lowering, so I stare straight ahead into the white prayer cap behind me and take in the sleek, bare lines of this tiny church, its plain windows looking out onto the rolling summer fields of corn and beans.

Inside, the congregants' faces are as weathered as the church pews. The men, dressed in solid black trousers and jackets without lapels that button high under their chins showing just a flash of their white shirts near their faces, kneel on the right side of the church, shepherding their smaller sons close to their sides. Near the front of the church, the older children sit by themselves, boys on one side, girls on another. The girls, like their mothers, wear their hair long and swept up into buns at the back of their heads. The boys, like their fathers, wear theirs mid-ear in "bowl" cuts attended to at home by their mothers. The men's necks and faces are deeply tanned, their foreheads and ears a distinctly lighter shade from the protection of their summer straw hats. The women, with their younger daughters tucked close, are garbed in pastel dresses, white, pink, blue and green, cut from the same pattern—puffed sleeves, pleated bodice, and full skirt. The minister stands at the front of the church on a raised platform. Nothing adorns this space but an oak lectern where his Bible rests.

I have come to church with my neighbor as an act of friendship and solidarity, Esther's gesture of welcoming me to the eastern Iowa farm community where I now live. I watch the stalks bend and sway in the morning breeze, thinking about my years of Catholicism, my knees imprinted with the lines of tongue-and-groove boards from hardwood floors, and realize what an odd thing I'm doing—kneeling down backwards in a Protestant church, this very strange act probably a statement of dissent against my own religion.

* * * *

I am on my knees praying with the Manning, Iowa, Sacred Heart Church congregation, facing forward toward the huge cross that hangs over the altar, lips just beginning to recognize a few words of Latin—*Dominus vobiscum.* ... It is 1956 and I am six years old and wedged in between my mother and grandmother on the left side of the church. Closer to the front, older children sit by themselves, boys on the right under the statue of St. Joseph with his blossoming staff, girls on the left under the serene pose of the Blessed Virgin Mary. My hands are folded, pressing against the pew, fingers pointed straight ahead toward the Lord the way I was taught in Catechism class, my right thumb draped on top of my left.

Over my shoulder, I wear a strap dangling a tiny white patent leather purse that holds a tiny white rosary and pipe cleaners. The adults around me keep their gazes fixed on the altar and beat their fists to their breasts at the ringing of the bells, but I slump back against the pew seat and take in on one extreme, the Stations of the Cross carved from oak depicting the bloody crucifixion, and on the other, the life-sized statue of the Christ child dressed by the women of the Holy Rosary Society in a long, flowing lace gown and golden crown.

Sun pours through the stained-glass windows, the deep red and blue rays brightening the flicker and glow of the rack of votive candles, casting a tint across the faces of the women in their pastel dresses, the men in their dark sports slacks and short-sleeved white shirts, collars open. An usher, his neck and arms tanned a deep brown, his brow and face ghostly white in comparison, reaches up with a pole to unlock and open one of the windows. It tilts toward me. Cooler air and a fly rush in and I make out the lettering on the pane: *In Loving Memory of Mr. and Mrs. Edward Signall* ... my great-grandparents.

My great-grandparents, who homesteaded near this small town of just fifteen hundred people in Carroll County, donated the land on which this ornate red brick church was built and helped hammer together the small plain wooden structure that came before it. They also donated the plot for the Catholic cemetery, a piece of pasture they fenced off where they had buried their nine-year-old daughter, the youngest of their ten children. My grandmother, who drops her envelope into the basket at the offertory, is donating money for the erection of yet a third church, a sleek, new modern one that will look like a gas station. Our Lady of the Pumps.

My grandmother was the sacristan for the original edifice, opening up its doors and building a fire in its wood stove when a missionary priest happened to come to town to say Mass, washing and ironing the vestments and altar cloths, polishing the brass candle holders and chalice, mopping down the floors, and even painting the building outside and in before her own wedding. Now, she often still takes a turn at laundering the priest's chasuble, the long flowing white garment with its golden cross embroidered across the back flapping in the breeze from our clothesline on clear spring days.

I have been taken to church by my family as a member of

our nuclear unit, as a part of our larger rural community, as an initiate into the mores and customs of our Irish tradition. We are here because this ritual of Sunday Mass feeds our need for a spiritual center to our lives. But we are also here because this ritual affirms our place in the order of things. It links us to other townspeople with similar values, beliefs, and heritage. It links us to other congregations in the diocese, throughout the state, the country, and the world.

"We believe in one catholic and apostolic church," we pray at the confiteor. We believe in the universality of our religion, but we know that on a smaller scale, it provided a memory of home for my immigrant great-grandparents, a piece of the old country, a social context to their lives. Even at six, I know that we often spend more time outside the church visiting with relatives and friends after Mass than we do inside praying. During the early settlement days on the prairie, when there were no phones or cars, when families lived in relative isolation during the week, the trip to town to church on Sunday was a crucial rite.

Edward Signall, my Episcopalian great-grandfather who converted the week before he died so he could be buried in the same cemetery he donated, piled his wife and ten children into the buggy every Sunday morning, driving through mud, blizzards, and thunderstorms to make it to Mass on time. It was a sin *not* to go to Mass, but incentives also abounded. Gossip was exchanged there, business deals cinched, marriages arranged. My family had a deep respect for the church, but also cautioned not to take it too seriously.

"Those priests and nuns," my grandmother used to roll her eyes while she wrung vestments through her wringer washing machine. "Don't get too thick with them."

My grandfather, an old country doctor, used to rise and genuflect, leaving the church to be "available to his patients," at the tail end of Mass before the priest launched into what could be an interminable sermon. When the homily was moved to the beginning of the Mass, he kept his same habits, exiting every Sunday after a mere ten minutes in the pew.

Agnus Dei ...

Even at six, I recognize the bond that religion creates. I do not yet understand the terrible gulf and hatred it can also engender. Secure but bored with my scenario this Sunday morning, my mind wanders to Saturday cartoons and cowboy shows. I take out my rosary and wrap it around my neck like a lasso. I fashion a pipe cleaner into a horse and pretend that I am Mary, queen of the heavenly Wild West, riding out through the gates of my celestial ranch.

* * * *

A horse gallops into the yard outside my grandparents' house in Perry, a man in a long flowing white gown carrying a torch. Other men, in white hoods, their eyes peering out of holes like Halloween ghost costumes, erect a huge cross wrapped in straw, quickly pounding its point into the ground. It is near midnight, the spring sky dark, the air clear, a breeze blowing the rag my grandmother uses to clean the line still clothespinned to the rope. The man with the torch bends down and sets fire to the cross, flames bursting into the night.

"Papists. Foreigners," he yells.

It is 1920 and my mother is six. She is the first one awake, her bedroom window facing the front of the house in the attic of their stucco bungalow. She stares through the glass, her body shaking in her flannel nightgown. She hops out of bed, watching the backs of the heads of the hooded men charging down Main Street toward her father's office. He has been in practice but a few months, after having left Clifden, Ireland, marrying my grandmother and completing a residency in Chicago.

"Papa," she calls and dashes downstairs through the dark to her parents' bedroom, her bare feet cold on the hardwood floors. "Papa, Mama!"

My grandparents light a lamp, toss on their robes and rush out onto the porch just in time to see the wind pick up a flame and carry it to the clothesline where the rag catches on fire.

"My God, they'll burn us out!" My grandfather bellows in

his thick brogue, my grandmother already filling a bucket of water at the pump.

But soon the flames in the yard are doused, the rag stomped into the ground, the wooden cross nothing but a skeleton of ashes, and my grandmother scurries down the street to the office to check on its security, bucket in hand, as she does every morning at dawn to clean and mop down the examining rooms. Inside the house, my grandfather puts my mother on his knee, trying to comfort her sobbing.

"Why did those men come and start a fire?" She cries and he wraps his arms around her.

"They are hateful people."

"But why do they hate us?"

"We're Irish Catholics," he tries to explain.

"And they want to burn us up?"

"For hundreds of years certain groups of people have hated us."

"Why?"

"People learn to hate one another. But you must be strong—strong in your faith and yourself."

My grandparents stay in Perry only another year, just long enough for a Catholic medical practice in Atlantic to open up. Then they move farther west and live within the shadow of St. Peter and Paul's Church.

* * * *

Black-and-white snapshot #1: I am nine and we have moved to Davenport all the way across Iowa to the eastern border of the state on the Mississippi River. I am dressed in white, my crinoline slip fluffing out the skirt of my polka dot Swiss dress, a garland wound with daisies in my hair, my patent leather purse slung over my shoulder, the pipe cleaners inside replaced by a small daily missal. I stand just outside St. Paul's parish church where minutes before I've made my First Communion. It is May, the magnolia bushes behind me in full bloom. My hands are folded, my face peaceful but for the wrinkle of lines above my brows where I squint into the bright sun.

Snapshot #2: Minutes later, tongue out, thumbs in my

ears, hands waving fiercely at my tormentor, my face is scrunched into a grotesque scowl. One of my Protestant schoolmates from public school has ridden by on his bicycle, jeering at me. He stops and pitches a rock in my direction. I pick it up and throw it back at him.

"Why are they throwing rocks at me?" I sobbed in my mother's lap one day after school earlier that year.

I had gone to my new second grade, earned all S's on my report card, learned new jump rope chants, *Down the Mississippi, down the muddy Mississippi, where the boats go push,* became playmates with Bobbie, the Jewish neighbor girl down the street with the Stop and Go earmuffs, but never became integrated into the class. Head down, I worked hard, then walked home alone, many of my classmates' mothers forbidding them to play with me because of my religion. Then, throughout the spring of the year, I was dismissed from class three days a week for two hours of special training in preparation for my First Communion. I rather enjoyed the sessions of instruction with the young priest who laughed a lot and drew pictures of the Holy Trinity on the blackboard, but I dreaded leaving public school at ten in the morning, fishing my coat out of my locker and walking across the playground with taunts of "mackerel snapper" and the sting of small pebbles grazing my back.

"People learn to hate," my mother tries to explain.

"Why?"

"It's been going on for hundreds and hundreds of years. You must be strong in your faith and yourself."

The next day I walk home from school with Bobbie, tell her about the rock throwing, the talk with my mother. She tells me what her mother has told her about pogroms in Russia, about Nazi Germany and the Holocaust. My eyes widen and I stop still in the middle of the sidewalk.

* * * *

Twenty young girls and boys dressed in white, their families following closely behind, parade down the sidewalk in Clifden, Ireland. They trail after a priest who leads the procession through the narrow, winding streets, a crucifix held high on a pole. Acolytes carry banners and a censer bobbing back and forth on a long golden chain, smoke rising into the air. The sun illuminates the faces of the townspeople who pour out of their houses and cheer the young parishioners with a radiance that warms the entire scene.

"'Tis a lovely day," they say, craning their necks up at the heavens in wonderment that the rain held off long enough for the young people to show off their white outfits before donning slickers and galoshes. It is late May, the windflower blossoming. A man with a horse-drawn cart clops up the street, the mare whinnying in delight at the spring perfumes.

"Oh, they must be making their First Communion," I say to my companions, a family from Belfast. I am twenty-six and hitchhiking through Ireland for the summer.

"Aye," the husband says from the front seat of the station wagon. We are on a day's outing, eventually going to the Cliffs of Moher where we will stand in awe at the power and majesty of the sea crashing against the rocks, the wind blowing so fiercely that we hang onto each other for fear we, too, will be swept away.

"Aye," the wife smiles and admonishes Dermit, her smallest son, who is sitting in the far back of the car, to keep his voice down.

In Dublin's fair city, where the girls are so pretty ... he belts out.

The husband stops to let the procession cross the street, lifting his right foot off the pedal onto the brake. The young boys and girls begin to sing, their voices intertwining in a sweet sounding purity with Dermit's raspy notes.

Holy God, we praise thy name ...

There lived a young maiden named Molly Malone ...

"Dermit, please," his mother says.

The husband's left leg lies limply against the seat, his foot a prosthesis. Several months before he had bummed a ride home from a pub in Belfast with a friend, and as soon as the ignition turned over, the vehicle exploded, the husband's left foot blowing off and landing fifty feet away. Since then, the husband has had a "nervous condition," and now the family is on holiday in an attempt to get away from their strife-torn city for a few weeks.

Infinite Thy vast domain ...

She wheels her wheelbarrow through streets wide and narrow ...

"You always remember days like that," the husband says, staring out at the children streaming by. "Your First Communion. Such innocence."

The horse pulls up right beside our car, its nostrils flared.

"Aye," the wife answers. "To be that age again."

Everlasting is Thy reign ...

And that was the end of sweet Molly Malone.

* * * *

I am sitting on my Old Order Amish neighbor's porch swing, both feet dangling, my toes brushing the floor boards, back and forth, the seat squeaking *eeek, eeek,* creating its own rhythm and breeze. It is early July, the corn across the road knee-high and a deep, iridescent green. I am thirty-nine years old and the temperature eighty-nine degrees. Earlier, I had walked my dog around the corner and knocked on Moses and Miriam's door for a visit. We decided to congregate outside as the house, with its kerosene lamps and lack of fans or air-conditioning, was stifling.

Now the leaves of the Norway maple tree in the yard rustle faintly with an almost inaudible stir, the sun setting, casting a magenta glow across the flat western horizon that stretches taut and secure as the twine wrapped across the bales of hay stacked in the barn. There, the stray cat has nestled in to deliver her litter of scrawny kittens that come in all colors—calico, fluffy white, solid grey, tiger stripes. A litter of cats can have several fathers, and this one looks like it's been fertilized by several denominations. In the morning, Miriam will cook oatmeal especially for these wanton creatures, half of whom will die in a few weeks of distemper, and Moses will carry the dish out to the barn where the mother will slink up close, always on alert, always suspicious as any wild animal instinctively is, her nipples almost dragging on the ground, and lap at the cereal with her rough tongue.

The cicadas in the windbreak of pines begin their chorus, raspy and chant-like. Tonight, my dog, who usually loves to chase and terrorize cats, takes a jaunt through the barn, but leaves the new mother alone. Instead, he circles round a spot in the yard and settles in for a good chew on an old bone he's found under the maple. A horse and buggy spin by, gravel clicking against the wooden wheels, the battery-powered reflector light blinking in the dark.

"Who's that going there?" Miriam asks, perched on the swing next to me in her nightgown and robe, her cheeks sunken into her face, a light chiffon scarf loosely draped over her grey hair that falls down around her shoulders.

"Fannie," Moses says, flapping open the screen door with a huge bowl of popcorn he's fixed in the kitchen. "Sure, that's Fannie Yoder."

Fannie waves from the buggy, the horse slowing slightly.

"Fannie? That's not Fannie," Miriam says.

"Well, sure it is."

"Where's she going then so late at night?"

"I don't know. She didn't tell me." Moses jokes, scooping out popcorn from the larger bowl into smaller ones, handing one to his wife.

"I won't have any. Don't have my teeth in. But did you bring napkins?"

"Yes, I brought the napkins."

"Fannie? She's got church at her house tomorrow. You'd think she'd be at home getting ready."

"You go to church?" Moses turns to me.

I nod, not wanting to expound on my "recovering Catholic" status, the troubles I've had all my adult life reconciling many of the tenets of the church with my own convictions, the pull and tug I've felt between staying with and leaving an organization I've found at once stabilizing and repressive.

"Where do you go?"

"In Richmond."

"Richmond?" Moses swings around and stares me in the eye, knowing that there's only one church in that nearby town. "You're not a Catholic, are you?"

I nod again. "I was raised a Catholic."

Moses drops his hand into the popcorn bowl and Miriam stops still in the swing.

"Well," Moses says after several seconds' silence. "That's all right. That's all right, too."

* * * *

The horses on the cover of our history books in the convent school are decked out in flashing armor, metal covering their whole bodies, their tails poking out on one end, their eyes on the other. Knights in matching armor perch atop the mounts, swords in scabbards slung across their waists. A knight in the foreground dressed in blue carries a crucifix held high on a long pole, the knight next to him in red hoisting a banner into the air. They are galloping off across the continent of Europe to attack the Muslims and attempt to secure the Holy Land.

"The Crusaders were searching for the Holy Grail," Sister Mary Aquinas says standing in front of my fourth grade class. "The Turks had stolen it and the Pope sent his army to fight to bring it back."

My parents have given up the fight and sent me to Catholic school, not the overcrowded parish school near our home but a more exclusive one in Rock Island, Illinois. They can ill-afford the instruction I receive in the Villa de Chantal, this gothic structure modeled on a French castle. Philosophically they object to its elitism but hope that it will provide not only refuge from the stone-throwers, but an excellent education that includes French and piano lessons. So every day, I climb into a green bus and ride forty-five minutes each way, through the bustling Quad Cities and up over the draw bridge that spans the muddy Mississippi.

"Pope Urban II promised that the journey would count as full penance for each knight's sins," Sister says, and even at that young age I wonder how killing someone else can absolve you from all the other bad things you've done, and raise my hand to question this logic.

"In the church, we have what's called the 'The Just War Theory,'" she tries to explain, launching into a winded explication of the doctrine. Confused, I stop listening and realize that there are some contradictions I will never understand. Take Sister Aquinas herself, for example. She has no thumbs. And while she teaches us history, she also teaches us penmanship. That's right. *Oval, oval, oval* ... She writes beautifully, though, and we all emulate her, holding our pens between our index and third fingers. Push-pull, push-pull, push-pull and off.

After history we have French and curtsey our *bonjour, ma soeur* to Sister Mary Ignatius who lays out the streets of Paris on the blackboard to a bunch of second-generation Irish and German girls whose Midwestern accents will give them away even when, in their early twenties, they navigate through the city as if they've lived there their whole lives. For now, my life is centered here where a crucifix hangs above every door, the nuns' long black habits swish across the marble floors, and the strains of *Frère Jacques* float out the window, down the bluff toward the water that winds southward through the United States, flows into the Gulf of Mexico, and mingles with all the great oceans of the world.

Inside the blessed womb of the Villa, the world is safe, although during the years that I am there, the outside world begins to stir. The Civil Rights Movement is born, Kennedy is shot, and Vietnam becomes news. Sister Aquinas has us write term papers on world affairs, and everyone it seems, "justly" or not, is fighting everyone else over race or religion. It isn't cool to be different, neither inside school nor in the world at large. In eighth grade I finally shift my pen to rest next to my thumb.

* * * *

Outside my boyfriend's eighth floor dormitory window at Georgetown University, a National Guard helicopter hovers, dropping tear gas on Pete Seeger and other protesters below. Cambodia has been invaded, students at Kent State University gunned down, and Washington, D.C., is filled with striking students who are demonstrating against President Nixon and a government that has once again escalated the Vietnam War.

I'm in Washington, D.C., because all my life I've longed to get a bigger picture on the world than Iowa has to offer, and at this moment this city is a vortex for the currents of a troubling but exciting historical time. I attend Georgetown, founded by John Carroll, brother of Charles Carroll, signer of the Declaration of Independence and namesake of Carroll County, Iowa, because it has long been touted as "the Catholic Harvard."

My boyfriend and I are just back from a protest at the Washington Monument, and from seeing my childhood friend, Bobbie, off at the train. She had come down for the weekend from her college in Massachusetts for the demonstration. It is early May, 1970, the cherry blossoms in bloom. I am twenty and still wearing a black arm band, still feeling the press of people surrounding me as we linked arms and sang *All we are saying is give peace a chance,* the scent of dope smoke in the air, the warm sun pouring down, some people out of their clothes and standing naked in the throng. National Guardsmen were stationed atop all the surrounding buildings, their rifles aimed down at the crowd.

Eugene McCarthy spoke, then George McGovern. Then a white-haired bespeckled man took the platform, opened his arms, as if he were embracing us all, and boomed into the microphone, "My children." We roared with laughter and applauded Dr. Spock. Next, Jane Fonda took the stage, a movie star I'd only known for her sex-kitten roles, and I was astounded to hear her talk about Vietnam and the Women's Movement in the same sentence.

"The oppression of people everywhere is linked together," Fonda said. "The killing of a people of a different race, religion, and political philosophy in Southeast Asia is linked to the killing of civil rights workers at home. The oppression of blacks in America is linked to the oppression of women throughout the world."

My boyfriend and I slam the window against the tear gas and lie back on the bed, our feet dangling on the floor. We are exhausted from the walking, the chanting, the emotional charge of the day. A life-sized poster of Ronald Reagan hangs from my boyfriend's closet, the governor of California riding a horse, dressed in cowboy boots and hat, his pistol drawn. REAGUNS, the caption reads.

My boyfriend and I wrap our arms around each other and vow we will study this evening. We do not know yet that exams will soon be canceled, the entire university as well as universities across the country shut down. I worry about writing a long paper for my theology class on the Just War Theory, the doctrine my Jesuit professor had so aptly debunked a few weeks before.

"There is no such thing as justified killing," he said, standing before us in his collar and black shirt and slacks, his hair covering his ears, a large crucifix dangling around his neck, his feet in sandals. "Violence stems from aggression and aggression is all around us. People are aggressive all the time and it grows in increments. Pick up the newspaper and all you read about is aggression. People jostled me in line at the supermarket last night. That's aggression on a smaller scale. People honked and darted in front of me in traffic this morning. And that's aggression, too.

In place of aggression, Father McSorley lectures on nonviolent resistance, Martin Luther King, Ghandi, and conscientious objectors. He takes us off to a retreat in a meeting house in Maryland to plan a protest to lay our bodies down in front of buses that will transport draftees off to boot camp. There, we join hands with Quakers and Mennonites in a prayer for peace.

* * * *

The large white truck, MENNONITE DISASTER SERVICE stenciled on its side, is parked in the lot of St. Joseph's Church. Life jacket, slicker, and wading boots thrown into the back of my truck, I drive through a foot of water to find my Kalona neighbors, Amish and Mennonite volunteers who have come to Chelsea, Iowa, to help pump out basements in this flood-ravaged town. It is 1993, I'm forty-three, and this is the third time this summer that the waters of the Iowa River have rushed through the streets and forced the evacuation of all 376 of Chelsea's residents.

Now, the waters have receded enough so that you can drive to the fire station and pick up cleaning supplies, but the town still has boats tied to front porch railings, carp swimming in large puddles in yards, and the rotten smell of sewage in the air. Here on a journalistic assignment, I slip my tape recorder into my pocket, sling my camera around my neck, and find my way into the Catholic school which has been converted into a Red Cross Center.

It is dinner time, and three grey-haired women in hairnets scoop hot dogs and beans onto plastic trays in the gymnasium, my neighbors in their plain clothes sitting at one long table under the statue of St. Jude, patron of lost and hopeless causes. Chelsea townspeople rummage through the free-clothing boxes set up in the corner of the room, plop down at tables with food, stare at the television on one wall tuned to the local news station showing shots of their own homes, and stare into space. Children sit docilely beside their parents, too confused to move. Parents try to attend to their children but their energy has been drained out of them like the air from a flat tire.

I interview a young couple who carried their four children high over their heads out of their flooding home, the water up to their necks.

"We can't break down," the couple says in hushed voices. "We can't cry in front of our children. Instead, we fall back on our Catholic faith, our faith in God."

I interview the town mayor.

"This is an old Czech town. Catholic. I know I might catch heck for calling in the Mennonites, but they know the job and have the equipment, see?" Suddenly, the mayor looks up at me nervously, realizing I'd come to town with the Disaster Service and might also be a Mennonite.

"They're my neighbors. I'm an old Catholic."

"Oh," the mayor relaxes back into his chair.

I interview one of the Disaster Service volunteers, a woman in her thirties.

"Are you getting a sense of the town?" she asks. "Catholic." Her voice and eyes take on a hint of tension that she quickly fights off. "You might want to talk to the priest. He knows everyone and everything that goes on here."

I thank her and head down the long corridor to find the pastor. The cornfields that come right up to the edge of town are brown and stunted, having stood in water a good month of the summer. Sofas and canning jars, piles of magazines and newspapers, photo albums and books—all the things that people keep in basements—are dumped in wet slimy clumps on the boulevard. Clothes that have been washed three and four times but never come clean hang from the lines like dirty rags.

I am at once amazed and encouraged, amazed that this town still exists at all, having flooded over and over for as long as its oldest residents can remember, amazed to think that after a hundred years, its religion is still its center and that center holds. I am also amazed that in the midst of such a disaster, religious prejudice could still crop up, could still be considered an issue in lieu of the leveling power of nature before us. Still, I am encouraged that here today, two groups, Catholics and Protestants, whose antipathy runs deep, are working side by side.

Now I have come full circle, facing backwards and forwards, from one part of the state to the other, from one part of the country, one continent to another. I am facing backwards and forwards, understanding how my small experience with prejudice in my small state opened up my consciousness toward a larger world. I am facing backwards and forwards, wishing that we could still retain our sense of community without built-in bias toward others. Now I am leaving St. Joseph's School, the doors flung wide. Now I am wading through water toward a church, a cross on top that I see bursting into flames.

SINCE HIS MARRIAGE to an Iowan, Richard, Lord Acton, finds himself in an annual migration pattern between London, where he sits in the House of Lords, and a home in Cedar Rapids. He grew up in Rhodesia, the eldest son of ten children, while the region was a British colony and, after Zimbabwe gained its independence, served as a senior law officer in the Ministry of Justice. (Touring America on a cultural exchange program, Acton was made an honorary citizen of Nebraska, an event we shall acknowledge and pass by with charitable silence.) In between his African lives, Acton donned the frock coat of the Queen's bank and the wig and gown of a London barrister.

A graduate of Oxford with a bachelor's and master's degrees in history, Acton has become an avid student of all things Iowan and has written articles on his adopted state for the *Annals of Iowa*, *The Palimpsest*, *The Iowan*, and the *Des Moines Register*. His comments have appeared in *The New York Times Book Review*, the *North American Review*, and *The Economist,* as well as on Monitor Radio's "Weekend Edition" on National Public Radio. And yes, he is related to the author of Acton's Law. It was his great-grandfather, the first Lord Acton, who stated, "Power tends to corrupt, and absolute power corrupts absolutely." He and his wife Patricia, who teaches at the College of Law at the University of Iowa, have coauthored (and remained happily married in the process) a broad, fascinating, and delightful legal history of Iowa, *To Go Free: A Treasury of Iowa's Legal Heritage* (ISU Press, 1995).

During the compilation of this essay collection, Richard occasionally called my office at Living History Farms where the receptionist instantly recognized the British accent. She would then buzz me and query, "The Lord is on line 2. Are you free or shall I tell him to call back?" I always took the call.

Much of what nineteenth-century Europeans knew about the American Midwest came from letters from immigrants writing home to family and friends. Acton has adopted that format to describe his impressions of the Hawkeye state and its people. He is indeed the gift that Robert Burns begged for to help us "see ourselves as others see us."

A BRIT AMONG THE HAWKEYES

Richard, Lord Acton

DEAR EDWARD,

Well, here I am in Iowa ... safe, sound, and married. You asked me to write from time to time and describe my reactions to Patricia's state, and I will do my best—but you know I am an unreliable correspondent.

Before I left England, I surveyed everybody I met on the subject of Iowa. Ignorance predominated; most people just looked blank. A few muttered about Iowa potatoes. In fact, only two had anything concrete to say—a journalist mentioned the Iowa presidential caucuses, and Uncle Guy praised the Iowa Writers' Workshop.

Soon after I first came here, I was made to realise my own hopeless ignorance. I was reading about the Black Hawk War, which led to the dispossession of the Sauk and Meskwaki Indians and the settlement of Iowa. The book said of the great Sauk war chief: "Black Hawk crossed the river."

I had no idea *what* river. I asked a university professor, who collapsed with laughter and said, "The *Mississippi*, of course." Only the river every British schoolboy dreams of—and I hadn't the faintest notion I was within a thousand miles of it!

Your ignorant brother,
RICHARD

Dear Edward,

I must explode a myth: Iowa is *not* flat. *Kansas* is flat. Kansas is the scene of *The Wizard of Oz*; Iowa is the scene of *The Music Man*—and quite definitely is not flat.

Our house sits on top of a very real hill. We look across rolling bluffs and corn fields. Our lane is extremely steep—I puff up it like an ancient steam engine when I walk to collect the post.

Do you remember Felix Salten's *Bambi*? Well, I'm actually living in Bambi land. Cotton-tailed deer wander across the lawn in the morning and evening. A flock of wild turkeys scatters as we go down the drive. We have raccoons and possums and woodchucks. To Patricia and other Iowans, these don't seem in the least exotic. To me, they represent so much that I imagined of America when I was a child.

Love from the hillside,
Richard

Dear Edward,

Everything in Iowa seems to be called "Hawkeye"—the state itself, masses of shops, endless sports teams, and all of their fervent fans. I was driven quite mad because nobody—including my Iowan-born wife—knew *why* it was nicknamed the Hawkeye state. So I spent weeks investigating this weighty historical matter, and am now ready to make a pronouncement.

Just before Iowa became a territory in 1838, a Burlington lawyer called David Rorer coined the name. He wanted to block a horrid nickname like the "Suckers" of Illinois or, still worse, the "Pukes" of Missouri. He chose "Hawkeye"—the name of the hero in *The Last of the Mohicans*, the best-selling novel of the era. The "Hawk" part also had a ring of the great Black Hawk (of Mississippi River–crossing fame).

Rorer was a clever fellow. During 1839, he wrote wildly

popular letters to newspapers in Dubuque and Davenport, eulogising Iowa and referring to its people as "Hawkeyes." He pretended to be a traveller from Michigan (a Wolverine) and signed himself, "A Wolverine Among the Hawkeyes." And Hawkeyes they have been ever since.

Now I'm thoroughly hooked on Iowa history. Obviously you must write to me by my new nom de plume ...

A Brit Among the Hawkeyes

Dear Edward,

Do you remember how full Uncle Douglas was of wise sayings? One of his best was: "If you sent a telegram to every man in London that said, 'All is discovered, flee at once!'— at least half would start packing."

The Iowans I have met simply don't give one that feeling. Of course, Iowa has its share of problems. All of the modern nasties exist in its cities, though probably to a lesser extent than in many parts of America.

But in the sheltered life I lead, people seem much steadier than in London. My theory is that America is like an airplane with its wingtips in New York and Los Angeles. Those extremes plunge and soar, but the body in the middle stays relatively stable, and Iowa is the middle of the middle.

In England, church-going seems to be a rare occupation. In Iowa, a lot of people still do go to church. Every city has a host of churches and the whole gamut of religions. There's no established church like the Anglican in England, but more people seem to believe and practice their many religions, and maybe this adds to the stability I feel here.

Another reason could be age. Iowans have a high average age, and I suppose that the older people get, the steadier they get, although I've never really noticed that happening to me.

Anyway, for whatever reason, I think if Uncle Douglas had sent his telegram to the people *I've* met in Iowa, he would have been disappointed how few rushed for their suitcases.

Perhaps I am wrong. Perhaps Iowa is secretly a seething cauldron of depravity—but somehow I doubt it. I think I'll unpack my bags permanently.

Love, RICHARD

DEAR EDWARD,

I have just finished a week's course on essay writing at the Iowa Summer Writing Festival, and I'm high as a kite. Our group included people from Pennsylvania and California. We had a librarian from Van Horne in eastern Iowa and a playwright from Waukee in western Iowa. The ages ranged from the twenties to the sixties.

Our teacher was an Iowan essayist and poet. In fifteen minutes, she had brilliantly turned us into a unit, roaring with laughter together. We spent our time writing and talking about our writing. We wandered off to Iowa City restaurants and book shops.

Have I mentioned my favourite Iowa City book shop, Prairie Lights? I've haunted book shops all over London, and I really think there isn't one to touch it. The people who work there have actually *read* the books they sell, and many are writers themselves.

This is a wonderful place for writing. Apart from the Writers' Workshop, Iowa is the home of several first-class literary reviews. The state is littered with best-selling authors, fine poets, Pulitzer Prize winners, and above all, hordes of enthusiastic would-be writers.

I've come away from my class stimulated to read hundreds of books in the next year. Goodness knows there is opportunity enough. Cedar Rapids has a splendid public library, which puts the English equivalents to shame. The University of Iowa library is superb, but I'm at my happiest in the State Historical libraries in Iowa City and Des Moines. Nothing equals the bliss of losing yourself in historical research.

I feel inspired to write to you more often.

Love, RICHARD

DEAR EDWARD,

Today is a day of dark despair. It is the Fourth of July. Iowans are thinking about marathons, picnics, and fireworks. They are thinking about Independence from Britain and the birth of their nation.

I, on the other hand, feel more intensely English than ever. I feel totally alien. I spend as much of the day as possible with a pillow over my head, and the rest *wishing* I had a pillow over my head.

Nobody wants to begrudge these kindly people their celebration. Yet my heightened sense of patriotism makes this a day I can't wait to end.

Yours from under the pillow,
RICHARD

DEAR EDWARD,

One of the things about life in Iowa is that you do more or less everything by motor car. For example, you drive up to a bank-telling machine to draw some cash, then you drive to one of the innumerable fast food places to buy your breakfast. If you want to go to the cinema, you just drive across town and park immediately outside. Think of London and the effort in actually getting to the cinema!

My car has become an extension of my feet. I've never once traveled by bus or train here, and I walk so little that I've grown into a fine figure of a man.

You know what a neurotic driver I am in London. Well,

I'm slightly less nervous in Iowa. The state is nearly the same size as England, with only a fifteenth of the people and hence a fraction of the cars. I always maintain that two cars in Iowa is a traffic jam, which isn't quite true—but when you think of the hell of London on a Friday evening, driving is wondrously easy here. The only problem is that Iowans *will* drive on the wrong side of the road.

Iowans think nothing of driving vast distances in one go. We have been to Council Bluffs on the western border and back again in a single day. I suppose we did 550 miles in eleven hours, but we lived to tell the tale. Such a journey from London would land you somewhere in the north of Scotland and take the rest of your life.

That's enough for now. I'll just pop over to the post office and drop this letter in the drive-up post box.

Love, RICHARD

DEAR EDWARD,

Iowa life is full of mysteries. For example, the word "Iowa" has at least a dozen possible meanings. Undoubtedly the state is called after the Ioway Indians, and one translation of their name is "dusty noses." But a popular meaning is "beautiful place," and I am happy to settle for that—because it is.

Equally, I'm puzzled by the name "Des Moines"—the state's capital city. The town was preceded by the Des Moines River, which gets us nowhere. Somewhere I read that "Moines" is/are connected with monks, who are said to have lived in huts near the mouth of the river. But the general guess seems to be that "Moines" is a French abbreviation of an Indian place called Moingona.

The pronunciation is also shrouded in mystery. The French would say "Day Mwa." The English would pronounce it all out: "Dez Moinz." The Iowans end the first word something between an *e* and an *i*: "Deh" and the second word, "Moin."

I love going to "Deh Moin." It is our big city, and I get something of the same lift when I see its State Capitol building and insurance towers rising in the distance as I do when the train pulls into London.

With love from Deh Moin,
RICHARD

DEAR EDWARD,

I have decided that Americans in general—and Iowans in particular—are obsessed by temperature.

When I first visited America in 1966, I was straight from colonial Rhodesia. Everybody I met asked: "What is the mean temperature in Rhodesia?" I had *no* idea, but I would gamely volunteer an answer. I would say: "23 degrees," or ... "*1*23 degrees." People looked slightly puzzled, but relieved to have the information.

I put their questions down to the American thirst for statistics (oh, how Americans love statistics!). But Iowans are genuinely and wildly overstimulated by the daily temperature.

The winters are very cold (but not as damp as in England), and the summers are very hot (something like our summers in Africa). That seems to me to be all that one needs to know.

But no, life is not like that here. You rise in the morning and the local "meteorologist" dominates the television. The meteorologist—who carries star billing—reads the runes and pronounces on the day's weather.

With this infallible prediction ringing in your ears, you dress accordingly. Then you set out for the day, stopping for petrol or a doughnut. Everybody you meet says: "It's going to be a hot/cold one today." You agree and drive on.

As you drive, the radio meteorologist tells you endlessly what the temperature is all over Iowa. By now you pine for a fresh topic, but all you get on other radio stations is yet another meteorologist telling you yet another set of temperatures.

When you arrive at your destination, you park and walk down the street. Outside every bank a sign displays the current temperature. I can't think why—it's far too late to change your clothes.

I once saw a man muttering outside a bank. I couldn't hear what he was saying, but I suspect it was, "66 degrees, and the meteorologist forecast 67 degrees!"

Have a hot/cold one.
Love, RICHARD

DEAR EDWARD,

If I could put any one thing that I have come to love about Iowa in a box and keep it forever, it would be Thanksgiving.

Just as I loathe the Fourth of July, I *adore* Thanksgiving. It's quite unlike any holiday I've ever met.

Americans cross the continent to be with their families and friends. Thanksgiving, unlike Christmas, is not too commercial—it is tranquility itself. People are so warm that, despite the foreignness of the rite, you feel a part of it.

The traditional dinner is *celestial*. My girth already forces me to patronise a clothes shop in London called "High and Mighty," but the Thanksgiving feast expands my figure to new dimensions. Turkey and pumpkin pie predominate. The latter sounds inedible to English ears, but as made by Patricia's mother is one of the great delicacies of the world.

At Christmas I squirm with embarrassment when Tiny Tim recites, "God bless us every one." At Thanksgiving, I gladly chorus, "Which of us is not thankful?" without a tremor of a squirm.

Your grateful brother,
RICHARD

DEAR EDWARD,

One of the discoveries I have made here is the joy of the supermarket. A chain of supermarkets called Hy-Vee is strung across the state. Our local one seemed to spring up overnight. I returned from London and a huge white temple of consumerism rose from a vast tarmac car park.

We duly attended the grand opening, and the first person we met was Miss Teen Iowa. Like most Iowans, she was friendly and open and had nothing about her that said, "I am a star."

Our supermarket is roughly the size of Alaska. Endless shelves in endless aisles groan with every sort of food and household convenience, an astonishing contrast to the bare shelves in Zimbabwe. I assumed that to get about I would need one of those little electric trolleys that cart elderly people around airports.

But you soon get used to the size and profusion, and our Hy-Vee has become a home away from home. You run into masses of people you know, and you stop and chat and nosily eye their shopping. I've decided that Hy-Vee is the modern equivalent of the medieval village.

Hy-Vee has a cafeteria legendary for its 99-cent breakfasts. You give your first name to order breakfast, so everybody greets me with "Hello, Richard." When Cedar Rapids had an ice storm and my car slithered to a terrifying halt on the hill nearby, I took refuge in that cafeteria for *nine hours*—possibly a world record.

I wheel my trolley from the cafeteria to the bakery. When I was writing an article about the Dvořák centenary in the Iowa Czech town of Spillville, the key problem was the spelling of the greatest Czech pastry. The consensus at the Hy-Vee bakery at 6:00 A.M. one Sunday morning was that strictly speaking "kolach" was more accurate than "kolach*e*."

The manager is a staunch ally. He has rescued my bank card when swallowed by the nefarious banking machine, and my car when the stupid owner left the lights on and flattened the battery. "Hello, Lord," he always says.

The greatest miracle is the check-out counter. Unlike

England, you don't have to pack up your own purchases or carry them to the car—everything is done for you. And best of all, the cashiers are enthralled by my accent. "*Please* go on talking," they say. "We just *love* your accent." After a lifetime of people trying to silence me, I oblige with gusto.

Love from your garrulous brother,
RICHARD

DEAR EDWARD,

You ask me how I like my double life in England and Iowa, and what it is that makes me want to spend so much of the year here.

Well, the worst thing about dividing your time between two worlds is the awful jet lag. The great advantage is that you're constantly getting two different points of view. I hope my experience in Iowa makes me speak and vote slightly more sensibly in the House of Lords, and that my English life helps me develop as a writer in Iowa.

What is it that makes me so happy in this far-away place? Obviously, Patricia is the reason that I'm here at all—and you don't need a panegyric on marriage. But the people of Iowa are also a great draw-card. They are straightforward and they are kind. Long ago I concluded that "kind" is the most important word in the English language.

When I was younger, I craved excitement. But when I found it, really it was most disappointing. Now that I am deep in middle age, peace is what I want—peace tinged with stimulus. That is precisely what I find in Iowa.

If you are happily married, enjoy the people, and at last find peace, what more can you possibly hope for?

From Iowa with love,
RICHARD

IN 1984 David Ostendorf made it onto *Esquire* magazine's list of "one of the persons under 40 who is changing America." Today, Ostendorf no longer qualifies for anybody's "under 40" list, but he has never quit trying to change America. Starting in the 1970s, he has been tireless in his efforts to organize people and build coalitions to revitalize farm and rural communities. He was a regional director for Rural America and then a co-founder and executive director of its successor organization, PrairieFire Rural Action. During the farm crisis of the 1980s, he was on the front lines. He holds a master's degree from the University of Michigan and a Master of Divinity from Union Theological Seminary. A minister in the United Church of Christ, Ostendorf has worked hard to promote political, economic, and racial justice throughout Iowa and the Midwest and has written extensively on rural issues.

In 1994, Ostendorf left Des Moines and returned to his home state of Illinois to launch a new national initiative to revitalize congregations, community, and democracy on the margins of urban and rural society. The Center for New Community, founded in 1995, continues his commitment to forge links between rural and urban people seeking justice and human community. Ostendorf, his wife Roz, and daughter Kyra lived and breathed the Farm Crisis, as Roz served as the Human Needs Program Coordinator for the ecumenical Inter-Church Agency for Peace and Justice throughout the decade. Dave asserts that Roz and Kyra's love, vision, and enduring commitments to justice have sustained him through his 40+ years.

IOWA'S RURAL CRISIS OF THE 1980s: OF DEVASTATION AND DEMOCRACY

David Ostendorf

IT WAS A STEEL-COLD Iowa prairie day as the crowd of two hundred farmers, townspeople, and clergy gathered to hammer white wooden crosses into the frozen grounds of the Wayne County Courthouse in Corydon. One by one the seventy slat-constructed crosses—each representing a farm or small business lost to the economic disaster of the 1980s—were pounded into rows as people visited quietly and respectfully.

Despite the cold and severity of the occasion, the crowd stirred and cheered as speakers decried the disaster and called for action. Then, in solidarity, many walked together with farmer David Grismore and his family into the courthouse for their bankruptcy hearing. The time had come when farmers and townspeople hard hit by Iowa's worst economic crisis since the Great Depression would no longer keep their quiet.

The Wayne County protest that October of 1984 was one of the first of many throughout the state that tapped the growing frustration and anger of rural Iowans. It would be followed by countless peaceful actions and protests reminiscent of the 1930s. Machinery and forced farm sales were stopped by coalitions of farmers and workers, galleries at the Capitol were packed in silent protest during the governor's opening message to the 1985 legislative session, and more than sixteen thousand farmers and ranchers would gather later that spring in Ames from across the plains and prairies in one of the largest agrarian protests of the decade.

For months, the American farm crisis was the lead story in media throughout the nation and the world. The white crosses, born of a meeting of farmers who helped plan the Wayne County protest from the small back room of a southern Iowa shed, came to symbolize both the devastating loss and the relentless hope of a people whose lives and communities had been ripped apart by an economic crisis unparalleled in fifty years. It was a decade that would change Iowans and Iowa forever.

Unheeded Warnings and Sounds of Silence

Although the number of farms has been declining steadily for most of the twentieth century, historians will look upon the 1980s as the period when the structure of American family farm agriculture was finally shattered. Farming became a full-blown, capital-driven industry tied only incidentally to the land and its people, and powerful corporate interests secured their domination over all aspects of food production and distribution, from the ground to the grocery store.

We had been duly warned about this possibility, but did not take heed. From the prophet Isaiah's admonition to those who add field to field, to the agrarian principles that shaped Thomas Jefferson's vision of democracy; from nineteenth-century Kansas populist Mary Lease who urged farmers to raise less corn and more hell, to Iowa farmer Mary Jane Weisshaar who led Union County opposition to industrial hog operations in the late 1980s—we had been warned about the devastating social and economic effects wrought by consolidation of control over the land and food production.

Beyond profit margins and net income, beyond capital and technological advances, and beyond even the millions who have left the land this century—including my own family—there is at the heart of this shattering of family farm agriculture a profound, fundamental challenge to democracy itself. Though we are two centuries removed from the fledgling agrarian beginnings of the American experiment, widespread ownership and control of land, its productive capacity and use are still at the heart of the democratic ideal. Whether in the countryside or the city, those who control land control people. And those who control food control nations.

Farms are not hardware stores or steel plants: they don't get better by getting bigger. Land is not a commodity: it is a gifted resource that carries a history and a future tied to the very social fabric of society.

As the '80s drew to a close, I was invited with representatives of Iowa farm groups to meet at the governor's office with a delegation from the Soviet Union. There was much discussion about strengthening the agricultural ties between our people and particularly about how Iowans could teach and support Soviet farmers as they made a transition to "modern" agriculture. Toward the end of the meeting one of the Soviet leaders talked of his nation's emerging land reform policies, which included a massive redistribution program that would transfer control of agricultural land from the state to individual farm families. He made clear to us that such a program was central to his nation's economic and political reform, as if he had read Jefferson himself. There was silence in the room. Noting the irony of his comments in a state still reeling from the fallout of the '80s and still presuming it could teach others about agricultural reform, I suggested that perhaps Iowans themselves might learn something from this exchange. Perhaps the Soviets could share their land reform experience and policies with us so we, too, could begin to move in similar "new directions" and thereby undergird our own deteriorating family farm structure.

This time there was dead silence in the room, and then the meeting politely continued. We had bumped up against our own contradictions and did not want to deal with them; we had scratched through the veneer of politeness that covered anticipated opportunity and had come up squarely against ourselves and those democratic principles that we do not wish to be reminded about. It was a disturbing but fitting commentary on a decade of devastation.

The Great Unraveling

In the 1970s an illusion of unending prosperity in American agriculture took hold. The Russian wheat sale of 1972 spurred the new optimism, which was fed by the secretary of agriculture's call for "fencerow to fencerow" planting to meet the food demands of a growing world population. Virtually every player in the agricultural infrastructure—state and federal government agencies, lenders, universities, farm organizations, manufacturers, and suppliers—joined the push for farmers to expand their operations. Land values climbed accordingly, even if crop, livestock, and dairy prices lagged behind anticipated increases.

But the façade of family farm agriculture began to show cracks in the late '70s when tractorcades descended on Washington to protest low commodity prices. Iowa farmers joined the national protests but not in significant numbers. Most simply rode out the decade and then voted in large numbers for Ronald Reagan and the economic and political change he promised in the 1980 presidential campaign.

And change they got. Committed to breaking the back of rising inflation and to controlling federal spending (at least in the early '80s), the new administration permitted interest rates to soar. Farmers, relying on borrowed capital to put in crops or to purchase land, took a heavy hit at the banks as the cost of money began to soar on increasingly heavy debt loads. By 1985, farm debt had grown to $215 billion nationwide, representing a 400 percent increase in debt since 1970.

Simultaneously, the price of land began a steady, then precipitous, decline as its inflated value dropped some 60 percent by mid-decade. Farmers who relied on their land as collateral to borrow money thus took another heavy hit as its value eroded like topsoil from hard spring rains. Moreover, commodity prices held at levels well below the cost of production while the price of farm machinery and inputs increased. The economic crisis in agriculture began to take its toll.

It was a quiet and largely unnoticed toll at first. By the fall of 1982, producers with Farmers Home Administration (FmHA) loans began to question the treatment they were receiving from the government agency whose mission since the '30s had been to help hard-pressed farmers stay on the land. Some farm operations considered at risk by the agency were told to pay off their FmHA loans in full, while others were sent foreclosure notices with little warning. Within the next several years, producers who relied on their partnership with the Farm Credit System or commercial banks joined these early voices and began to question national economic policy that was allowing—indeed, accelerating—their forced displacement from the land.

Among those early voices were Gary and Rosie Barrett from Stuart. The Barretts ran a five hundred–acre grain and hog operation, quietly and unassumingly trying to make ends meet as the economic crunch descended on their family. The FmHA did not like the looks of the Barretts' declining economic standing and their ability to repay the funds they had borrowed. The agency decided to foreclose on the family's farm, but in doing so the FmHA ignored its own rules to assure due process in foreclosure proceedings.

The Barretts began to raise questions about the agency's actions. As word of their situation spread, other farmers across the state and nation came forward to reveal similar treatment they had received at the hands of the federal agency. The farmers began to hold meetings to discuss these problems. They began to organize to challenge the agency's actions. And much to their surprise and consternation, they were stonewalled.

In the early years of the decade, those who challenged the policies and politics of the new administration were labeled "bad managers" by "successful" producers and farm organizations committed to the new administration and its "free market" philosophy that would "get government off their backs." Numerous Iowans in key leadership positions joined the chorus of condemnation aimed at these failing farmers, refusing to examine and analyze the political and economic decisions being made that would soon encompass the state in a farm and rural crisis that would take many of them down with it. Denial was rampant and widespread.

But the Barretts and the growing number of farmers organizing in response to the crisis were not to be deterred. In 1983, Gary and Rosie Barrett became plaintiffs in a national class action lawsuit against the FmHA that was destined to stop the agency's foreclosure proceedings across the country. In Federal Court in Bismarck, North Dakota, the agency was exposed for ignoring due process in its foreclosure proceedings against the Barretts and other farm families and was enjoined from any further foreclosure actions until it developed new rules for dealing with financially distressed farmers. The Barretts and thousands of other FmHA borrowers were given another chance while the agency attempted to get its house in order. The dam of indifference about the spreading crisis in agriculture and the federal government's role in it had been broken, but only after a long and arduous court battle waged against a federal agency whose mission had been redefined by the new farm politics.

By the mid-1980s the farm crisis had swept across the state and region, devastating tens of thousands of farm and rural families and entire communities. Farmers who entered the decade relatively debt-free escaped the economic turmoil unscathed in most cases. But the combination of declining land values, high interest rates, and low commodity prices exacted widening losses. Even debt-free farmers could lose everything when they faced unexpected family health care bills, when farms of sons or daughters they helped finance sank into debt, or when their lenders called for loans to be paid in full as the value of their collateral plummeted. Countless farmers who thought the Reagan era would yield untold prosperity were, by 1985, flooding the Farm Crisis Hotline with calls for assistance.

And then the banks themselves started collapsing, and untold millions were lost. By the end of 1986, some twenty-four Iowa banks had failed. More would follow, and the Federal Deposit Insurance Corporation became one of the state's biggest growth industries. The scope of the crisis widened rapidly. The Farm Credit System had to go to Congress for financial help to stave off its own collapse. Countless small businesses went under in rural Iowa. Machinery dealerships failed. Farm implement manufacturers laid off thousands of workers, and houses in cities like Waterloo were simply given back to lenders as workers and their families joined the massive outmigration from the economically ravaged state.

THE MOUNTING TOLL

The '80s was a decade when many Iowans affected by the economic crisis lost whatever innocence they had left, when the social fabric of long-standing personal and community relationships built on mutual trust and common purpose unraveled in the heat of economic chaos and unleashed market forces. Farmers and lenders who once closed deals with a handshake and minimal paper work turned to attorneys to be sure that the detailed agreements they now signed adequately protected their interests. Business and personal relationships between and among farmers, merchants, and lenders were strained as the financial crunch led to missed payments and mounting debt. Bankruptcies became commonplace as debt was restructured or liquidated. And antagonism grew deeper among neighbors in the countryside and in towns as blame was cast on those falling to the crisis.

Events unheard of in the contemporary era took place. On the action of a Chariton bank, a mounted posse of armed sheriff's deputies ran down, rounded up, and shipped off for "protective custody" a herd of prize cattle belonging to a respected area farmer who had run into financial difficulties. A major lender called in its loans to a Master Farmer who had served with distinction as a school board member and community leader, compelling him to pay his entire debt immediately and in full, and forcing him out of farming. Hundreds of distressed farm families participated in food stamp sign-up days at local welfare offices to demonstrate their plight, and to their own surprise were found eligible to receive assistance. Farmers turned out to support locked-out implement workers in Waterloo and striking meatpackers in Ottumwa, just as union workers turned out at farm protests across the state to demonstrate their support for farmers.

Some farmers, seeing no way out of their problems, simply packed up and disappeared into the night, never to return. Others faced with deeper despair and hopelessness took their own lives. In Johnson County in late 1985, a farmer killed his banker, his wife, and a neighbor before shooting himself in a tragic rampage that shocked the nation.

In desperation—and in one of the uglier chapters of life in '80s Iowa—some fell prey to bigotry and hatred. The economic crisis lured and encouraged those quick to blame its ills on Jews and people of color. Jews, it was alleged, controlled the Federal Reserve, the banks, and the media and now were out to wrest control of the land itself. On the heels of these bigoted and anti-Semitic views came the racist conspiracy theories of a gaggle of extremist groups and individuals, some of whom openly advocated violence. In the volatile and often chaotic mix of the period's politics, even these ideas got the attention of some Iowans. And interwoven with such notions were a plethora of fraudulent schemes and scams that bilked hard-pressed farmers with false promises of quick fixes to their mounting economic problems.

An affront to the overwhelming majority of farm and rural people who suffered through these difficult years, such bigotry prompted strong and effective countermeasures by the state's religious community. Many farm, labor, business, and political leaders put aside their differences to stand united in opposition to the rising tide of intolerance and threats of violence. In 1985 and 1986, numerous media and public education initiatives were launched to remind Iowans that racism, bigotry, and hatred were not to be quietly tolerated or politely ignored, lest they sink even deeper into the fabric of American life. It was work fraught with risk, and I will never forget the cold, hard hatred I saw and experienced, the threats made against PrairieFire staff and leaders as we sought to expose and confront this sickness, and the sense of disbelief and disappointment I felt when Iowans succumbed to it.

Ironically, in a decade when the rhetoric and politics of "family values" entered and often dominated public debate, the economic policies of its proponents probably destroyed more Iowa families than were ever strengthened by it. The crisis in Iowa took a severe human toll on those men, women, and children who faced the devastating loss of generational ties to the land. As farms that may have been in a family for generations were put on the auction block, the sense of loss and responsibility was too much for many to bear. The crushing weight of personal failure and self-blame fractured families beyond repair and led too many farmers themselves to suicide. Strained and broken marriages, spouse and child abuse, and alcohol and drug abuse became more common in the countryside. And with dreams shattered and hopes dashed, farm families in ever-increasing numbers openly began to discourage their sons and daughters from farming.

The crisis also forced more family members in rural areas into the wage-earning workforce to pay their bills and to secure, if possible, health care benefits that were otherwise unaffordable. Good jobs were hard to find, and desperation compelled many to take employment wherever they could find it. Long commutes into the cities became commonplace. Low-paying service sector jobs were taken unabashedly. Professional jobs held by members of the family were coveted. By the early 1990s the U.S. Department of Agriculture reported that some 60 percent of farm operator households relied on one or both spouses to supply off-farm wage and salary income.

With this particular change, traditional roles of rural women began to shift dramatically. Long considered the "silent partner" in farming operations—legally and culturally unrecognized—countless women became the primary breadwinners for their farm and rural families. As farmers, they worked two full-time jobs and were often, quite literally, responsible for keeping low-return farm operations afloat.

Betrayal and Change

As a result of the '80s, Iowa's self-image as a progressive rural and agricultural state underwent major transformation. The "virtue" attached to the state for its preservation of presumed traditional values, both mythical and real, was shattered as the powerful rules of commerce and the marketplace prevailed. Pastoral scenes of rolling farmland and vibrant communities that evoked the Iowa we believed in had turned to Depression-era images of forced farm sales and boarded-up towns.

Early in the decade, many Iowans still saw themselves as the very incarnation of the values of neighborliness, trust, and community, and when the rules changed suddenly, they were stunned and shocked. Farmers were often bewildered at the behavior of those with whom they had long-established, multigenerational relationships—and others were equally bewildered at the behavior of farmers. Trust in government, never high, had traditionally been strong enough to lead Iowans to believe that "the government" at least understood that it was in the national interest to maintain and protect those who produced the nation's food.

But it was not to be. "The government" revealed itself completely as protector not of community, but of capital. A sense of betrayal set in. Even though every indicator for decades had pointed to the continuation, indeed the dominance, of agricultural and rural policy aimed not at sustaining the structure of family farming but at replacing its labor with capital and its efficiency with productivity, it took this disastrous decade to bring the reality brutally home.

Like those farmers shocked by the stonewalling from the FmHA, the ever-increasing number of Iowans affected by the spreading economic and social crisis was shocked that little was being done to rescue what remained of their rural history and culture. As predominantly white, middle-class Americans, many could not fathom why "the system" that had usually worked for them was ignoring their plea for help and the losses of generational ties to the land. Military veterans who had served their country loyally were especially incensed and bitter that their own sacrifices now meant nothing, that their land and livelihood could so easily be taken from them.

Not until the mid-term elections of 1986 did the Reagan Administration take any decisive action to respond to the crisis. Concerned about the storm of protests across the entire region and the potential impact of the crisis at the polls, it responded by pouring billions of dollars in emergency cash payments into farmers' pockets just before the election. It was a classic case of too little too late. By then the damage was largely irreparable and unstoppable.

But amid the growing cynicism and sense of betrayal, broader political and policy changes also were emerging from and being won by the grassroots rural organizing and coalition building that had begun in 1982. Out of the crisis, a new generation of farm, rural, religious, labor, and political leaders had grown to give voice and direction to the rural insurgency. Across the state, in small groups and large meetings, thousands from the farms and factories, the towns and cities had gathered since 1982 to organize in response to the growing crisis. By 1985, half the counties in the state had some form of grassroots committees and coalitions to address the crisis, most of which were organized under the auspices of the Iowa Farm Unity Coalition.

Organized by farm, church, and labor groups in January of 1982, the Coalition became the driving force for change and a crucible for articulate new leaders. Forged by hardship and bound in common purpose, these Iowans rose above their own losses and difficulties to give shape and focus to public policy and political change that might assure the survival and revitalization of family farm agriculture. And through their work and that of the thousands who had gathered under their leadership, they won significant changes that helped brake the losses.

Following several years of steady Coalition demand, backed by protests, vigils, and dialogue, the group succeeded in moving Governor Terry Branstad to use his authority to declare a state of economic emergency in Iowa in the fall of 1985. The declaration triggered a limited farm foreclosure moratorium under a 1930s Iowa law still in force and again brought the attention of the nation to the farm crisis. Concurrently, support for mandatory mediation before foreclosure was spreading and, with strong bipartisan support, was enacted by the legislature in 1986.

Other victories followed. A strong legal services program for farmers who could not afford an attorney was launched with state support. Farmers won the right to separate their forty-acre homestead from foreclosure proceedings on their farm land. In 1987, the Iowa Homestead Act provided new repurchase and redemption rights to foreclosed farm families. Tighter restrictions were won to control land takeovers by nonfarm interests.

To effect change in federal farm policy, these and other Iowans more than five hundred strong drove by bus, car, and van to Washington, D.C., in 1985 to work for passage of a strong Farm Bill. They gave leadership to the formation and passage of the Agricultural Credit Act of 1987, testified before numerous congressional committees, and then returned to Washington in 1989 and 1990 to work again for a better Farm Bill. By mid-decade many of these new leaders had begun to run for public office, winning seats on county boards and in the Iowa legislature.

In short, these Iowans brought about significant change, and in that process were themselves changed. Even in the midst of deep conflict and adversarial relationships, their work together across class, vocational, and party lines to confront the economic crisis engendered a sense of new-found power and possibility, and even respect from those with whom they differed on solutions.

Two Iowas

As the interminable decade finally drew to a close, it became clear that Iowa, with the rest of the nation, had been split by the great divide that now so characterizes life in late-twentieth-century America. The massive upward redistribution of wealth and power as a result of the public policies of the '80s is only now being understood. The rich got exceedingly, excessively rich. The poor were made poorer still. And the great middle was squeezed hard, losing livelihoods, jobs, small businesses, and land. Over the decade, the average salaries of those with incomes exceeding $1 million increased more than 49 percent, while the average wage earned by those making less than $20,000 (almost half of all Americans who had jobs) increased 1.4 percent, according to the *Philadelphia Inquirer*. By decade's end, 11.2 percent of Iowa's citizens were living below the poverty level, with the highest rates of poverty found in the state's small rural counties.

Since the late 1980s, intensified economic stratification and increased dominance by capital and corporations have been the hallmarks of American agriculture. The U.S. food manufacturing sector has become the nation's most profitable industrial sector as measured by return on stockholder equity, according to A. V. Krebs. The ten-year average return to the food manufacturing sector was 18.4 percent over the 1980s, while the return on equity to farmers during the decade averaged a *negative* 3.79 percent. So it is not surprising that over the course of the decade Iowa lost some 25 percent of the farmers who considered agriculture their primary occupation, compared with an 11 percent loss of full-time farmers in the 1970s. Between 1978 and 1987, financial distress eliminated 55 percent of Iowa's farm operators younger than twenty-five. The state's overall farm population declined 34 percent in the '80s.

The '80s accelerated the development of a two-tier structure of agriculture, with large farms getting larger, and small and medium-sized farms pushed to the margins of economic viability. In Iowa between 1982 and 1992 the number of farms of 1,000 or more acres jumped more than 50 percent to 4,733, while medium-sized farms of 180 to 499 acres dropped more than 25 percent to 33,988. Nationwide, less than 2 percent of all farms reap 40 percent of total farm sales. By the end of the

'80s there were fewer owners of farmland than at any other time in this century. By 1989, nearly half of all the nation's farmland was held by about 4 percent of all farmland owners, and more than 40 percent of the 833 million acres of private farmland was held by those who did not themselves farm that land. It is a pattern of land ownership and control that rivals that of any oligarchy and that reinforces the sharply divided economic and political structure that is Iowa on the edge of a new century.

Despite the experience of the '80s—or, perhaps, because of it—the corporate dominance in Iowa agriculture has continued unabated. While most Iowa farmers continue to express concern about the loss of rural community and the historical structure of family farm agriculture, in which those who farm the land own it and work it, they have ceded their shrinking political power and will to those very forces that would expedite those losses for their own advantage. In a state where agriculture was once the bedrock of both the economy and collective identity, reports are now issued that brazenly dismiss family farming as "economic folly," and politicians know that but one in ten Iowans earns a livelihood from it. And a state world-renowned for its hog production capacity now faces the imminent loss of that sector to massive, highly capitalized industrial hog operations.

The sheen is off Iowa; the "virtue" is gone. The great divide defines us and keeps us apart: rural from urban, haves from have-nots, farmer from farmer. Iowa's identity is no longer tied to the land and its people, or to the small towns it still claims when it has to. It tries to maintain the fading images of the old rural Iowa, with its implicit values of neighborliness and trust, but the mythical message doesn't play well these days.

In reality, it is a state where urban and urbane elites configure themselves in a "Golden Circle" to garnish more economic and political power. It is a state of small regions and competing powers vying for a share of the shrinking public pie. It is a state where "free enterprise" corporations compete at the public trough for tax dollars to build or keep open plants that often provide low-paying jobs with few benefits. It is a state that yearns for inclusion but does not know quite how to be inclusive. It is but one of fifty players looking for a quick-fix buck wherever it can find it, now thoroughly "modernized" with gambling and lotteries, crime and drugs, political scandals and dominant corporate powers. It is a state reeling from the '80s, still trying to find its identity in a time when chaos seems to reign midst withering community, and where the people of the land, the towns, and the cities seek to make sense of their lives and to recapture a vision of wholeness, possibility, and neighborliness that once defined them.

Creating Anew the Democratic Community

In hundreds of church basements and meetings halls spread across the prairies, I have seen the faces of Iowa full of despair and rich with hope. I have had the privilege of working with the state's people through one of the harshest periods of its history. I have stood with them against powerful interests and shared their victories and losses. I know their strength, their resilience, their possibility, their dreams. I have felt deeply their pain. I have been with them in death. I have cried with them in loss. I have laughed with them in spite of it all. And I have been given one of the richest of life's gift in the process—the opportunity to create hope, vision, and common purpose through collective action in the face of great adversity.

On a crisp, early fall evening in 1982 I gathered with a small group of farmers in Adair County to listen and learn and try to help them determine how they might proceed—go forward—in the face of great economic difficulty and growing pressure from the FmHA to simply get out of farming. Gary Barrett was there. Dixon Terry led the discussion, my wise and close friend and visionary leader who would rise to national prominence before his tragic death in 1989. We met in an old, ramshackle one-room schoolhouse on an overgrown township corner where a path had to be beaten through the high prairie grass to get in the door. Once inside we had to move the accumulated clutter from months of nonuse and misuse to set up the dusty, groaning benches for our meeting. As I looked out on the rolling land in the fading sunlight and visited with farmers before our start-up, I felt an irrepressible surge of remembrance and hope. For it was in places like this with people like these that history had been changed through the ages, where democracy is constantly reborn, where the people find in and with each other the strength, the resilience to carry on.

Out of that meeting came new ideas for reaching out to other farmers in trouble and need. Out of that meeting came new leaders to carry the message to others across Iowa and the nation. Out of that meeting came farmers and their families who carried on the struggle for economic justice in the '80s and who fought a successful effort in the federal courts to stop foreclosures across the nation. And out of that meeting came families who worked together to survive and to farm into the '90s.

In *Democratic Promise,* his epic history of the populist movement in America, Lawrence Goodwyn warned that this century about to end may become known as one of "sophisticated deference"—a time when in our passivity we failed to confront the consolidation of political and economic power that so directly affects and controls our lives and undercuts the fundamental principles of democracy itself. As Iowa moves toward a new century, its people would do well to reflect on the wrenching experience of the '80s and to consider how we might, indeed, begin to move beyond such "sophisticated deference" to fundamentally reshape our state, ourselves.

While we cannot recapture that which has been lost, we can reshape that which remains of the most basic values we have historically laid claim to—neighborliness, civility, trust, and community, rooted in a sense of place on the land—and thereby create anew a democratic commonwealth of communities working together to revitalize the countryside and the cities. The emerging economic structure of rural life will not and cannot survive over the long haul, and we must lay and sustain plans to rebuild underneath it, to create new and vital social and economic relationships that will inevitably flourish as the dominant system collapses.

It was a harsh decade, the 1980s. It did, I believe, change Iowa forever. But out of the crucible of that experience came hope and possibility and promise. Out of adversity came refreshing and energizing awareness that the often-overwhelming magnitude and complexity of the problems sweeping this state and nation can be confronted by people working together to recreate democratic visions for a new era. After 150 years, that re-creation of democracy in Iowa is still not an easy task, nor one that will come to fruition in our own lifetimes. The principalities and powers are strong and seemingly insurmountable, the market culture exceedingly dominant in our midst. And race and class continue painfully and unconscionably to separate and condemn us.

But the tasks of creating a new state, a new nation in twenty-first-century America cannot be ignored. The rebirthing of democracy is a never-ending, dynamic process. It must be undertaken especially by Iowans, who at least retain the memory and the contemporary experience of standing up to power and holding their ground and who believe that they can indeed change the world.

LIKE MANY OTHER IOWANS, Mohamad Khan is a farm boy. Unlike many other Iowans, Khan's homeplace was the family farm in Guyana in northeastern South America that grew rice, coconuts, fruits, and vegetables. There, Khan first discovered his love of growing plants, an interest that would become a lifetime vocation. In 1966, Khan traveled to Ames to earn a diploma from Iowa State in technical agriculture. In 1968, he completed a bachelor's degree in horticulture from Southwestern Louisiana University and returned to Iowa State for a master's in agricultural education in 1970. For five years Khan taught high school vocational agriculture in Oelwein, Solon, and Jefferson. Since 1975, he has been on the staff of the ISU Extension Service, where he is now a horticultural specialist. Many central Iowa residents recognize Khan's voice on his popular Saturday morning talk show as he patiently answers callers' questions about lawns, gardens, ornamentals, and house plants. The recipient of numerous Extension and horticultural awards—and the Governor's Volunteer Award in 1994—Khan is the author of many publications and articles for horticultural journals.

Khan is also the imam, the spiritual leader, of the Islamic Center of Des Moines. Like Scandinavian Lutherans and Irish Catholics a century earlier, Muslims from North Africa, the Middle East, and elsewhere have brought their religion with them to Iowa. In recent years, many have been attracted to the state colleges and universities.

On the afternoon that Mohamad came to my office to discuss his essay, I learned for the first time that the first mosque in the United States was built in Cedar Rapids. I also learned that the plants in my window had spider mites.

IN THE NAME OF ALLAH, MOST GRACIOUS, MOST MERCIFUL: BEING A MUSLIM IN IOWA

Mohamad Khan

ON FEBRUARY 15, 1934, the first Muslim house of worship was opened in the United States. This mosque was located in Cedar Rapids, Iowa. In 1992, to commemorate that opening, the Iowa legislature passed a resolution that designates February 15 as Islamic Day in Iowa. Yet, although Muslims have lived in Iowa for more than a century, the general public is still, even today, ignorant about Muslims and the religion of Islam. Most Iowans did not know anything about Islam until political activities brewed in the Middle East in the 1970s. It is a most unique and challenging experience for a Muslim to live in Iowa: unique because the practices, customs, and traditions are unlike most other religions and often attract attention and curiosity; challenging because it is not an easy task to practice the religion freely in American culture. Muslim youth are especially affected, and a larger burden is placed on them at school where there may be activities they cannot participate in because it may not be acceptable in Islam.

The first Muslims in Iowa were a group of young men, mainly from Lebanon, who migrated to seek a better life by farming. Later these people moved to the city where they established the first Muslim community, now known as The Cedar Rapids Islamic Center, and built their mosque. In 1948, these industrious and creative Muslims established the first Muslim National Cemetery as a result of a generous donation of land by William Aossey, one of the first immigrants. Eventually, these pioneers moved to a new location, leaving the old structure, but the original building has now been renovated and renamed The Mother Mosque.

Today's Muslim population in Iowa stretches across the state in all the large cities and on college and university campuses. Because of the rapid increase of immigrants, students, and converts as well as through intermarriage, Islam is growing in Iowa, and there are small pockets of Muslims in small towns and rural areas. At least eight thousand Muslims now live permanently in Iowa or attend public schools or institutions of higher learning. Because of these students, many Iowans have had some contact with Muslims, but most have had little or no exposure beyond what is portrayed in the media. Many Iowans learned about Muslims and Islam when the Black Muslim groups were active in the fifties and sixties, but they found out later that this was a different brand of Islam than that practiced by most Muslims around the world.

Many Americans are still confused about the God Muslims worship. Some think that Muslims worship Muhammad and usually refer to them as Muhammadans or Moslems. They do not know that Islam means total and absolute submission to one God—Allah, in Arabic. Therefore, a Muslim is one who worships one and only one God and prefers to use the Arabic name Allah because the English translation "God" does not suffice. There is no plural in the name Allah, and Allah has ninety-nine attributive names.

In addition to the belief in and worship of one God, the Muslim believes in destiny, the Quran (or Koran) and all other revealed Scriptures, all the Prophets (Muhammad being the last), all the Angels, and the Day of Judgment (or the hereafter). If one professes to be a Muslim, then he or she should practice the five Pillars or fundamentals of Islam, namely, (1) *Shahadah,* testifying that no other god deserves to be worshiped except Allah, and that Muhammad is the Servant and

Messenger of Allah; (2) *Salaat,* performing the five daily prayers: before sunrise, at midday, at midafternoon, after sunset, and at night before going to bed; (3) *Siyam,* fasting during the month of Ramadan, the ninth month of the Islamic year; (4) *Zakaat,* almsgiving to the poor—2½ percent of what is left after household bills are paid; and (5) *Hajj,* making a pilgrimage to the city of Mecca once in a lifetime if one can afford it.

A Muslim must be prepared to perform these obligatory duties on a regular basis because Islam to a Muslim is a way of life. Because most Iowans are not accustomed to observing Muslims perform prayers in public, it becomes quite a curiosity and sometimes brings jeers and ridicule as individuals and families perform their prayers at rest stops or other public places. During the fasting month, people who are not informed about fasting may try to get Muslims to eat or drink something, but after some explanation, most people understand and respect the religious customs. In fact, I have always been surprised and thankful to my coworkers for the respect and dignity shown me during my religious practices.

My children, however, have not always been as fortunate when at school or in public. Even though many of their fellow students, friends, and teachers have been understanding and kind, many have showed prejudices. My children experienced such prejudices not only in elementary and high school; they were more pronounced in college, even from some of their instructors, although most institutions were teaching courses in diversity.

My family was subjected to the worst prejudice, name-calling, and bigotry during the Gulf War. We received some anonymous phone calls and threats during the Iranian hostage crisis, but not as many as during the Gulf War. Many Muslims with names such as Hussain and Sadam had to change their telephone numbers because of threats and harassment. My children were also exposed to this ugly display when they were confronted by some adults at the local grocery store and told to "go back to Iraq where you belong." Of course, my children were all born in the United States and are not acquainted with any other lifestyle.

Holidays, special services, celebrations, and congregational prayers can lead to some problems, especially during working hours and school time. Friday is the day for congregational prayer, which takes the place of the midday prayer after a short sermon. Even though it is only a half-hour event, it does not fit in everyone's schedule. Muslim schoolteachers, for instance, have no flexibility in their schedules and therefore have to sacrifice this obligatory duty to keep their livelihoods. I am sure most Muslim employees would be delighted to make up lost time if given the opportunity to attend Friday services.

Since the Muslim calendar is based on the lunar system, obviously the month begins when the crescent (moon) is first sighted in the west. Therefore, our holidays and special events may occur on working or school days, making it almost impossible for a working Muslim to participate. However, in some cities in the United States where large Muslim populations live, holidays have been given in schools and other public institutions during the *Eid-ul-Fitr* (celebration of the breaking of the fast) and the *Eid-ul-Adha* (celebration of the Feast of Sacrifice).

However, some recent developments have made it easier for Iowa Muslims to practice their faith. Foods are one example. For Muslims, some foods are *halal,* permissible, and others are *haram,* forbidden. Like Jews, Muslims are prohibited from eating swine or the blood of any animals. Beef, chicken, and lamb are *halal* if they have been slaughtered in an approved manner so that the blood is drained quickly. Foods that are labeled kosher for Jews are acceptable for Muslims. Better labeling on prepared foods makes it easier for Muslims to find *halal* foods. For example, a Muslim can eat a product made with vegetable shortening but not lard, so complete labeling is important. In addition, Islam forbids the use of anything that harms the body, such as alcohol and cigarettes. Other items can be added to the *haram* list if we learn that they harm us. In addition to foods, Muslims have benefited from interfaith religious programs, diversity programs, and efforts to practice tolerance of groups different from one's own.

Ramadan

Ramadan, the ninth month of the Islamic calendar, is the month of fasting and is considered the holiest by Muslims around the world. As stated in the Glorious Quran: "O you who believe! Fasting is prescribed for you as it was prescribed to those before you, so that you may learn self-restraint." Muslims, therefore, begin fasting at the sighting of the crescent and continue until it is sighted again the following month. This period lasts for twenty-nine or thirty days. Fasting begins each day before dawn, about one and one-half hour before sunrise, until sunset. No eating, drinking, sex, or smoking is allowed during this time. Every Muslim, except the old and feeble, the chronically ill, the young, and the insane, is required to fast during this month. The temporarily ill, travelers, women in childbirth, nursing mothers, and women during their menstrual period are exempt but must make up the lost days at a later time. At the end of the fasting month, Muslims celebrate the *Eid-ul-Fitr,* or breaking of the fast. Traditionally, Muslims visit each other all day long or sometimes for several days until each family of the congregation is visited, but if the holiday falls on a working day in Iowa, this tradition is forfeited. Such traditions are difficult for Muslims to practice in American society.

Salaat (Prayers)

The five daily prayers, the most important of the five Pillars of Islam, should be practiced in congregation, preferably in a mosque. It is very inconvenient for Muslims in Iowa to attend the mosque during the day. It is allowed, however, for them to perform the prayers in any clean place. Some Muslims practice at their working place, but for others, it is difficult because conditions may not be conducive or appropriate. For instance, the workplace may not be equipped with ablution facilities, prayer area, or privacy for concentration. Some Muslims working night shifts are not able to take time off when sunset prayer arrives, and teachers cannot leave their classrooms for midday or midafternoon prayers.

Refugees

The recent influx of refugees from Bosnia-Herzegovina, Somalia, and other war-torn countries has been a rare but complex opportunity for Iowans. Many Iowans with unparalleled generosity have welcomed the refugees with open arms and assisted them in resettling in their new homes. Refugee Muslims coming to Iowa have been fortunate to have friends who poured out their hearts to make sure that the settlers had a good start in their new lives.

The first three families from Bosnia arrived in Des Moines in February of 1993. Now, more than five hundred Bosnians live in the Des Moines area. Several weeks after the arrival of a number of these families, the 1993 summer flooding began in Iowa and continued for several months. The city had no water for several weeks. Some of these same families had experienced similar situations in Bosnia because of the war there; however, in Iowa these families assisted in the distribution of food and water to flood victims through the Islamic Center of Des Moines.

Refugees may arrive here speaking little or no English. As a consequence, many educated people settle for unskilled labor. Local sponsors help families learn the language, customs, traditions, and most of all, the "ropes" of a successful life. Almost all Muslim refugees are gainfully employed within one to three months after arrival, thanks to their Iowa friends.

Because the extended families of refugees can be split, life in Iowa can be difficult, especially during holidays and festivals. A lack of family togetherness dampens all celebrations, especially for children. At this point, children may lose interest in their family's traditions and cultures and begin to adopt American customs and non-Muslim holidays. Even though there is much to be gained from other cultures, it is unfortunate to watch new generations of Muslim immigrants lose much of their own heritage. It is indeed painful that, because of religious and cultural differences, many refugees are robbed of their holiday traditions and ceremonies.

The Future

As the population of Muslims increases, Islam could be the second largest religion in Iowa by the end of the decade. There are more than eight million Muslims in the United States, making it the nation's second largest religion. Because of differences in culture, religious activities, and holidays, I anticipate the establishment of many more Islamic schools and other institutions of higher learning. Early Muslims who migrated to Iowa at the beginning of the century learned to assimilate to their new society, as will the new immigrants.

Like any other religious community in the world, Muslims try to group themselves socially according to nationality. However, they do participate in religious activities and prayer services as a Muslim community. As the number of second- and third-generation Muslims increases, nationalism and ethnicity will eventually disappear.

As Iowans become more aware of the beliefs and fundamental principles of Islam through numerous books, pamphlets, the media, and contact with Islamic communities throughout the state, there should be a better understanding of the many similarities among Islam, Christianity, and Judaism. I anticipate that there will be less stereotyping and a better appreciation for Iowa Muslims as the various groups dialogue with one another.

Despite the negative publicity from the media, Islam is still the fastest-growing religion in the United States and the world. Most converts to Islam indicate that they are impressed with its simple and uncompromising way of life. With the deterioration of today's society, Islam is attracting the young, the confused, and those searching for good moral values.

THINGS THAT HAPPEN everywhere in general happen somewhere in particular. Such is the case with the changing opportunities and expectations for Iowa women in the last three decades. Elizabeth Block graduated with honors from the University of Iowa in 1963, the same year that Betty Friedan's *Feminine Mystique* demanded horizons for women wider than home and family. A native of Storm Lake, Liz married a fellow Storm Laker, raised two children, completed her doctorate in child development at Iowa State, and took a job in Ames as a kindergarten teacher. Her daughter Erin is also an honors student, graduating top in her class at Ames High School in 1993. Erin grabbed headlines all through high school as a champion cross-country runner and is currently enrolled at Iowa State studying to enter medical school.

In this essay, Liz and Erin compare their experiences across the decades. Liz also adds her observations on the kindergarten children she teaches. While in some ways the Iowas in which each grew up are light years apart, in other ways the issues they confronted as girls and then as women are remarkably similar.

Liz and Erin live in Ames with their husband/father Dave (a mediocre card player on his best nights), son/brother Nathan, currently a medical student at Iowa City, and a houseful of cats.

TWICE UPON A TIME IN IOWA

Elizabeth and Erin Block

LIZ SAYS: It was the best of times. Period. My Iowa childhood remembered seems an endless summer interrupted only by the necessity of showing up for school. But then, my parents didn't really raise me as a girl. They raised me as a child. Consequently, my inner life knew no limits, and my outer life knew only the routine of mealtimes and the length of the sunwashed days.

In the Storm Lake of 1950, a child could ride a bike anywhere in town. Once I mastered my two-wheeler, the streets and sidewalks were mine, and in those disciplined days, streets and sidewalks offered only an occasional tree-root bump or railroad track to trouble the safety of a small person on her way Somewhere. On summer Saturday afternoons, the neighborhood kids rode downtown for the weekly installment of the *Black Hawk* serial at the Vista Theater. We parked our bikes, which had never known locks, out in front, paid our dimes, and entered the cavernous building. The theater during a Saturday matinee for kids was all ours—a barnful of happy, noisy younglings, feeding on Black Crows, Jujyfruits, popcorn, and pop, bouncing up and down on the worn springs of our seats, cheering for the hero, tossing popcorn at the bad guys, immersing ourselves in the blend of screen and kids. Emerging from the darkness after the movie, we were always surprised to find the bright, ordinary day still there, the sidewalk sparkling white in the sun, our dog Tippy snoozing loyally beside our bikes. Still fired by the Black Hawk persona, we'd ride the two miles home as combat heroes, gradually emerging as ourselves as we neared our neighborhood, where our moms were hanging out clothes and our own dads were mowing the lawns.

On hot days we'd ride to Sunset Beach to go swimming off the big horseshoe-shaped dock, the smaller kids splashing around inside the horseshoe and the older ones, the actual swimmers, paddling out beyond the dock to the raft. The bottom of the lake was rocky and silty—a real incentive to swim, float, or tread water—anything to keep from touching bottom, even in four feet of water. When we needed a break, we'd pry the nickels from the knots in the corners of our towels and stand at the candy counter for cherry popsicles, our bare feet uncomfortable on the warm cement eternally sticky with popsicle juice. When the afternoon ran out, we'd tie our towels around our necks like Superman capes and argue the possibilities of *Superman and the Mole Men* on the way home.

Those sunlit days of my Iowa childhood may not have dictated *what* I would eventually become, but they contributed to the best and bravest part of *who* I would become. It was a free and fine spirit that played kick-the-can in the summer dusk until the fireflies came out and our mothers called us home. That tired, dirty kid-body trudging home across the backyard playground of clipped grass, garden rows, and clothesline poles carried one more day's worth of fidelity and peace.

Seeking the Prince

And I was to need it all, because eventually, I started junior high. My world became a lot bigger but at the same time infinitely smaller. The focus switched irrevocably and with astonishing suddenness from what I expected for myself to what some ill-defined Other expected of me. I had always been unthinkingly at ease in my skin. Now I was searching the faces of others to see who I might be, how I might be doing.

From the first day of junior high I recognized a new set of

priorities, and I entered armed with fresh pencils, white bucks, can-can slips, and my first deodorant. Certain things were now Important and would require a great deal of attention until that unconsidered and distant time when I would be married and my troubles would be over. The boys, who for seven years had been my fellow explorers, now floated away across an invisible moat, acquiring mystery and desirability in the process.

A boy was to be desired not so much for himself as for the status he conferred. A boyfriend was the American Express card of junior high; he was accepted everywhere and gained for you a level of admittance that nothing else—not looks, not clothes, not talent, certainly not brains—could guarantee. Actually, a lot of that system climbs up to adulthood with us. The social economy of Iowa (maybe of everywhere) is still based on the Couple.

Junior high blurred into high school, and at some point, boys became attractive for their own sakes. A few girls could always attract any boy they wanted, but most of us spent endless hours cross-legged on our beds, reading *Seventeen* and plotting, plotting, plotting. I stayed relatively virginal not so much by vigilant parents as by the pervasive moral climate of small-town Iowa, a climate that my friends and I had thoroughly internalized. In those days, "they" were all in it together: the coalition of parents (all of whom knew you by name, family, and church affiliation), the churches (that preached abstinence from a lot of things), the movies (one of my first dates was to see *The Ten Commandments*), television (father knew best), and the print media (*Seventeen* told you how to attract boys and then say "no," in a nice way, of course).

High school led, for me, to college. I arrived at the University of Iowa in the fall of 1963, when girls were required to live in dorms, and girls' dorms had hours. We were all safely locked in by 10:00 P.M. weeknights and by 1:00 A.M. on weekends. When the Student Senate held a referendum to abolish hours, we girls voted to keep the system. For us, it was a trade-off: although we had to tear ourselves away from the boys we liked, we had a handy and legitimate excuse to unload the boys we didn't. (Boys, of course, had no hours. And they had maid service!)

The girls' dorm was our sanctuary and prison—a fortress in perpetual danger of being stormed. The head housekeeper actually advised us, in the event of the dorm being breached by boys, to heat up our irons to keep them at bay (the boys, not the irons). I imagined nervous, middle-class college boys in a police lineup, being identified by iron-shaped scorch marks on their madras sport coats.

For almost every woman I knew—in my generation, my mother's generation, and her mother's generation—marriage and motherhood were the natural and desirable goals. Unmarried women and childless couples were objects of pity. Some of that value system still lurks within my nooks and crannies, popping out at odd moments to startle me and irritate my daughter. I can't help it; I was raised in the 1950s.

Today, my kindergarten girls of the 1990s have absorbed these values to varying degrees. I have noticed that, year after year, the brightest, most capable girls are the least sex-typed in their behavior, sometimes standing and watching in disbelief as less liberated little girls twitter about, giggling over inventively spelled love notes to embarrassed and/or disgusted little boys. The little girls who seem the most desperately smitten with the concept of "boyfriend" are those who seem to have a space to fill in their lives. This isn't to say, however, that the Prince is dead. *Cinderella* is still popular, and the *Princess and the Pea* is still well-received as a life plan. I once asked my kindergartners whether *Beauty and the Beast* would be just as good a story if the Beast had been a girl. They couldn't conceive of it. It was laughable, literally. Who could love a Beasty Girl?

ERIN SAYS: Before middle school, boyfriends were for show and to assert my popularity and maturity. My first date was in fifth grade when a friend, a boy, and I went to a movie together—alone! All things considered, this first relationship was probably the most mature of all my twenty years, because he was my friend, and we had fun. He had a tree house, a trampoline, and an actual stage indoors. Now he has a pool, so we're still friends.

Seventh grade, in 1987, was the pinnacle of my dating career in terms of sheer quantity, which was the most important goal in those day. The first boy who asked me to go out with him called me every day and even gave me a rose. A week later, when my rose had withered, so had our love. On to the next, I thought. Each short-lived romance lasted about as long as that first rose. Seventh grade also saw my first kiss. We kissed at a party, which was important because we could impress many people at once. My girlfriends threw Skittles at us and snickered. That's what I remember: the Skittles, not the kiss.

If eighth grade was a dry spell as far as boyfriends were concerned, my freshman and sophomore years were droughts. Not that I cared; I always managed to get myself a date for homecoming. Besides, I was much too busy and self-centered for others. I had school, cross-country, track, and friends—no extra energy for a relationship. I had my mile time to worry about!

In my junior year, I dated my older brother's best friend, over whom I had been pining since my freshman year when he was a senior. The "older man" was in college, which was exciting, but unfortunately that college was in Minnesota. We began our romance by going to see *Beauty and the Beast.* He asked me out after we had gone for a run together, and I could hardly speak for all my excitement (or perhaps from the run, during which I maintained, in order to impress him, a pace much faster than I could actually handle). Our year as a couple was interrupted by long periods spent in bordering states, but I look back fondly at that relationship. Our fairy tale first date set the tone for a peaceful relationship. Maybe that was the problem. In any case, we drifted apart but remain friends today. I guess the glass slipper just started to cramp my foot. I'm not Cinderella. We run together from time to time, and he and my brother are still best friends. We are all living happily ever after.

In contrast, my most recent relationship ended with only one of us riding off into the sunset. I met him at a cross-country meet. Half Jamaican, he spoke with a British accent and was exotic and intriguing. (My mother describes my affinity for men who don't fit the "Ken doll" mold with the statement, "She likes to date nice guys, but nice guys with a five-o'clock shadow.") We dated for almost two years, gaining insight into the other's lifestyle and attitudes. He was of a different ethnicity, and religion—basically of a different world from my Iowa one. Any conflict mainly served to broaden our minds. I didn't give much thought to our difference in race—a fortunate consequence of being born to my generation. My parents wouldn't have had the luxury of dating someone of a different color without facing condemnation and contempt from friends, community, and even family. My boyfriend and I encountered little of this opposition. My parents were more concerned about the gap in our age and background than our difference in race.

Once, an elderly woman approached us as we were sitting in McDonald's. Fearing that she was about to give us a speech on the sins of interracial dating, I was surprised and pleased when, instead, she asked my boyfriend where he was from in England. She had traveled abroad years ago and was interested in our young lives, not in the difference in our race.

Barefoot in the Ballroom

LIZ SAYS: In the black-and-white photo of my first grade class, there are thirty kids, all with the faces of innocent heroism of children everywhere. The little girls sit primly, ankles crossed, in beribboned and beruffled dresses. All except for one, who sits primly enough, but in a pair of shorts and a white blouse. Oh, I was a plucky scrap of social defiance in those days. Somewhere between kindergarten and first grade, I'd reached the conclusion that there was some connection between wearing pants and being a person, and I adamantly, and out of all proportion to any real power I held in the family, refused to pull a dress over my head. My mother must have been frustrated, torn between loving me and lamenting over the spectacle I was making of myself. My teacher, Miss Stump, lectured my class about my row of pretty dresses in the closet at home that I refused to wear because of my selfish and shameful attitude. Aflame with humiliation and fury, I put my head down on my desk and fought back the tears. Miss Stump's campaign went for naught. I lasted out the first grade in jeans and shorts. But in my second grade picture, I'm wearing a dress.

Until the 1960s, girls wore dresses. Or skirts. Or jumpers. Something you could see up. Something that forced us girls to choose whether "skinning the cat" on the monkey bars was worth the risk of flashing our panties to the boys. When we swung on the swings, the boys would lie in the grass and make offensive remarks as our dresses flew fore and aft. During the coldest months, we were allowed to wear slacks under our dresses, but we had to remove them before class, which entailed our gingerly pulling them down, taking care not to hitch our undies down with them, and keeping our skirts carefully arranged so as to reveal nothing private in the process.

Steamy Iowa summers offered their own dress-code miseries. At the Presbyterian Church camp on Lake Okoboji, a vespers service was held under an open-air canopy every night. Boys could wear jeans and long-sleeved shirts, but girls were required to wear dresses, exposing our suntanned, sticky flesh to thousands of mosquitoes that arrived, astonished at their good fortune. The strains of "Wade in the Water, Children" were soon accompanied by the sounds of slapping, smacking, and scratching. On one occasion, the Mosquito Wars became so noisy and distracting from the spiritual ambiance that the camp director gave us girls ten minutes to run to our cabins and change into long pants. Oh, the joyous flurry that ensued! We flew to those cabins, threw our dresses wildly in the air, flung our slips over the bunk beds, kicked our patent leather shoes out of the way, and yanked our jeans in one motion over little fatless fannies. Suppressing our unseemly joy, we raced under the darkening trees back to the canopy. It was as though we had changed out of borrowed clothes back into our own elastic skins.

The constraints of floppy little dresses seemed negligible, however, once we were introduced to the world of Undergarments for the Grown-Up Girl. When I retreated to my bedroom to unwrap and try on my first garter belt, I was awed and a little bewildered by the task at hand. "What do *fat* girls do?" I wondered, gazing at the wide band of unforgiving rubber and fabric that was only about fifteen inches around. My hips were probably about twenty-eight inches around in those happier times, but there was still quite a bit of compression involved. The garter itself was a funny contraption designed to grip the top of a nylon stocking, but, because of a disconcerting design flaw, it occasionally slipped from its mooring and snapped to the floor. I witnessed this event once at a Rainbow Girls' Spring Formal at the Country Club. We were all dancing romantically, handsome teenaged couples dressed to the nines, when suddenly—poing—a garter zapped to the wooden dance floor from some poor girl's Parts Unknown. We small-town Iowa teens of the early 1960s did not have the easy comfort with things personal that today's youth seem to enjoy. Frozen with embarrassment at the sight of The Object on the floor, we tried nervously to ignore it. The thing lay unclaimed in our midst. Brave couples began giving it hesitant little kicks. Skittering around the floor, it became a zippy projectile in an unacknowledged pinball game. I imagine it lying there still, forgotten under an aging Coke machine, a fading testament to the days before pantyhose.

The little girls in my kindergarten class are, for the most part, sensibly dressed for the messy business of childhood. They wear shorts in hot weather, long pants in cold weather, and dresses when the mood strikes. Their tastes run to rainbows, flowers, baby animals, and all things that sparkle. Most of them are unaware of brand names, but status accrues in other ways. "Theme" outfits (everything Minnie Mouse, for example) are much admired, as are clothes reflecting career choices, such as the little ballerina's selection of tights, tennis shoes, tutu, and Ninja Turtles shirt. Perhaps remembering the humiliation of Miss Stump's "Why-won't-Elizabeth-wear-a-dress" speech, I let the children in my class wear whatever they want as long as they're not freezing, falling down, or running into door frames. Against the whiteness of a winter playground, the neon colors of their nylon snow gear create a December garden so vital and beautiful that it sometimes makes me ache with tenderness.

ERIN SAYS: My mother had to wear a dress to school every day. I, on the other hand, was lucky if I had underwear on. (A slight exaggeration, though I did go through a phase in which I questioned the moral necessity of underwear since no one could actually see it.) Family photos show me in the first years of my life wearing either a diaper and no shirt, shorts and no shirt, my older brother's brown plaid pants with some hideous off-brown velour shirt and navy socks, or a frilly Easter dress and bonnet. Never any shoes. When I entered elementary school, my fashion sense matured rapidly. I wore a shirt nearly every day, and often even shoes. Sometimes I even wore a dress. There is a picture of me heading off to school on the first day of kindergarten. I am waving from the sidewalk in front of my house, in a pink and white dress, white tights, and little brown Mary Janes. My hair is fake, I think, having that rare plastic-doll-hair look that apparently was the fashionable style because every other little girl in my class had similar hair that first day.

In the years to come I survived several other clothing trends. For two years straight I wore terrycloth one-piece playsuits with a zipper up the front. These resembled a tank top and shorts all-in-one ensemble, a "must" in the wardrobe of any active girl who couldn't be bothered with taking the extra time to find both shirt and shorts, let alone ones that matched. What a contrast to my mother's struggles against the dress establishment! For shoes, the choice was simple. At Kinney's, my brother and I could choose between blue and red. His had four white stripes because he wore bigger sizes, and mine had three. I eagerly awaited the day when my own shoes would have four stripes.

Middle school changed everything. My fashion world had one focus: name brands. If your jeans had a question mark inside a triangle on the back pocket, the result was instant popularity. My parents could be persuaded, albeit reluctantly, to pay the high price that came with purchasing shirts that had popular names written across the chest in bold and easily distinguishable writing. I survived this fashion show unscathed, during which I thought money could buy popularity. Many were not so lucky.

The high school years brought the fun back into outfitting myself. While the girls of my mom's era were trapped in skirts and garter belts, freshman girls in my class sported sweatshirts made for powderpuff football (the annual grade-versus-grade female football matchup) with the letters R.A.W. on the front. Until now, what these letters stood for has been a well-kept secret: Rompin' Ass Women.

My female classmates and I began as well-dressed girls in carefully planned outfits, trying to impress the upperclassmen or at least avoid their ridicule. But as we progressed from being freshmen to seniors, we became more confident that our character and actions could speak for themselves. Dress became more casual. Of course, that is the politically correct version. One might also identify the root of the transformation as laziness. Regardless of the explanation one chooses, the result was the same: in my senior year, jeans and a sweatshirt were the uniform. If I wore a sweater or a button-down shirt, I was looking exceptionally classy. My senior year had a few occasions that called for a dress: the awards banquet, the prom, commencement. Reluctantly, I answered the call. Generally, I try not to wear a dress except in extreme situations—and I still don't like to wear shoes.

You Can't Run in Glass Slippers

LIZ SAYS: In 1950s Iowa, there was a curious division between big schools and small schools on the issue of girls' sports. The small-town and country schools offered interscholastic basketball and softball for girls; the big-town and city schools didn't. I don't know why. It's not as though the little schools were reticent about their girls' teams. If a girls' basketball squad went to the state tournament, the little town affiliated with that school decorated itself and most of its rolling stock, closed the town, and traveled en masse to Des Moines. (I'm telling this as if it's part of some quaint past, but the same thing happens today.) The *Des Moines Register* printed up a patronizing story describing the farm kids and their families to the city folk, as though the latter were some enlightened British upper class amusing themselves with anecdotes from the provinces.

Since I grew up in Storm Lake, which had self-defined its way to Big Town status, we didn't have interscholastic sports for girls. I believe some of the adult population took pride in this, as though by refraining from watching our girls play basketball, we were somehow more sophisticated, almost Des Moines-like, in our restraint. Consequently, the physical development of girls was left to gym class, presided over for most of my growing-up years by Miss Peabody.

Miss Peabody was a very large woman, and she was neither jolly nor quietly dignified in compensation. She may have been kindhearted and patient and supportive, but we girls were not on the watch for those characteristics, and I don't remember them leaping out to surprise us. What Miss Peabody was was consistent. She always wore a big, shapeless dress; she always sported her ear-splitting whistle; and she always offered the same sports in the same order. That's probably why it came as such a shock to us one day when Miss Peabody decided to Demonstrate the Trampoline. Now here was something different!

First of all, Miss Peabody appeared before us in shorts. You need to understand that Miss Peabody rarely demonstrated anything, much less in a pair of shorts. We girls were dumbstruck. Miss Peabody clambered aboard the trampoline and edged her way to the center. She told us to gather around the rim to observe and "spot" her. These instructions were unnecessary for two reasons: One, nothing short of a flash fire could have prevented us from observing, and Two, nothing but nothing could have induced us to try to break her fall had she come flying off. We were a bunch of eighty-pound middle schoolers, too well brought up to dispute a teacher but not so stupid as to stand in the way of an airborne Miss Peabody. Had she shown signs of toppling, we would have scattered like marbles on a downhill slope. As it was, we clung to the frame and watched wide-eyed while Miss Peabody slowly gathered momentum. As the height of her bounces increased, the blasts of air shooting out from under the trampoline on her descent gathered force. My thin cotton gym shirt flattened against my stomach with each "ker-whoosh" of the tramp, and we sneaked nervous peeks under the frame to see if the trampoline bed would bottom out on the gym floor. It didn't, and after a few more commanding bounces, Miss Peabody climbed off the structure, and the lesson was ended.

There were other lessons over the years—a little softball, a smattering of basketball, a few slow walks down to the tennis courts in the spring. In high school we could join the Girls Recreation Association and play intramural badminton before school. The Presidential Fitness Tests rolled around every year to offer incentive to those of us who through some happy genetic accident had acquired a level of all-around fitness. Cheerleading was available for a handful of girls, but for that you had to be elected by the student body, and the judgment of that assemblage was not always guided by purely athletic considerations.

I didn't mind not having sports in high school, in the same way that children everywhere accept whatever *is* as being the natural order of things. My mother had been a chaperone for a girls' basketball team in the 1930s, and she felt that all the emotion, nervous hysteria, weeping, and wailing that she had witnessed were arguments against girls' competition. It was also widely felt that athletic competition was unladylike. When I was in grade school, we were discouraged from doing full-length push-ups for fear we would "damage our female organs." I have now carried two babies to term, and I'm pretty sure that if childbirth doesn't damage female organs, a few push-ups aren't a serious threat.

Having watched my own daughter grow up as a jock, I suspect that I may have missed out on something good. It's not because I think that team sports are the golden key to leadership, scholarship, and character. And it's not just the fitness aspect, though that is definitely a plus. No, I'm for girls playing sports because they deserve a chance to experience the rush of a young human body operating at its peak. And I'm for girls playing sports because it gives them the chance to go toe-to-toe in self-esteem with the boys. You can't be a cheerleader all your life.

ERIN SAYS: My mother and the other girls of her day jumped up and down on the sidelines yelling for the boys on the field or the court. One chose between a life in a cheerleading skirt or a life in ... just a skirt, I guess. I scoffed when my high school made cheerleading a varsity sport in which one could receive an athletic letter. I know, my attitude is snotty and colored by my participation in "real" sports, but I still breathed a sigh of relief when two of my best friends who had been cheerleaders as freshmen saw the light of day and joined the cross-country team. (Before I further offend card-carrying members of the National Cheerleading Association, I must reveal one of my closely guarded secrets: I harbor no real contempt for those who dedicate their sporting lives to the pursuit of excellence in the field of cheerleading. It's my duty as a runner to make fun of cheerleaders just as it's the farmer's duty to complain about the weather. Yet, while I commend these young women, I have two words for them: think gymnastics.)

I began my athletic career playing soccer in the days when soccer teams weren't divided by gender, so our team had about an equal number of boys and girls. As the years passed, however, the number of girls dwindled until I was the only girl on my team. I didn't mind as long as I saw playing time. The boys on my team treated me as an equal: they tripped me and teased me just as they would any other team member. My other memory from my early soccer career is the only rule difference for girls: a female can cover her chest with her arms for protection from an oncoming ball without being called for "hands," while a male cannot. This rule was an enigma to me at the time. Eventually, I decided not to go out for soccer. Had there been all-girl teams then as there are today, perhaps I would still be playing soccer.

Because my father had been a gymnast in college, I inevitably tried the sport myself. Initially I loved it. I was small and light, so the spotters could throw me into the air and flip me around, giving me the impression that I was performing perilous tricks. As I grew older, I realized that I would someday be expected to perform *all by myself* those same tricks mastered earlier with the aid of trampolines and the powerful arms of spotters. I discovered a new and foreign emotion—fear. I quit gymnastics soon after my sense of weightlessness and joy were replaced by gravity and the fear of injury.

I participated in a variety of other sports throughout grade school and middle school: volleyball, basketball, and softball. I enjoyed each, especially the team aspect. Always being a bit of a show-off, however, I chose the sport in which I had the greatest early success—track. At first I was a sprinter, as are most children. I could beat all of the girls and most of the boys my age. Gradually, as my running style became more efficient, I began to find myself drawn to longer and longer distances. I think a sport that depends so much on preparation and dedication, rather than mere talent, appealed to me. As early as fifth grade, I trained on a two-mile loop around the neighborhood to prepare for summer races. It was fun, and I gained a lot of confidence and notoriety. I was hooked.

By the time I reached high school, I was a specialist. Except for intramural basketball, I concentrated on training for long races. Cross-country and track became my passion, indeed, very nearly my obsession. I trained religiously and spent nearly every waking moment thinking about practices and races. I made my closest friends in cross-country and track, and still do today. I got a lot of attention from classmates, coaches, teachers, parents, and the media for my accomplishments. Much of this attention, especially my freshman year, stemmed from the fact that I was barely five feet tall and weighed a mere seventy-eight pounds. The press loves to see the victory of the underdog, or in my case, the underweight. I thrived on the attention, even though it got to be almost too much to handle at times. I felt a lot of pressure to succeed, from both others and myself. All things considered, though, cross-country and track were one of the, if not the, most influential and positive aspects of my life. My happiest memories are of green golf courses accented by hundreds of runners in uniforms of various colors warming up, stretching, racing, and celebrating; meets interrupted by hail that caused the athletes of opposing teams to huddle in a small locker room talking and singing together; and early morning workouts when the last interval had been run and it was time to gather at a friend's house for breakfast. It has been said that the race is not always to the swift but to those who keep on running. I intend to keep on running (and to convert as many cheerleaders as I possibly can while I'm at it).

Dr. Princess, Ph.D.

LIZ SAYS: When I was about six years old, I set off on my tricycle one fine morning dressed in only a pair of shorts. It turns out that the policy of "No shirt, no shoes, no service" didn't apply in that instance, because my mother serviced me right back into the house repeating, "Oh, honey, no, little girls don't do that. Just boys can do that." It turned out that there were a lot of things that little girls couldn't do that little boys could do, aside from peeing on trees. In the 1960s a friend of mine named Dallas applied to Iowa State University's College of Veterinary Medicine and was accepted. When she showed up in person for registration, she was discovered to be—whoops!—a girl, and was promptly unaccepted.

My own career choices have charted a zigzag course guided by accident and circumstance as much as by design. When my generation of Midwestern girls was young, our mothers encouraged us to have a career plan to "fall back on" in case our husbands failed to materialize, died, or turned out badly. As a small child, my plans were centered on the cowboy life. For birthdays, I wanted cowboy outfits and guns. Neighbor moms would ask with concern, "Don't you mean a cow*girl* outfit, sweetie?" Well, no, I didn't mean a cow*girl* outfit. I meant a cow*boy* outfit. I watched the Roy Rogers show. I knew where the action was. While Roy was thundering along on Trigger and Pat Brady was clattering close behind in Nellybelle, Dale Evans was stuck in that damn cafe, waiting for news from the Western Front. Phooey on that.

As I grew older, around seven or eight, I refined my aspirations and settled on the goal of becoming a Royal Canadian Mounted Policeman. To my mother's credit, she ignored social convention and outfitted me as a Mountie for Halloween. The Neighbor Lady, ever clueless, gushed, "Oh, what a darling marching band suit!" Words failed to express my contempt. I bless the memory of my parents for allowing me to follow my heart in those days. I guess, in their wisdom, they figured that the rangy backyards of a small Iowa town were big enough to contain whatever happy wanderings a wiry little Mountie could chart.

In junior high I decided that, like half the people in the world who need counseling, I wanted to be a counselor. In high school, further conforming to my assigned sex role, I envisioned myself as a nurse. In college I majored in psychology for three years, tacking on a degree in secondary education only when it dawned on me that I might actually have to have a job some day. From that point on, nearly all my work experiences and my lengthy stints in graduate school have been dictated by the serendipitous edicts of chance and opportunity. Strangely, I've enjoyed almost every job I've ever had, from driving an ice cream wagon to teaching college classes. Although I resent the constant intrusion into my time, I like the working world. I think most of us need a team to play on.

The career aspirations of my kindergartners are not so very different from those my classmates might have entertained in 1950. The boys still have visions of themselves as firemen, football players, and construction workers. The girls see themselves as teachers, mommies, nurses, and ballerinas. The difference is that today those few little girls who dream of paleontology, medicine, or electrical engineering actually have a decent shot at it. If my friend Dallas was to be accepted into the veterinary college at Iowa State today, she would be joining a class that is 50 percent female. The times they are a'changin.

Still, if I had to offer some advice to a baby girl starting her trip through the world in 1995, I'd have to say that there is something to this Marriage and Family thing. I'd have to say that if you're lucky, you'll marry your best friend and have kids you're totally crazy about, and all the rest will be gravy.

ERIN SAYS: I'm currently a sophomore at Iowa State University pursuing a degree in biology, with a possible double major in psychology. I hope to follow in my brother's footsteps and attend medical school. I haven't thought much about this decision in terms of gender. People never said to me, "Don't you mean you want to be a nurse?" Just fifteen years ago it was probably uncommon to encounter a brother and sister who wanted to be the same thing when they grew up.

Everyone involved in my education has been supportive of my goals and has encouraged me to work hard to reach them. Perhaps this is because of my upbringing in an affluent college town with an excellent school system, but I have never felt oppressed in the classroom because of my gender. I don't feel that I've been discouraged from pursuing excellence in math and science. As far as I know, I've not been ridiculed or shunned by boys who are threatened by my intelligence. (Maybe my intelligence is not so threatening.) If differences do exist in the manner in which teachers treat boys and girls, these differences could be in response to higher levels of assertiveness displayed by boys. Are boys innately dominant and girls submissive? Do teachers subconsciously treat boys and girls differently? I don't know. In any case, I believe that female students can escape many negative consequences by simply asserting themselves. If you want the teacher to call on you, it helps to raise your hand.

The problem I foresee is not a lack of young women working toward professional degrees and entering high-powered careers but the absence of a compensating revolution by young men. It's still mainly the woman who is forced to choose between career or family, or else try to juggle both. Besides being unfair to women, the lack of shared responsibilities can be devastating to children. Just as girls should be encouraged to achieve their professional dreams, boys should be taught that work done in the home is vital and important.

The women in my extended family for the past century attended college and went on to become teachers. Being a teacher was acceptable (until you got married, that is). Then there were babies to be born and housework to do. My mother is also a teacher, but a teacher with a Ph.D. (although she doesn't require her kindergarten students to call her Dr. Block). My grandmothers had few career opportunities, my mother a great many more, but I feel my opportunities to be unlimited.

Happily Ever After: Are We There Yet?

LIZ SAYS: During one discussion of this essay, Erin was doing tae kwon do moves back and forth in the kitchen. Erin does these with some accuracy because she has taken tae kwon do and can do things like break boards, which she says is no big deal unless you can do it with your head. Erin and I are not always impressed by the same things, nor do we always agree on what is best for each other. I admire Erin for her dedication to running, but I think a little moderation in that area might be called for. Erin responds, "Total dedication is always appropriate. Moderation leads to mediocrity." For her part, Erin says that sometimes I'm not open-minded enough about alternative lifestyles, to which I reply, "I spend half my teaching day trying to repair children who have been damaged by enduring their parents' alternative lifestyles." And while we're on that subject, I wonder who, after we've all liberated ourselves out of the house, will raise the children? Erin wonders the same thing.

Erin feels that I've lowered my sights over the years because I sometimes say things like "Oh, I used to be smart." She's probably right. It seems as if other things came along and took over my priorities—things like Erin. I wonder how she'll deal with it when her single-minded pursuit of her laudable goals conflicts with the needs of people who love her or need her. Erin says she plans to link herself up with people who have no needs. I hope she's kidding.

The trend from my generation to hers seems to be one in favor of greater self-fulfillment for girls. And maybe my mother's generation was more selfless than mine. When my mom died last October, I was overwhelmed with admiration for the women, her peers, who gathered to say good-bye and to offer strength and comfort. They were such fine people, finer than the current standard, it seemed to me. These women in their late seventies and early eighties have dealt with the Depression, wars, illness, and all the rest. As my brother-in-law put it, "No whining." They were taught to carry their share of life cheerfully and gracefully, and it seems to an outsider looking in that this is pretty much what they did. Going through Mom's things, I found P.E.O. membership lists from the 1940s. Many of the women on those lists came to Mom's funeral. For thirty, forty, even fifty years, those generous and lovely faces smiled, talked, laughed, and cried with my mother, forming over the seasons an unbreakable circle of support, courage, and love. In our headlong rush toward liberating our daughters, I hope we can hang on to the sacrifices of our mothers.

I don't want my daughter, who lit a fire with her SAT scores, to spend her life whipping up casseroles. But neither do I want her to spend her life having no one to share casseroles with. Ideally, I'd wish for her work that engages her head, her heart, and her humor. And I'd wish up a nice guy for her to marry and some kids who could play kick-the-can through a cricket-orchestrated Iowa dusk. That would be enough for me. I wonder if that will be enough for her.

❋ EXCEPT FOR HIS four years at Dana College in Blair, Nebraska, Steve Berntson has always lived on the family farm in northwest Iowa near Paullina. In some ways, Berntson is a typical Iowa farmer, active with his wife Joanne in community and church affairs and concerned about this year's crops and next year's prospects. But Berntson is also a freelance writer. He has followed up his bachelor's degree in English and humanities at Dana with a list of articles in the *Des Moines Register, Draft Horse Journal,* farm co-op publications, and other agriculture magazines, as well as a chapter titled "A Year in the Life of a Family Farmer" in the Smithsonian's *1991 Festival of American Folklife.* He also serves on the editorial board of a West Des Moines advertising agency that handles agribusiness accounts. In 1988, the Iowa Press Association presented him with its Service to Agriculture Award for his series on farming in *The Northwest Iowa Review.* In 1993, NBC's "Today Show" selected Berntson to give a commentary on how Iowa farmers feel when they watch their fields flood and juxtaposed his remarks with the thoughts of a Virginia farmer whose crops were withering in a drought.

In *Walden,* Henry David Thoreau explained that he "went to the woods to live deliberately." Berntson has stayed on the farm for the same reason. He and Joanne, who has a degree in elementary education, are home-schooling their son Daniel. When I was on a trip through northwest Iowa, I took up Berntson's offer to spend the night in the guest house where his grandparents had once lived. I had read the first draft of his essay, which begins with his description of the farm looking east, and that panorama first greeted me when I walked out in the spring morning. It was indeed a beautiful sight, and I could understand his affection for his place and its stories.

DEEP ROOTS, GENEROUS CROWN

Steven Berntson

LOOKING EAST from the sunporch of our ancient farmhome's new addition—built in 1935, forever the new addition—you will see first of all the barn, corncrib, and hoghouse, all built in 1905, a triumvirate bent now into the headwind of old age. And from those buildings your eye will take you up a winding lane to the highest spot on this farm. As a four-year-old, my son Daniel decreed it to be "the most beautiful spot on Earth" and delighted in taking his friends to see it. I have never questioned his judgment.

From there, the land dips to the head of the hollow, past a knoll a family of badgers has called home for at least the four generations my family has lived here. Beyond that is the southeast twenty acres, the lumpy lap of the farm. In the early 1900s it was permanent pasture with a creek good for fishing. Today, after several tile lines were dug in by hand by immigrant Norwegians eager for a toehold in the new land, and after a larger tile line was more recently installed with the aid of a laser beam, the land is all cropped.

But this bottomland was also the farm's beginning, where an early, unknown pioneer built the first of four houses on this farm. Like most pioneers, he built near water and timber, but settlers valued high, dry ground, and thus the farm's last three houses were built on the higher, west side.

From the bottomland the view ascends to a neighbor's

farm, particularly to its board-and-batten, post-and-beam red barn, rising high and holy like a cathedral on the eastern horizon. And finally, then, the land rolls on, like the swell of the sea, to that faint, clean seam of earth and heaven. It is a view of which I can never tire, though I have been looking at it for forty years. A prized snapshot while I was yet a toddler shows me sleeping on the swing of that sunporch, lulled to sleep by the methodical whirring of the windmill. It is indeed a cinematic frame of my earliest and deepest connections to this farm and this world. The fusion of past and present. The collision of history and progress. The defining window of our family.

It is a room with a view.

* * * *

A place is not a place until its people have been born there, come of age, known the *joie de vivre,* shared their sorrows, and died there. A place is not a place until its people have shaped it, and in turn, been shaped by it. A place is not a place until it has a story. I cannot speak of my place apart from my story, nor can I speak of my story apart from my place. I cannot tell you of my sense of place apart from my place of sense.

It has been my good fortune not only to be a farmer—and I say that, and mean it, even after the buzz-saw farm economy of the 1980s—but to have grown up on an extended family farm of three generations: my parents, sister, brother, uncle, and grandparents. We always stuck by each other; occasionally we were stuck with each other as well.

Among my treasured memories of those growing-up years were the rainy afternoons of storytelling by my father, grandfather, uncle, and occasional neighbor or salesman. Sometimes we would sit on the swing in the sunporch, more often in an oddball assortment of cast-off rocking chairs in the garage, which in its first life was the one-room country school my father attended. But here I learned things never taught in school. They told stories about themselves and each other, living again in their own memories and thus keeping their memories alive. Some were about family, friends, and neighbors whose passions, nuances, and complexities were seldom smoothed over. Many were hilarious, some touching, often described with pointillist detail. Through them I came to know my grandfather, my father, my uncle, and something of myself.

And I learned about the nature of story itself. There is, first of all, the story the public knows. Within that there is the story the neighborhood knows, and within that neighborhood story is the story the family knows. Finally, at the core, is a story we seek to find and understand, but it remains largely beyond our ken.

Though these stories were spun over and over, they never lost their punch or power. They had the force of parables, the grip of epics. They are the stories that scar and sustain me yet today. I am the son of immigrants, and their stories have become part of my inner moorings.

You cannot begin to know what a person means until his or her story can be told, and a story cannot be told unless you know its beginning. It is an iron law of narration. In a more specific sense, you cannot understand the story of my family apart from the SW ¼ of Section 25, Dale Township, O'Brien County, where our own story begins. The *1924 Atlas of O'Brien County and the World* (a title I've always found half-perceptive and half-amusing) describes the farm as "a fruitful place." In the curious way that a farm owns a family generation upon generation, it has certainly been that.

Though I speak of this farm as the place of my family's story, it is more precise to say it is the place of many stories set within that larger story. Today, Iowa—in the year of your 150th birthday—I share with you two of those stories, of my grandfather the pioneer and my father the settler.

My grandfather's story begins a full century back and half a world away, when he and his father, Lars Berntson, bundled their bravado and belongings in a rosemaled emigrant trunk at the port of Kristiansand, Norway, leaving forever the *vaterland.* On that May day in 1883, they joined that vast wave of emigrants flowing to a country brimming with promise, chasing the long and elegant dream of land. But it was a dream denied, a tragic fealty. The gleaming geometrics of fields of wheat, oats, and barley lured Lars and his family to Minnesota's Red River Valley, where land lies as flat and rich as a slab of chocolate. Three consecutive years of crop failure drove them to Iowa, crushed and broken. He never farmed again.

But the dream was then fulfilled in his son, my grandfather, Bernt Krisstian Berntson, a man stern in determination and purpose, indomitable in spirit. It's the character quality my Finnish friends call *sisu,* a word not readily translatable, but if you can imagine the thistle-persistence required to endure and survive deep-woods Finnish winters, you know what *sisu* is.

After several years as a hired laborer, he rented forty acres and then purchased an eighty-acre hill farm near Marshalltown. When pouring rains washed out his newly planted corn, he vowed never to farm a hill again. The next year he sold the eighty, and, mortgaging his heart on hope alone, purchased a farm near Paullina. Then, in the miserable depths of the Depression, at an age most men would be thinking retirement, he again geared himself for the bold stroke, buying a second farm and mortgaging the first. All that is *sisu.*

My grandfather had the good fortune, foresight, and fortitude to buy at opportune times—first in 1906, then during agriculture's Golden Age (1911 to 1915, the time frame on which the concept of parity is yet based), and again just before the prosperity that accompanied the Second World War. And yet his was not a simple story of success. It was, rather, a long, hard pull, as tough as any immigrant story, with a litany of hardships and struggles.

He went from the Old Country to the New World, from four-legged horsepower to four-wheeled horsepower. His life spanned a time without antibiotics to the day of the heart transplant. It can be reasonably argued, I think, that no generation on earth has ever seen or will ever see such fundamental change.

He was the Pioneer, never looking back, ever searching for the New Land. Though my father's farming was joined to his father's farming, it was in many ways different. My dad was the stay-put, stand-pat guy, the settler whose roots went deep on this farm. In this age when it is almost quaint for family members to live in the same time zone, Dad lived his first seventy years in the same house in which he was born. Seventy years! Imagine that! Who does that anymore? Some would say one of his biggest moves in life was when he moved from an upstairs bedroom to a downstairs one.

He began farming just as the Depression crept its crippling way into the heartland. Though he lost only a small savings account when the local bank collapsed, the Depression left an invisible but deep scar within him. Thus he became the quintessential self-contained man, as many sons of those dark days did. Never a dollar in debt. He was an insurance agent's worst prospect. He has spent hardly a day in the hospital. He still drives the only pickup he has ever owned. If he ever participated in a government farm program, it was against his principles of self-reliance. (In an ironic twist of fate, the road past our farm was recently named Roosevelt Avenue, in honor of the father of many of our social programs.)

Early on, my father declared his personal war on poverty. Psychologists tell us that as adults we stockpile what we did not have as children, and in my father's case, to put it bluntly, that was money. And so, in addition to inheriting this homeplace, through small economies, diligent hoarding, and careful management, he built a mountain of cash, which has sheltered him from every financial storm. Part of his success, I think, was that he accepted a reasonable boundary of land and a logical perimeter to his life. Call it contentment, if you will.

If I admire my grandfather as a man of boldness and vision, my admiration for my father comes from a kind of faithfulness almost unheard of these days. That faithfulness began with this farm but did not end there. It extended to his bachelor brother Les, who never could have farmed alone. But my father took him as a full partner and simply made the situation work.

Dad was not only the loyal brother but the good son as well, who kept his aging, ailing parents here on the homeplace they loved until their deaths only seventeen days apart in

1968. And now, at eighty, he continues as the faithful husband, caring for my mother after a debilitating stroke.

These lessons have not been lost on me.

Iowa, I do not hold up the stories of my grandfather the trailblazer and my father the steady one because they are so remarkable or unique. They are neither, for there are a multitude of stories like them. But they are my stories, our stories, Iowa's stories, the important stories, the family reunion stories that need to be told and retold.

And they are farmer stories that have something important to say to this farming state. They speak of the vocation (from the Latin *vocare,* "to call"), the calling of the farmer, which is the calling to be faithful in the midst of struggle. And don't farmers struggle! If it were possible to write a job description for a farmer—and after being a farmer for two decades I'm not at all sure it is—I would head up that description with this: farmers will struggle.

They battle heat and cold, drought and flood, blizzards and hail. And always the wind, the unrelenting wind. (But then again, even if farmers controlled the weather, I'm not sure they would succeed.)

They struggle with a short crop one year and a surplus one the next. When grain prices are low, their cash flow becomes a cash trickle. When grain prices are high, they can't afford to feed their livestock.

They contend with pigs that scour and plows that won't.

They must deal with government farm programs that, in the name of doing something *for* them, are just as likely to do something *to* them.

And when they occasionally prosper, they up the ante, purchasing more land and machinery, taking on more debt.

If that struggle is eternal, it is often addictive and seductive as well. In our nation's collective psyche, the farmer's struggle is portrayed in mythical, heroic proportions. (Perhaps that is why, in the Farm Crisis of the 1980s, polls showed greater support for agricultural subsidies from city dwellers than from farmers themselves.)

That calling to be faithful in the midst of struggle is akin to the marriage covenant itself, with all its great promises and dire warnings. In sickness and in health. For richer, for poorer. For better, for worse. The land is always here, but we come and go. And the people who love it and understand it are the only ones who can ever be faithful to it, in our fleeting moment. It is enough, I think, if somehow you have kept a sense of yourself, of who you are as a farmer, and bequeathed that to your children. It is, in the end, the sole property we can call our own, the only property we truly own free and clear in our brief authority here.

Do we need farmers? Do we need their stories? Or is the memory of the family farmer and family farm enough in this modern world? Geneticists tell us that in the near future we may be able to manufacture much of our food rather than grow it. For example, we may produce orange juice in factories conveniently located throughout the country. But can you imagine a world without orange trees? I can't. We need the orange trees and the farmers who tend them as much as we need the orange juice itself.

In Iowa, we take great comfort in the old and persistent imagery of red barns, white farmhouses shaded by spreading elms, chickens scratching in the gravel, Mother working in the garden, and Father pursuing a high and holy calling, even when he's hauling manure. All's well with the world.

But this image, this memory of the family farmer, is not enough. We need to know, perhaps on an almost primeval level, that farmers can yet draw their lives and livelihoods from the soil and nurture and nourish their families on it until one day they themselves are planted in it, their final seed. In the curious alchemy of soil and soul, we care for the earth, and are in turn cared for by it. The longing to return to the land is inborn; it is part of our humanity.

We need our farmers—as custodians of the dream of land, as keepers of its stories and as caretakers of the countryside.

* * * *

In the beginning, this place and this story chose me, just as a place and story choose each of us. But one day—and I scarcely know when—I chose this farm and this story as my own. It was as though I took the Benedictine vow to stability, to make this my home, to let the place happen to me. This has been, as C. S. Lewis once said of Christianity itself, "a good and blessed infection."

Part of calling a place home is to know where you are; a bigger part is to love what you find there. I am a child of the prairie. Born from its soil, I will also die into it one day. And as my life has grown from the soil, and into it as well, I have come to know the inexhaustible abundance here, the grace in this place, which is really the grace in any place and every place. In speaking of our mortal transience, the Bible says in Psalms 103 that "a man passes away, and his place shall know him no more." His place ... his place ... his place. ... Unremarkable as this place is, I yet wonder: Was any man's place more his place than this farm has been the place of my grandfather, my father, and now me?

For many years my walks have taken me around this farmstead and across its beloved acres. Often they are inward treks. They remind me of the events and companions of my life; I revisit them. Many voices, some silent, speak to me in many ways.

Walk with me today around this farm. This isn't just another blocky white farmhouse with a pair of porches and a trumpet vine climbing its south wall and a couple of thousand board feet of hardwood floors and woodwork. No, this is home, where hired men would swing on the sunporch, waiting for dinner. Where Grandma carried the eggs down the basement steps and the milk to the separator—dutifully, daily. Where children giggled and romped and played.

And this living room, with its great etched windows, where my own son now plays—this was, in that grim spring of 1919, a funeral parlor. Burdette and Beulah, brother and sister to my father, lay in state, plucked in the bloom of childhood by scarlet fever. The lilacs on the northwest corner of the house bloomed that sad spring, as they do now, planted at the birth of each child, an old custom. The flaming poppies—perhaps the poppies of Flanders Field itself—belong to the end of the war that was to end all wars, to a simpler day, when the flag was a matter of allegiance, not debate.

We know these trees. We have planted some, fallen out of a few, mowed around them all. And here are the great rows of towering ash, protecting the farmstead like unyielding bodyguards. Only God in His blue heaven knows what pioneer in utter faith stuck those rooted sticks in the ground and watered and prayed and watered and prayed—all for the next generation.

This shop is the reconverted one-room schoolhouse. It still teaches. In it you will learn the history of mechanization on an Iowa farm—a story told in spare parts, old tools, nuts, bolts, cast iron, chains, pulleys, broken parts, spark plugs, and mounds of watchamacallits and thingamajigs. Behind it is the multigenerational Disappointment Heap of inventions that never quite made it.

Among the tools is a tinsnips made by my grandmother's uncle, a pioneer and homesteader on the North Dakota prairie. He made not only the tinsnips but the forge that made the tinsnips. Is there a better definition of self-sufficiency?

The grove is a cemetery littered with the ancient carcasses of unused, outdated machinery. Here is what's left of the farm's first mechanical cornpicker, a one-row, side-delivery model. Over there is the Pride of Port Huron, the neighborhood threshing machine that must have heard a wealth of stories. How I wish it could talk! And there are old plows, disks, dump rakes, mowers, wagons, and windrowers scattered about. There's even a bobsled.

In life, machinery often gives the farmer status. In death, it's more the reverse: the farmer's character, whatever he had, electrifies each piece of machinery with a story. When you live within your history, the shadows and echoes of the past are everywhere. Here I see a faithfulness to a place and in a place. Here I see a faithfulness to a story and in a story. This is for me a fruitful place with a useful story. I am the custodian of my forebears' dream of land and the inheritor of that place and its promise. And yet, in a larger and truer sense, we are all keepers of the story, for the blood that flows in our veins is the blood of immigrant forebears who sacrificed mightily to carve a new life in a brave, new world.

Like this farm, Iowa is a fruitful place with a useful story.

It is also, I am sorry to say, a troubled state, particularly in its countryside. When F. Scott Fitzgerald wrote some seventy years ago in *The Great Gatsby* of the "lost Swede towns" of western Minnesota, little did he realize how accurately his words would shadow forth the rural areas of the late twentieth century. We live in a diminished, debased countryside. The marks of decay are all around us. Towns wither. The great barns and cribs and blocky farm homes—monuments to a builder's skill—are abandoned and stare at us with vacant, hollow eyes. Fences, well and tightly made, like lines of good poetry, are ripped from the ground.

Our culture is prejudiced not only against things rural, but against the land itself. Even it disappears. When Iowa was first settled, topsoil measured two feet. Scientists tell us we average only eight inches today and continue to lose about an inch a decade.

And for the farmers who yet remain on the land, this is not the good old farming of man and machine and soil and seed and God sending the rain and all that. No, as the prairie garden has become a production factory, farmers are more and more merely extensions of their creditors, agents of the marketplace and tools of technology. Farmers become carriers for profits shared between the supply side of farming (chemicals, herbicides, seed, machinery) and the multinational grain dealers and food processors, seldom enjoying those profits themselves. As farmers have bought into the outside economy that is slowly strangling them, they have thus often connived in their own ruin.

All this is sequence, not cycle. Even in the Great Depression, when farms failed in epidemic numbers, the way of life of the farmer was eventually reclaimed and restored. That is unlike what is called the Farm Crisis of the 1980s (but would be more precisely termed the Farm Debt Crisis of the 1980s). As a result, we are now simply missing a generation of farmers, because farmers were forced out and would-be young farmers are scared off from even starting. Young Farmers programs sponsored by local elevators now typically include forty-year-olds.

Farmers have been hurried off the land for a long time. Now, as my neighbor says, we have been hurried off a little faster. This is the Dakotaization of Iowa. We, too, have more towns, schools, and churches than we can sustain. It is a disintegration in progress for so long that now it is established, accepted, and even respected as the norm. We have been too slow, I believe, to acknowledge our losses and too quick to write them off as the price of so-called progress. How has this happened? To blame our predicament on outside forces, even admitting our own culpability, is too easy an answer. External predation could never have succeeded were it not also for internal disaffection.

For many years I have sought to gain some understanding, some vision of what this land was while it was yet young. I have wanted to know what it was like to come to such an inviting but hostile place, and what kind of commitment to community and family life was required to conquer the new land. One year ago that quest took me to Norway, to the earliest roots of my family and our story. There, life goes on much as it always has. My people farm the ancestral acres that have belonged to our family for at least five hundred years, milking a few cows and gathering a little grass hay in the summer as they have always done. Their home dates from the 1600s, the old moss-covered stone fences from who-knows-when. The generations are practically built-in to the place.

If this place is not particularly productive, it is nonetheless immensely fruitful in its abundance of generous memories. It protects gifts and honors ancient bonds of people and place. And its farmers, as much as anything, are keepers of their stories and caretakers of the countryside—with their government's blessing.

As I see this Norwegian farm in my mind's eye, and as I hear again in my memory the stories of its people, I come to an understanding of the generations who have called it home. In the way the world measures wealth, they were poor, as country people often have been. The working energy of the farm came from themselves and one horse, which they shared with other cousins and neighbors. Their economy was an economy of the most authentic kind: centered within the farm and home itself. (The very word economy comes from the old Latin *economicus,* meaning "of the household.") Because they were not dependent on an outside economy—or what we call economy—they were not vulnerable to exploitation. They were at once safe and free.

They were also rich—in the things that matter. They had their own economy in which they had each other. They had each other's comfort when they needed it, and they had their stories, their history—all together in that one place, *their* place.

Norway's Odal laws, which virtually guarantee the succession of the generations, and generous subsidies (Norway's farmers receive four kroner from the government for every one they actually earn) have combined to make it, as one Norwegian told me, "about as hard to get out of farming in Norway as it is to get into it in the U.S." The *landesflyktning,* the leaving of the old mountain farms for the flat land of the New World, a story repeated countless times, is long over. As a third-generation Norwegian American, I now ponder the ironies of our times.

The great tragedy of the people who left the misty hollows of the Old Country and booked all they had into steerage was that in the new land, where they sought to create a New Norway for their children, they instead discovered that they needed to prepare their children for a life to which they themselves could never belong. The good fortune of those who did not leave Norway is that their farms, while small, are deeply rooted in their society, and thus their future is settled and secure. American agriculture, with its bias to the large and mobile, has made the life of the Iowa farmer tentative and tenuous.

We have begun to scratch the surface of knowing what place change and language change have meant, thanks to writers such as Ole Rölvaag, Vilhelm Moberg, Sophus Keith Winther, and Johann Olaf. But we are just beginning to learn—personally, communally, and nationally—what the loss of story means. We are seeing hints of it in the wanton violence of our cities, the fracturing of the family, and the aimlessness of the culture. When we do not know each other's stories and what they mean, and when we—even as family—are not connected one to another by those stories, then we become, to use Rölvaag's term, "vagrants." We cannot trust each other, and when trust is gone, we cannot be of much helpfulness and comfort to each other.

The ancient rule of neighborliness gives way to the modern mandate of tolerance. When applied to our cities and urban areas, the whole notion of community and the stories necessary to nourish community becomes so large and metaphorical as to be practically useless. The idea of a nation—or the world—as a community is meaningless unless first there are smaller communities that are safe, sound, and stable, lots and lots of them.

When children depart, generation after generation, a community, and a place, loses its story, the useful memory of itself. In the industrial world, to which farming more and more belongs, the pattern for parents, when their children come of age, is to kick them out of the nest, figuratively speaking. In a society that honors place and story, the norm is just the opposite. The children kick the parents out of the nest, succeeding them in place and thus preserving the story as well.

As the local continuity of the generations is broken, succession gives way to supercession. Children do not so much learn from their parents as outmode them. Schools, in their careerist zeal, consider it secondary to pass down a cultural inheritance unimpaired, preparing their students rather for a provisional future that has little to do with place or story. In this way, the leaving of the land becomes the norm, institutionalized through schools which seek to remove children from their parents and homes as quickly and fully as possible.

Finally, then, the local history—story and memory—if it survives at all, loses its place.

What is the prognosis for Iowa's farms and country towns? Because I am a farmer, I am necessarily a man of some faith and hope. But I am also a realist. It is evident, I think, that we cannot expect too much help from large corporate bodies—huge agribusiness firms, universities, the government itself. For they have largely viewed the heartland as the colony of the coasts and the cities, all too willing to exploit and sacrifice its raw products—commodities, soil, and even its people—for the so-called good of the national economy. It is not that they do not understand our problems; they are simply on the other side.

Whatever regeneration we see will come not at the behest of bureaucrats nor on the advice of visiting experts. Rather, it will be a resurrection from the inside out, accomplished mainly by those who know both the predicament and promise of rural life. Already we are seeing some encouraging signs. Young families, some simply weary of the city, are taking a second, countercultural look at a very good place—the countryside—and finding an astounding quality of life there. So, too, are small manufacturing and business concerns, who have learned to value the rural work ethic. There are some pockets of agricultural vigor. Our neighboring county, Sioux County, with the smallest farms in the state, has a stunning vitality.

And in the near future, with the rise of what sociologists call the telecommuter (the worker who works in the home but is connected to faraway offices by fax machines, computers, telephones, and satellites), Iowa may hold even more promise as an inviting place.

* * * *

An ancient spreading elm once graced our backyard in my boyhood days. In cold October it exploded into gold. Deep roots yielded a generous crown. Those leaves, however, needed to be returned to the earth from which they came, to build soil.

So, too, we must collect stories as they fall through time and preserve them in their place, to build story and thus community. They must be turned to account. And when they are, we can then say, without apology and within a culture that denies feeling, that we have come to love our place and our story.

We can gladly accept the responsibilities, affections, and allegiances that place and story demand, which are, as *The Book of Common Prayer* says of marriage itself, "fearful, joyful and unending."

If I hold dear this farm and the story of my people, and if I treasure Iowa's countryside and its stories, it is because they incarnate for me what I cherish most: the wish to be home, the love of precious things, and the abiding rhythms that move us ever onward.

RANDALL BALMER moved with his family to Des Moines as a teenager when his father accepted a pastorate at the Westchester Evangelical Free Church. A "preacher's kid," Randy absorbed the cleanliness/godliness connection early in his life and while still in Hoover High School started a janitorial service called Blue Ribbon Maintenance. Although he earned a doctorate from Princeton in 1985 and has been a professor at Columbia University ever since, he continues to think of Des Moines as home, making sojourns annually for Van Dee's ice cream and the Iowa State Fair. In addition to his teaching duties, Balmer writes a column on religion for the New York Times Syndicate and has written and hosted several documentaries for public television. In 1989, Balmer documented the revitalization of evangelical Protestantism as a major political force in *Mine Eyes Have Seen the Glory: A Journey into the Evangelical Subculture in America* (Oxford University Press). He followed that in 1995 with *Grant Us Courage: Travels along the Mainline of American Protestantism* (Oxford).

As his essay points out, religious roots go deep in Iowa, where diverse faiths have competed not only for members but the right to impress their own vision of "the city upon a hill" on the political and social landscape. Balmer combines solid academic training with an insider's sensitivity to the hopes and fears that provide the momentum for this religious renaissance of evangelical energy.

"A GREAT EXCESS OF UNDENOMINATIONALISM": RELIGION IN IOWA AT THE SESQUICENTENNIAL

Randall Balmer

ON THE EVENING of May 31, 1972, at the graduation exercises of Hoover High School at Veterans' Auditorium in Des Moines, my father rose from his chair on the dais and strode purposefully to the lectern to deliver the invocation. I remember holding my breath, not at all certain what would follow. My father, an evangelical minister, had never prayed from a prepared text in his life. In the best Protestant tradition, he believed that prayer should be a spontaneous, unrehearsed conversation with God. But my father's prayers, as I knew from long experience, could also be admonitory, addressed equally to his auditors as well as to the Almighty: "Lord, I pray most of all that my children will turn from their sins and embrace you as Savior, that they might live their lives uprightly before you."

What would he say on this occasion? Here was a captive audience, nearly five hundred members of the class of 1972 and several times that many grandparents, parents, and siblings. That surely represented too great a temptation, even for a minister. Would he seize the moment and issue an altar call, inviting my classmates to come forward and give their lives to Jesus right then and there?

My father acquitted himself admirably, speaking in tones

more anodyne than admonitory, and it was a proud moment—for both of us, I think, although adolescents rarely discuss such matters with their parents. The selection of my father to deliver the invocation struck both of us as significant because we, as evangelicals, never felt part of the establishment. We were the outsiders, the religious insurgents engaged in a hopeless struggle against the Protestant mainline, which had the wealth, the influence, and the status that we simultaneously resented and coveted. They belonged to the Rotary Club and sipped whiskey sours at the country club outside of town; they sat on the school board and the city council. Members of the Protestant mainline, we suspected, were only dimly aware that we evangelicals even existed, and whenever they deigned to consider us at all they talked of us in hushed and condescending tones, much the way that embarrassed family members might speak about an addled cousin.

My wonderment at the selection of my father to deliver the invocation deepened when I recognized that there was at least one other preacher's kid in the class of 1972, a perfectly respectable Lutheran. And I have since conjured the scenario of my high school principal arriving at the office one bright spring morning only to be informed by his secretary that the commencement program had to go to the printer that day and he needed to choose someone to offer the invocation. Being told that there were two candidates, my father and the Lutheran, the principal flipped a coin and when it came up tails—my father—he muttered a mild expletive and decided to close his door and go for two out of three. When the toss came up tails a second time, the principal, a fair man, decided to relent, and as my father approached the lectern on that balmy May evening, the principal too held his breath.

Shortly after those commencement ceremonies in Veterans' Auditorium, I (like too many other Iowa youth) left the state for college and graduate school. When I returned in January 1988 to write about Pat Robertson's run for the presidency, however, I found that the religious energies were shifting from the Protestant mainline—the Presbyterians, Methodists, Disciples of Christ, Congregationalists, Lutherans, and some Baptists—to the evangelicals, those—like my father—with conservative views on the Bible, morality, and, increasingly, politics. Evangelical congregations, many of which were either independent or affiliated with smaller, lesser-known denominations, were making their play for cultural and political influence, especially within the Republican party. I attended three churches on the Sunday before the Iowa precinct caucuses: the venerable St. John's Lutheran Church in downtown Des Moines, First Federated Church in northwest Des Moines, and Westchester Evangelical Free Church, my father's former congregation, across the street from Hoover High School. Robert Dole and his wife Elizabeth attended First Federated, and Jack Kemp made a whistle-stop at Westchester Evangelical Free Church. No presidential candidate had St. John's, the mainline congregation, on his itinerary.

The shift of religious energies and influence that was just beginning to become apparent in January 1988 had been building for some time and was part of a larger shift in Iowa's religious landscape. Just as Iowa has been politically schizophrenic, swinging between prairie populism and reactionary conservatism, so too various religious affinities—which might roughly be categorized as evangelical, mainline Protestant, and Roman Catholic—have vied with one another for cultural ascendance. Most significantly, the moral reform impulse that once animated mainline Protestants has been commandeered by conservative evangelicals.

In 1850, despite a high concentration of clergy (most of them missionaries to the frontier), Iowa had the lowest rate of religious adherence of any state in the Union. A hundred years later, however, when the mainline Protestant journal *Christian Century* designated twelve congregations in the United States as "great churches," two were located in Iowa.

As much as any state, Iowa has a rich and colorful religious past, beginning with the Native Americans and extending to the various groups late in the twentieth century who provide color and texture to the term "multiculturalism." The history of religion in Iowa might be characterized, as one fierce partisan of Congregationalism described it in 1911, as "a great excess of undenominationalism." Iowa's religious landscape has sustained the Mormons, the Icarians, the Society of True Inspiration, and various ethnic groups (Antonín Dvořák spent the summer of 1893 in the Czech town of Spillville, played the organ for St. Wenceslaus Church services, and composed much of his famous elegy to America, *Aus der Neuen Welt*). Despite the presence of these diverse and colorful groups, however, most of Iowa's religious history has been dominated, at least until recently, by Roman Catholics and mainline Protestant denominations, especially Lutherans and Methodists, with smatterings of Presbyterians, Congregationalists, Baptists, and the Disciples of Christ. One way to chart Iowa's religious landscape is geographical, with Methodists dominating the lower third of the state, Catholics in the eastern part of the state, especially the Northeast, and Lutherans in the Northwest.

Much of Iowa's religious configuration can be traced to the zealotry of missionaries animated by a desire to tame the rowdiness of the frontier. In 1838 Asa Turner and Julian A. Reed, two Congregationalist ministers, crossed the Mississippi to form a Congregational church in Iowa, a country that Turner found "so beautiful that there might be an unwillingness to exchange it for the paradise above." Turner, concerned about the incursions of Mormons into the territory, appealed to Congregationalist authorities back east for missionaries. Twelve men, all from Andover Theological Seminary's class of 1843, heard the call and became known as the Iowa Band. A few years later another Congregationalist minister heeded a different call. It was to Josiah Bushnell Grinnell, an abolitionist preacher in New York City, that Horace Greeley issued his famous dictum: "Go West, young man, go West!" Grinnell settled in the town that now bears his name, helped to establish a college, and remained active in the fight against slavery, even to the point of inviting John Brown to preach in church while Brown was planning his raid on Harpers Ferry.

The religious history of Iowa also includes colorful characters. After Billy Sunday's religious conversion and his retirement from professional baseball, he became an itinerant preacher. On January 7, 1896, the Iowa-born evangelist held his first revival at the opera house in Garner and then began barnstorming throughout Iowa and the Midwest at the turn of the century before launching his campaigns in larger cities. But the flamboyant evangelist did not always meet with success on what he referred to, often disparagingly, as the "Kerosene Circuit." After a rather unavailing visit to Eddyville, Sunday allowed that the "most low, God-forsaken town he was ever in was Eddyville, Iowa, and Morehead [*sic*], Minn." Sunday's sentiments provoked a spirited response from the editor of the Eddyville *Tribune*, who asserted that in Eddyville "the actual infidels to God, as we understand the term, do not exceed five."

Another religious development in Iowa was even less edifying. In March 1887 Henry F. Bowers and six associates gathered in Clinton to form the American Protective Association, an anti-Catholic nativist organization. Members of the association subscribed to the notion that Roman Catholics were plotting to undermine American democratic institutions and that Catholics were subservient to a "foreign potentate." The American Protective Association propagated these ideas throughout the Midwest, especially in rural areas, and claimed that half a million members had pledged never to vote for a Catholic, go on strike with a Catholic, or hire a Catholic when a non-Catholic was available.

Ida B. Wise Smith was also consumed by hatred, but a hatred directed against the liquor traffic rather than Roman Catholics. Smith, an ordained minister in the Disciples of Christ denomination, was a schoolteacher in Des Moines who went on to become a crusader for social reform—for women's suffrage, to improve the welfare of children, and to outlaw cigarettes and liquor. "I love God, my country, and little children," Smith declared once, summarizing her views. "I hate the liquor traffic and abhor all vice." Smith, together with other religious crusaders, such as the Reverend Claud N. McMillan of Sioux City, sought to eradicate vice from the state. In 1915, two years after Smith ascended to the presidency of the Iowa chapter of the Women's Christian Temperance Union, a state prohibition law went into effect. Some time later, however, Smith faced a more daunting challenge when she became national president of the WCTU in 1933, the year the Eighteenth Amendment was repealed.

The WPA Guide to 1930s Iowa, first published in 1938, estimated that one-half of all Iowans were church members. The contributors from the Federal Writers' Project also noted the critical role that religion played in Iowa society and culture. "From the time of the first settlements the church has furnished the meeting place for many of the social affairs of town and country," the *Guide* noted, "the box and pie suppers, the bazaars, the ladies' aid society meetings, the potluck suppers, and the church party or social." Churches were also recognized for their role in sustaining the arts. "In many communities the only outlet for musical expression is the church where choirs and orchestras are conducted," the *Guide* continued. "Many a talented farmer's daughter, or small-town girl, has first been heard at the organ or piano in the church."

When *Christian Century,* the mouthpiece for mainline Protestantism, designated two Iowa congregations among its twelve "great churches" in 1950, it was clear that religion—in this case mainline Protestantism—was a central and guiding force in at least two communities and, by extension, throughout most of the state. Appropriately, given Iowa's religious configuration, one congregation was Lutheran and the other Methodist. Washington Prairie Lutheran Church, a commanding presence from a hilltop outside of Decorah, played a major role in the community, from county politics and 4-H clubs to school curriculum and soil conservation. In 1950 students and faculty from Iowa State College (now University) queued along Lincoln Way in Ames, waiting for a seat at the eleven o'clock service in Collegiate Methodist Church.

Just as the Protestant mainline has fallen on hard times nationwide, so too the influence of Methodists and Lutherans in Iowa has waned somewhat in recent years. Battered by demographics, the aging congregation at Washington Prairie Lutheran now struggles to survive and no longer dominates social and political affairs in the community. There are no lines outside of Collegiate United Methodist Church on Sunday morning. Neither congregation would be considered a "great church" at the sesquicentennial.

Where have the religious energies gone? In an odd way, the popular Iowa politician Harold Hughes epitomizes the changes in Iowa's religious configuration over the last few decades. Hughes was a truck driver and alcoholic from Ida Grove, who found religion in the form of Methodism, mended his ways, and became both a politician and a Methodist lay preacher. Elected governor three times as a Democrat, Hughes won election to the U.S. Senate in 1968, briefly ran for president in 1972, but then retired from a secure Senate seat after one term because he wanted to devote his energies to an evangelical religious organization, Fellowship Foundation.

The Hughes analogy cannot be pushed too far, in part because his politics differ sharply from those of the Religious Right, but Hughes's movement from mainline Methodism toward a form of evangelicalism reflects larger shifts in the culture, both nationally and within Iowa. Church adherence within mainline denominations, including the Roman Catholic Church, has declined steadily since the mid-1960s in favor of evangelical churches, most of them located in the suburbs. In Des Moines, for instance, the rapid growth of First Assembly of God, First Federated Church, and Westchester Evangelical Free Church, which relocated from Highland Park to the northwest suburbs in 1970, underscores this reconfiguration of Protestantism away from the mainline toward evangelicalism.

The evangelicals of Iowa, like those across the nation, have not confined their activities to churches. White evangelicals, who for the most part were politically quiescent during the middle decades of the twentieth century, began to emerge from their cocoons in the middle of the 1970s. The presidential campaign of a Southern Baptist Sunday School teacher, Jimmy Carter, lured evangelicals out of the political wilderness, and Carter's success in the Iowa caucuses early in 1976 was due, at least in part, to the support he received from evangelical voters, many of them participating in the caucuses for the first time. Four years later, however, evangelicals had grown disillusioned with Carter, and, beginning with the Iowa caucuses, they looked to the Republican party for alternatives, settling finally on Ronald Reagan.

As evangelicals, together with conservative Catholics, began to mobilize politically, they contributed to the defeat of incumbent Democratic senators Dick Clark and John Culver in 1978 and 1980, respectively. As David Yepsen of the *Des Moines Register* has pointed out, evangelical activists in Iowa have made it virtually impossible for any Republican politician in the state to countermand their positions on major issues, especially their opposition to abortion and to the proposed Equal Rights Amendment to the U.S. Constitution.

The evangelical focus on issues relating to women was no happenstance. Many "traditional," stay-at-home women felt belittled by the women's movement, with its emphasis on professional aspirations over childrearing and its blurring of gender distinctions (at least in the early years of the movement). The rhetoric of evangelicalism, with its strict, unambiguous morality, resonated with many of these women who felt displaced by social and cultural changes. They were disturbed by what they regarded as a culture careening out of control in the mid-seventies, and they fastened on the Right's call for a return to "family values," including traditional gender roles and a celebration of the nineteenth-century cult of domesticity. These evangelical women began "lobbying from the kitchen table," in the words of one activist, expressing their sentiments about prayer and sex education in the schools, about gender issues, and about morality generally.

This reentry of evangelicals—especially women—into the political arena, moreover, signals the resumption of a long tradition of moral activism in Iowa history. Whereas mainline Protestants dominated the social-reform movements in Iowa around the turn of the century, that mantle has been assumed by evangelicals, particularly evangelical women. Evangelical activists such as Maxine Sieleman, head of the Iowa chapter of Concerned Women for America and a member of First Federated Church, can be seen as latter-day descendants of Ida B. Wise Smith, head of the WCTU. "Women will change the country," Sieleman told me in 1988. "Women are the real key for turning this country around."

Although evangelicals mobilized to defeat a 1992 ballot initiative guaranteeing equal rights to women, the height of evangelical political influence in Iowa politics came in January 1988 during the Iowa caucuses. As caucus night approached, Republican presidential hopefuls—especially Dole, Kemp, and Robertson—worked themselves into a frenzy chasing the evangelical vote. They and their surrogates visited evangelical churches, sought to curry the favor of antiabortion activists and leaders of Concerned Women for America, and trekked out to KWKY, the tiny but influential evangelical radio station situated amid the cornfields south of Norwalk. Evangelical political fervor in Iowa has ebbed somewhat since 1988, in part because of the bruising battles between Kemp and Robertson loyalists and in part because of greater mobilization on the Left, drawing on the state's long tradition of progressivism. Evangelicals, however, much to the consternation of longtime "country-club" Republicans, have taken control of the party.

What accounts for this reversal? Why have evangelicals seized the initiative in Iowa religion, culture, and politics from mainline Protestant groups? Protestantism in the nineteenth century flourished in Iowa (and elsewhere) precisely because of its energy and because it offered a critique of—and an alternative to—the prevailing social order, whether it was the lawlessness on the frontier, the drunkenness in the cities, or the calcification of social, political, and religious institutions. But as Iowa's sesquicentennial approaches, mainline Protestantism itself has become calcified, part of the establishment that cries out for reformation (as scores of Iowa officeholders have learned over the decades, Iowans are little impressed with seniority). Evangelicals have succeeded over the last several decades because they have brought energy, conviction, and devotion to the task of reforming society according to what they interpret as the norms of godliness, just as the

Methodists, Baptists, and Presbyterians had done a century earlier.

One of the great ironies of my life is that my office window at Columbia University looks directly across the street into the Interchurch Center, a hulking, nondescript building constructed in the 1950s to provide offices for the major Protestant denominations in the United States. This International-style structure, known almost universally as the "God Box" or the "Protestant Kremlin," has come to symbolize for me the indifference and insularity of mainline Protestantism in the latter half of the twentieth century. Even in a neighborhood of derivative and largely undistinguished architecture, the God Box stands out as the worst of a bad lot. President Dwight Eisenhower laid the cornerstone on October 12, 1958, an event that symbolized the fusion of mainline Protestantism with American middle-class values.

In recent years, however, mainline denominations have left the God Box—the Presbyterians to Louisville, the Congregationalists to Cleveland, the Lutherans to Chicago, the Methodist mission board to a location as yet undisclosed—in an attempt to reestablish contact with the grassroots and thereby to stanch the loss of members and income. It's too early to tell whether that strategy will succeed, but the fact remains that my office window in Manhattan looks across the street into a building now largely bereft of denominational headquarters. Mainline Protestantism, through some perverse combination of indifference, complacency, and a desire to affirm rather than to challenge the entrenched power structure, has lost its prophetic edge. The religious energies—in Iowa and across the nation—are being exercised at the margins of religious life. And at the God Box, that icon of the Protestant establishment outside my office window, nobody's home.

That's a delicious irony for someone who sweated through his father's invocation at Veterans' Auditorium more than twenty years ago.

FAMILY REUNION

An Album of Photographs

How was your day at the office, dear? Lord Acton at the House of Lords.

Dr. Randall Balmer, Professor of Religion, Barnard College, Columbia University.

Steve Berntson. A nap after lunch is always a good idea.

(Left) *Lizzie Block, the scourge of bad guys in Storm Lake.*
(Above) *Erin Block. Directing the world is a rotten job, but someone's got to do it.*

Not a Bronco nor a Mustang nor a Ram. Michael Carey drives a dalmation. Photo by Owen Carey.

John Chrystal, always a little more comfortable left of center.

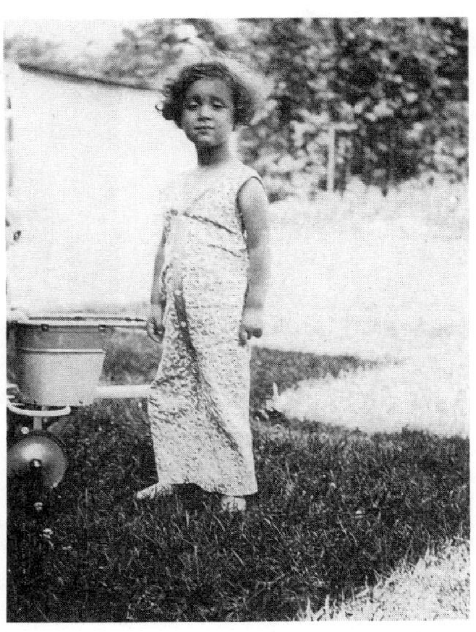

Barbara Higdon. Can world peace co-exist with just a touch of ornery?

The Fink family at Nathaniel's bar mitzvah (from left), *Benjamin, Steven, Nathaniel, Sally, and Miriam.*

Mohamad Khan (center) *shares a meal with two friends on the first day after the Muslim fast of Ramadan.* Photo by Jeffrey Z. Carney, courtesy of the Des Moines Register.

The Mata family at home: Bob, Kathleen, Nathan, and Belén.

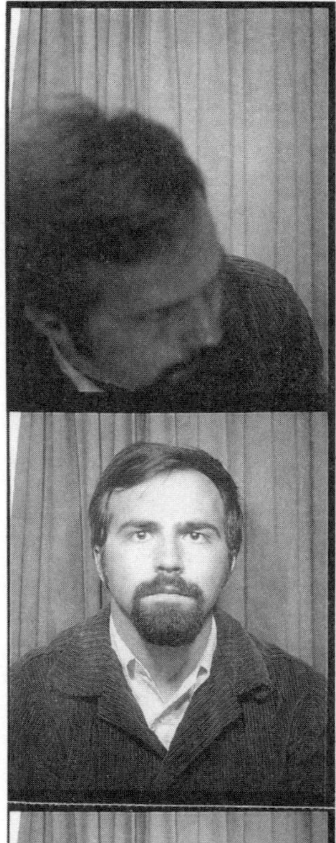

Tom Morain. If you look like your student ID, you're probably too sick to be in class.

Robert Morris in focus.

Connie Mutel and fresh rhubarb—two wonderful reasons to live in Iowa.

Dave Ostendorf (right) *offers support to a friend.* Photo by Bill Gillette.

Ken Pins, Dyersville newshound on the prowl.

Mary Swander. Faculty parking at Iowa State is always tight.

Dave Yepsen displays an early interest in journalism.

"Will Write for Food"
Authors' supper at Living History Farms, May 28, 1995

ROW 1 (left to right): *Dave Yepsen, Tom Morain, Mary Swander, Michael Carey;* ROW 2: *Liz Block, Vivian Morris, Connie Mutel, Steve Berntson;* ROW 3: *Robert Morris, Richard, Lord Acton, Randy Balmer, Bob Mata.*

IN 1979, Kenneth Pins returned to his hometown with a bachelor's degree in history and journalism to become news editor of the *Dyersville Commercial*. He describes his introduction to the profession this way: "I was photographer, reporter, laid out the front page, wrote editorials and was in charge of the company float for the St. Patrick's Day parade. Community journalism is much closer to the bone. The people who've known you since you were three don't care much for First Amendment explanations when you've written something that really ticks them off." From Dyersville, he moved to the *Des Moines Register* as bureau chief first in Dubuque and then in Ames (in both, the "bureau" was a one-man operation). In 1986, he began working in the *Register*'s Des Moines office covering political topics and writing the Iowa Poll. Since 1990, he has shifted to the newspaper's Washington bureau where, he notes, "I am not the only person in the bureau." Pins covers politics and economics and pokes around statistics in the census to discover things about us we never knew before.

IN THE STEEPLE'S SHADOW: THE PARISH TOWN IN A SECULAR WORLD

Kenneth Pins

IN THE MORNINGS before school we sat in the basilica for an hour, as the Mass made its leisurely way in Latin. The girls wore white lacy things on their heads, the names of which I've forgotten and which the church long ago ceased requiring. My mind would wander, and I remember staring at the colored light slanting through stained glass windows, trying to guess at the meaning of the German words inscribed there. It has been thirty years or more since then, and still I can't comprehend what the people who came before me were saying. Though a generation has passed and I've gained a different perspective, I can barely trust myself to describe how we were different from the Protestantism that dominated Iowa or from the Catholics who preceded us.

The first wave of German Catholic farmers to Dubuque County came fleeing Germany's mid-nineteenth-century upheaval, ignorant of English, with little wealth, knowing only that the church was helping to establish parishes west of the Mississippi River that were not unlike what they'd left. When asked the country to which they were claiming allegiance, my own immigrant ancestors arriving at New Orleans in 1852 responded "St. Louis," according to passenger records now on microfiche in the National Archives. They came up the river to Dubuque and settled on a farm as part of the St. Boniface parish at New Vienna.

It is, I think, hard to exaggerate the degree to which they placed their fate in the hands of the church, the mixture of dependence and devotion they must have felt. It is obvious in the architecture. Throughout northeast Iowa, parish towns are built around impressive churches, some of them native stone, others red brick, all of them, even those in unincorporated towns, distinguished by soaring steeples and stained glass that seem out of proportion with their humble surroundings. The public buildings are functional but unimpressive, most of them frame structures lost amid the storefronts. These towns were not centers of commerce first, nor government, but parishes around which commerce and local government evolved. While Dyersville was different—it did not begin as a parish but as an English settlement that was later overwhelmed by German Catholics—the basilica there is a remarkable edifice for a community of its size, a physical expression of the influence of a church that said that one's labors were not for personal gain but for something larger than oneself.

The basilica was the third church building, each one successively more grand. The final, Gothic church, dedicated in 1889, was built largely with local labor, and several farms were mortgaged to pay for its construction. Interior details were added later as money allowed. Two ornately carved butternut side altars were added in 1897, the carved butternut canopy over the main altar in 1899, frescoes in 1905, and the organ in 1913. It was no small feat. When the church was dedicated in 1889, six thousand people came from across Iowa to be there, which is something I can hardly imagine now.

What I could imagine, even as a young child, was how small and insignificant the individual felt sitting in that cavernous church (it seats twelve hundred), with the vaulted ceilings rising sixty feet overhead. This physical symbol implied several things. There was a burden of responsibility to sustain the community, especially its religious institutions, and opting out was not really a choice. I doubt that the first generation felt this as a burden to be shouldered.

The centralized focus also created a community in the true sense of the word. People were obligated to help those in danger of failing because of illness or some other reason—except sloth—and so ready to criticize those who presumed to rise above. Too much free enterprise was seen as gouging, because in a small community those who are rich (especially merchants) obviously are made that way at the expense of their neighbors. Ostentatious displays of wealth were not only in bad taste, they were bad business.

This is, of course, terribly oversimplified, but I think it's generally true. The earliest settlers established something there by a strong act of collective will that is hard to imagine today.

* * * *

It was 1960 by the time I was aware of my surroundings, and some of the superficial manifestations of that early German Catholic enclave were giving way to the homogenized global village being created by travel, television, and other marvels of a modern age.

The language was the first to go, as German Americans separated their identity from a nation that started two world wars and committed unspeakable atrocities in this century. I knew no one in my hometown who spoke German fluently, although German expressions and its peculiar syntax occasionally surfaced. Latin was on its way out, too. Our first missals prepared us for the change, with Latin on the left page and English on the right. Fasting eight hours before Communion soon was lifted, which meant that breakfast no longer had to be brought from home to be eaten after Mass at school desks.

But other things remained. There were no public grade schools or high schools in Dyersville or in the neighboring parish towns of New Vienna, Luxemburg, Petersburg, and Worthington, which must have had five thousand people or more collectively in and around them. It didn't strike me as unusual at the time, because I barely knew anyone who was not Catholic. The few non-Catholics I did know were enrolled at the Catholic school to be part of the mainstream. Most of the descendants of the English settlers were gone by this time, or had converted, and while there had been three Protestant churches in town in the nineteenth century, there was none in the 1950s and 1960s.

This had a peculiar effect. We were not self-consciously Catholic, because there was no one else around to make us self-conscious about it. The habits of Catholicism were part of everyday life. Everyone I knew ate fish on Fridays. The newspaper of the archdiocese published a list of movies that were deemed acceptable, and the local movie theater rarely strayed from it. There was no external challenge requiring us actively to defend our Catholicism.

The kinds of collective acts of will that built the basilica were now channeled into community projects, which became almost by definition an extension of the church. A painted thermometer fifteen feet tall in the business district marked in dollars rather than Fahrenheit the progress toward breaking ground for a local hospital. The leaders of the effort raised more than $900,000 in donations in two years and sold bonds for the remaining $700,000, and the imprimatur of the church was sought at every step. When it came time to break ground for the building, the pastor was there in the picture along with the leaders of the fund-raising. The hospital opened in 1969. Just three years earlier, the new Catholic high school, bringing together students from the parishes in Petersburg, New Vienna, Worthington, Earlville, and Dyersville, was opened after a long fund-raising struggle. Each parish was assessed a share of the school's support, not unlike a taxing body. No one could accuse people of retreating to their selfish interests.

In Dyersville, the St. Francis Xavier annual report helped them. It was one of the great levelers in the town. The contributions of every parishioner were published in the report and thus on display to everyone else. On the Sunday it was published, each person's contributions could be measured against the reader's notions (usually accurate) of what that person was capable of contributing. It was and still is a remarkably coercive document.

Also, in the 1950s and 1960s the state was rationalizing public education, pulling scattered rural schools together into organized school districts supported both by property taxes and eventually by income taxes paid to the state. Public schools got a foothold not in Dyersville itself but close by, and the parish was engulfed into the Western Dubuque school district, the largest in Iowa, covering five hundred square miles, with an enormous bus fleet to extract scattered public school students from that Catholic territory. Western Dubuque High School at Epworth, eleven miles east of Dyersville, was opened in the 1960s. A large public elementary school was built in Farley, just five miles east, in the 1970s, if my memory is correct.

The challenge to the old institutions became the subtle, incremental effects of time and growing material well-being that focused the mind on secular and personal matters. Individuals were taking more control over their lives. Families were smaller. Separation from the grind of labor-intensive farming created fewer but more prosperous farmers. Advances in medicine lifted the almost constant dread that scarlet fever or some other malady would carry off a whole family.

Religion still had a central place, of course, but people had more choices. The church was clear about the educational choices it wanted parents to make, but this was an era when people were asking more questions, and even the authority of the church was not as strong as it had been. Fewer young people were joining the priesthood or entering the convent. It is easier to run a parochial school when the faculty has taken an oath of poverty, but as the supply of nuns, priests, and Christian brothers dwindled, lay teachers—religious civilians—had to be hired, driving up salaries and related costs.

Divisions were forming among Catholics over their level of commitment. As tuitions rose, many parents opted for public schools, and the church's ability to dissuade them appears to have diminished. Busing and shared-time instruction agreements were worked out in the 1970s, shifting some of the costs of educating parochial students onto the public tax system. By 1974, there was a financial crunch, and a vote was taken to close parochial Beckman High School, which had opened just eight years earlier. The vote passed, but was then reversed after yet another massive fund-raising drive was launched—the third in a decade—this one to establish an endowment.

* * * *

What if this ongoing battle to preserve the institutions of the church, this separateness in education and in other ways, is lost? How would the community be changed?

A friend of mine—an Irish Catholic from Omaha—and I have a running argument about what I call ethnic and cultural determinism. He believes we are shaped by where we're from to a large degree and that we are helpless to change it. I argue that we have free will and that we become who we choose to become. If we adopt the cultural habits we learned when young, it's because we don't choose something else. He tells me I betray more of where I'm from than I admit to, or perhaps am even aware of.

In Dubuque County, five out of six people who claim a religion are Catholics, and in the western part of the county where I'm from, I'm sure it's more like nine of ten. There are many people I admire there. My family of course, but there are others who suggest themselves to my memory but who have no direct connection to me. They were the people who were not just going through the motions of Catholicism, but who appeared to have made an affirmative commitment to it and were quietly acting out that faith.

They were there when we served 6:30 Mass in the summer, when the town was not yet stirring. Bill Klosterman, the blind piano tuner, sat up front to the left near George Reicher, the parish groundskeeper. A dozen or so nuns occupied the front pews. A few widows and elderly couples were sprinkled about the front one-third of church. These were the truly committed, and the feeble echo of their voices singing in the immense, mostly empty church had a spiritual quality, I think now.

There were many others, however, whose religious expression was merely habit. The group consciousness didn't encourage individuals to make an exploration of religion. Passive acceptance was good enough to avoid being talked about in the hushed tones that were the fate of the fallen away.

College brought out of me a fierce rejection. A friend died. A philosophy course asked questions I had never before considered. The history and theology courses of parochial schools had not lingered on the crimes of the Medicis or the excesses that had motivated Martin Luther. Once eighteen years of religious assumptions were undermined, the pendulum swung hard in the opposite direction, and I looked too harshly on where I was from. I felt duped. Normal human weakness became evidence of hypocrisy. The all-or-nothing mind of young adulthood concluded that if this faith had elements it could no longer reconcile, the entire faith had to go.

Now things are less certain once again. Having acquired the freedom to make choices about religion, one that helps build and sustain a community has much to recommend it. On the East Coast, where I now live, there is little pretense of community, and individual expression and acquisition of wealth seem to be what pass for a theology. I was reminded of the differences recently on a visit home, when a new factory opened and a foreman was hired—someone obviously qualified but who already had a good pension from one of the big factories in Dubuque. "You would think they could have given that job to somebody who needed it," it was said. Jobs are for those who need them. Work provides both the ability to take care of one's family and the means to make a contribution to the community. These are the old values coming out. The sharp edges of capitalism are rounded off by the assumption that the economy is to pull everyone along, not widen the gap between success and the failure.

And yet a standard feature of every visit home now is the tour of the new houses that are filling subdivisions on the fringes of town. Some of them are truly breathtaking—not in their beauty but in their ostentation. The convent is now empty, a shocking development in one generation and tangible evidence of the decline in religious conviction. This continues to strain religious institutions that were built with so much personal sacrifice over so many generations.

The public schools are now filled beyond capacity, forcing students into drafty auxiliary classrooms, prefabricated buildings set upon blocks in the parking lot that were never intended to be anything more than temporary when they were built more than a decade ago. For now there is a stalemate. Bond issues to pay for permanent expansions of the public schools consistently fail. Those still stretching themselves to support the parochial schools see this, probably correctly, as a zero-sum battle that, if it passes, will only siphon off more students from the parochial schools. Some in the older generation believe the younger people aren't supporting the church and its institutions as they should. There is evidence all around: in the annual report, in the construction of new houses, in the exodus of Catholic kids to the public schools.

So where does this leave things?

I would not wish for a return to what came before. There is more than one way, I would insist, to look upon the world, and freedom of expression is more than just something to be celebrated on the Fourth of July.

And yet, what the secular, ambition-driven world has created—sharper economic divisions, an almost nihilistic popular culture—seems a poor use of the freedom it has obtained. In a way, the peril in which the old values find themselves makes the original commitment to them that much more admirable; they do not suffer by comparison to what has come after them. Ironically, there is now a popular rejection of government intrusion and popular culture, both of which helped pry people away from the influence of the church.

It isn't so much that the people who left the inscriptions on stained glass are calling us back to their lives. Perhaps they were left there to remind us that a life without commitment to something greater than ourselves isn't progress.

ROBERT MATA was born into a Latino family in a small farming community in the arid northeast corner of Colorado. He earned three degrees in education from the University of Colorado at Boulder, culminating in an educational specialist degree in curriculum, administration, and supervision. Pursuing a lifelong commitment to education, Mata has served as a teacher, director of federal education programs, staff development consultant, and academic dean for a private career college. The Matas moved to Mount Vernon, Iowa, in 1988 and then to Conrad when Mata accepted his current job as principal of Anson Elementary School in Marshalltown. He currently serves on the Iowa Commission on Latino Affairs.

Mata is a music collector and disc jockey *aficionado* (that's Spanish, of course, for a devoted enthusiast of something). And, in case you have some thing he could use, he also collects postcards of old Iowa schoolhouses.

OF SUNSETS AND TOMORROWS: A LATINO PERSPECTIVE OF LIVING IN IOWA

Robert Mata

THE SUN IS EASING its way behind the rolling hills of soybeans and corn. As evening approaches, cloud-wisps hover above the horizon. Shimmering strands of rose and purple-blue stretch out in all directions like fingers from a giant, outstretched hand. Very soon, thousands of lightning bugs will rise from the field and perform their mating dance rituals, giving no thought to the delightful show they will provide me as I watch in amazement from my deck. It is another beautiful Iowa summer evening.

It has been six years since our family moved to Iowa from Colorado. We have been residents of Conrad in Grundy County for several months, having moved here from Mount Vernon. Our home sits on the western edge of town. The backyard flows into a soybean field planted to take advantage of the natural contours of the land. I marvel at the beauty of this view, which has become the backdrop for family meals. This beauty is also present along the county roads I travel to and from work. The peace and serenity of the land could easily be taken for granted. I cannot fathom ever tiring of this landscape that I now call home.

I do not believe that the view I see with my brown Latino

eyes is very different from the view of those who live near me or with whom I work. I suppose I could be accused of indulging in the natural splendor of the area, being a fairly recent arrival to this state. However, it didn't take long for me to understand and embrace the rhythm of life I found in this wonderful environment. Members of my family, as well as many friends who still live in Colorado, wonder just exactly how long this "living in Iowa business" is going to last. After all, wasn't I the one who emphatically stated time and time again that I would *never* move to the Midwest? And, if in some mad moment I *did* make such a crazy idea become reality, it would not be to Iowa. Good grief, there aren't any large cities! What would you *do*? Six years later and living in a community of less than one thousand people, I find myself doing what my wife and I came to Iowa to do: raise our children, find a better balance between our professional careers and our personal family goals, and be more at heart's ease with ourselves.

I come from a family of eight children—five sisters and three brothers—raised on the plains of eastern Colorado. Until the age of fifteen, I lived on a farm. My father was a "hired hand" on the three farms I remember growing up on, and he remained as a helper even when we moved into town. I imagine he was content with his work, because he farmed up until the day he died. I recall my mother working outside of the home when I was in my early teens. A strong work ethic was instilled upon us at an early age. Everyone was expected to contribute to the well-being of the family. We had our chores, and we worked the fields in the summer, thinning and cleaning sugar beet fields for the man my father worked for as well as for other farmers in the area. When I was fifteen, we moved into town and I took a job with a supermarket and helped in the produce department.

Our religious upbringing was an interesting mix of doctrines. Some neighbors down the road thought it would be in our best interests to go to church with them on Sunday mornings. This is how we became Presbyterians—at least by day. By night, our parents "kept us in the fold" by taking us to their church, a fundamentalist group where we spoke only Spanish.

Needless to say, this was an interesting, if somewhat precarious, faith continuum.

Our parents deeply understood that the only way their children would have a better life was through education. I may have taken this too literally, as I tried to get on the school bus at the age of three, so determined was I to go to school. I did, however, promptly start first grade at the age of six and was faced with an immediate reality: I could not understand what the teacher or students were saying! It had not occurred to me that I would be attending a school where I could not communicate in *Spanish* to my peers, nor to the adults in charge. I'm sure my classmates and teachers were equally frustrated, yet we seemed to make the best of the situation.

I recall being seated next to a set of deep-red books with beautiful gold lettering. I don't exactly know how or when I made the connection between letters and sounds that year, but I do know the first word I learned to spell: e-n-c-y-c-l-o-p-e-d-i-a. With that breakthrough, I truly became a *public* school student, and the *private* language of our home, Spanish, quickly assumed secondary language status. Just how important this was to become was made clear in my second grade classroom when, on a sunny, early fall morning, I was working on a reading worksheet and "lapsed" into Spanish as I tried to talk myself through the paper. Out of nowhere, a shadow covered my desk. I looked up just at the moment a ruler was making its way toward my hands. There was a whooshing sound and then—*whack!*—across the fingers of my right hand. "Don't you *ever* use that language in this classroom again!" said the teacher. Two things became clear to me that day: in this world of good and bad, a line had definitely been drawn between speaking English and speaking Spanish. Also, the mind can be quickly programmed to accommodate aversions. To this day, I gingerly handle wooden rulers with metal edges.

I am thankful that much is changing in education with regard to second languages. The bilingual and English as a Second Language (ESL) programs established in the 1970s have never been free of controversy (what in education has been?), but these programs have at least created for students and parents a better sense of *belonging* and *participation* in the educational process. My parents never felt comfortable attending school functions because they had a difficult time speaking English, and no one was present (teacher, administrator) to assist them. So we, their children, became their "voices" when it came to school matters. This happens today when a child is asked to serve as an "interpreter" for his or her parent. Culturally, this changes the parent-child relationship, putting that relationship in a precarious balance. While school personnel may view this innocently as a means for helping communicate information, the dynamic of the parent-child role assumes a more "equal" status and can have far-reaching effects. Today, as a principal, I make sure that I am addressing the parent. I am thankful that I have the ability to speak Spanish so that the parent-child relationship is kept secure.

I have also observed that attendance at our open houses, school carnivals, and parent-teacher conferences has become more inclusive, with more Latino families present. I've asked a number of Latino parents about my observations, and they all have said that they feel better about attending because someone is there who relates to their struggle to participate in the lives of their children. Thus, my own experiences with my parents have allowed me to be more cognizant of the need to reach out to those who may feel disenfranchised with the schools simply because they do not feel they can communicate in ways that are comfortable for them.

The realization that education should be my vocation came to me when I was in fifth grade and was further enhanced by my seventh grade social studies teacher, a man whose teaching style and devotion to his students astounded me. I kept my dream alive through the rest of my secondary school years but almost got sidetracked my senior year when a counselor tried to talk me out of attending the state teachers' college. She suggested to me that someone of my *background* would do far better attending a vocational-technical training school. But I was very good academically, hardly ever missed school, was involved in a number of clubs, was currently the senior class president, played in the school band,

and worked part time. Throughout my school years I had dealt with misperceptions about my abilities because I was Latino. I *knew* what the counselor was referring to because of my own experiences: she felt that schools weren't ready for Latino men as teachers. I excused myself and never returned to the counselor's office.

Still, I persisted. The Spanish word for this persistence is *aguantar*: to sustain, to bear, to endure, to abide, to maintain. Having been raised in this spirit, I realized that I had to go on with my dreams and the dreams my parents had for their children. With the help of student loans, I completed my bachelor's degree at the University of Colorado and graduated with honors. Since that time, I have completed my master's and my educational specialist degrees. I expect to complete my doctorate in the next few years. I've taught on an Indian reservation, tutored college freshmen in mathematics, taught in summer migrant programs, administered federal education programs, worked as a staff development consultant, served as an academic dean for a private career college, served on a local school board, and now serve as a building principal. Education is my life. These experiences permit me to talk with students and parents alike about the importance of never giving up on your dreams *no matter what others might think of you.* This spirit is in every conversation I have with the students I work with, and it permeates my life's work with the various community groups of which I am a part. You *endure* because you *must.* In spite of any ignorance, prejudice, insensitive statements, and stares, you simply must keep looking ahead to realize the full potential of your hopes and dreams.

Perhaps my story is not altogether different from another person's. That's good. All of us face personal challenges; hopes and dreams abound. Do I think my life has been radically different because I am Latino? I sincerely believe that my life's composition, as a whole, has and continues to be an accumulation of many experiences—positive and negative—that serve to define who I have become. Over the years, I have taken a holistic, encompassing approach to my life that *includes* my cultural heritage. I have never had the viewpoint that everything I do, have, and am to become stems from being Latino. My life is enriched as a result of being able to pick and choose from the many philosophies, values, and beliefs available from the mosaic of people who live in the United States. It is unfortunate that Latinos are all classified under one visually identifiable cultural group. It is difficult for some people to accept the fact that there are many individual differences among Latinos. The degree of acculturation to the dominant group, maintenance of cultural traditions and customs, as well as how individuals view their level of acceptance within the dominant group all play into the diversity that exists among Latinos.

It is interesting to engage in conversations about the influence of Latinos in Iowa and hear that the Latino presence is considered a recent phenomenon in the state. A visit to the state's libraries and archives quickly dispels this thinking. What is now Iowa was once part of the Spanish land grants of upper Louisiana. Spain owned the region from 1770 through 1803, and there is well-documented evidence of trading among Spaniards, French, and Indian tribes. The Iowa Census of 1856 reported the settling of a Mexican immigrant in Lyons County in northwest Iowa.

Latinos have continued to move into this state and now comprise 1.2 percent of its population, according to the 1990 Iowa Census. The census uses the term *Hispanic* to mean people who classify themselves into one of the specific Hispanic origin groups listed on the census questionnaire, which include Mexican, Puerto Rican, Cuban, other Hispanic Dominican (Dominican Republic), Central American (including Costa Rican, Guatemalan, Honduran, Nicaraguan, Panamanian, and Salvadoran), and South American (including Argentinean, Chilean, Colombian, Ecuadorian, Peruvian, and Venezuelan). The report also indicates a "residual" category of "All Other Hispanic Origin" that includes people who reported any Hispanic origin group but were not tabulated under any of the above-mentioned groups. Because of the diversity of this group of people, there is no consensus on an "official" name (i.e., Hispanic, Latino, etc.). Although the terms are essentially synonymous, Hispanic tends to take into account European origins, while Latino focuses on Latin American roots.

The 1990 census reports 32,647 Latinos in Iowa. Of these, 75 percent list family origins in Mexico. Puerto Ricans and Cubans are the next two largest Latino nationalities from the diverse list mentioned above. Among Iowa Latinos, 60 percent are native-born Iowans; the remaining 40 percent have migrated from another state or from abroad. Although 60 percent live in metropolitan areas of the state, many Iowa Latinos live in small towns or rural areas. Communities with significant percentages of Latinos include West Liberty, Columbus Junction, Muscatine, Buffalo, Fort Madison, Davenport, and Sioux City.

Iowa Latinos as a group tend to be young and family oriented. The census indicates that the median age for all Latinos is 22.0 years. The number of people per household is 3.3, and the number of people per family is 3.2. For whites, the median age is 34.5 years, and the number of people per household is 2.5, with 3.0 people per family. For African Americans, the median age is 24.6 years, the number of people per household is 2.6, and there are 3.2 people per family.

Language remains a significant factor distinguishing Latinos. More than 40 percent of Iowa Latinos speak a language at home other than English. For whites, 3 percent speak a language at home other than English, and for African Americans, 6 percent.

Educationally, close to 65 percent of Latinos over the age of 25 are high school graduates, and almost 14 percent possess at least a bachelor's degree. There are 384 Latino teachers, school librarians, and school counselors in Iowa; 40 percent are elementary and secondary school teachers.

Approximately 73 percent of Iowa Latinos 16 years and older are in the labor force. The areas of employment with the largest number of Latinos include manufacturing, retail trade, professional and related services, and business and repair services.

A report printed in 1993 by the Guadalupe Center, Inc., of Kansas City, Missouri, titled *Hispanics in the Midwest: A*

Growing Presence, provides further insights into the Latino experience in the Midwest (a region identified in the report as the states of North and South Dakota, Nebraska, Kansas, Minnesota, Iowa, Missouri, Wisconsin, Illinois, Michigan, Indiana, and Ohio). For example, most Latinos came to the Midwest for economic opportunities, not because of political and social oppression. Contrary to public perception, Midwestern Latinos predominantly speak English, and many are bilingual. Seven in ten (70.6 percent) Midwestern Latino families are married-couple families, which compares with 44.5 percent for African Americans and 83.9 percent for whites. Only one of five (20.2 percent) Midwestern Latino families is headed by a single female. For African Americans, it is almost one in two (48.1 percent), and for whites, one in eight (12.1 percent).

From a national perspective, a larger percentage of Midwestern Latinos are college graduates (10.1 percent Midwest versus 9.2 percent nationally), and more Latino women (59.9 percent) are in the work force than African American (57.1 percent) or white (57.3 percent) women. Similar to their national Latino counterparts, Midwestern Latinos continue to experience low levels of educational attainment, high participation in the work force, and high poverty rates. Because of their small numbers compared with the overall population, Midwestern Latinos do not comprise a majority or even a clear plurality in any metropolitan area, major city, or county and have historically been underrepresented in the political and policy-making processes at all levels of government compared with Latinos in other parts of the country (John Fierro, Robert Aponte, Marcelo Siles, *Hispanics in the Midwest: A Growing Presence* [GCI Policy Analysis Center, 1993], pp. I-3, 13–18).

Both of the documents mentioned above indicate that the Latino population is young, diverse, and rapidly growing. Another report, *Population Projections of the United States: by Age, Sex, Race, and Hispanic Origin: 1993 to 2050,* predicts that nationally, the race/ethnic group adding the largest number of people to the population in the United States will be the Hispanic-origin population. This report does not address the population of the country by regions; however, it would appear certain that the number of Latinos in Iowa will continue to grow at a faster rate than has been experienced over the previous decade.

As part of my efforts to gather information about Latinos in Iowa, I interviewed and surveyed several individuals to determine what being an Iowan and living in the state means to us today. This very informal process was an attempt to discern whether there are common threads among the diverse Latinos in Iowa. I selected three individuals to provide the reader with a sample of their views.

* * * *

Mary's parents came to Iowa (and Minnesota) from Oklahoma. They were migrant workers who settled in the Des Moines area in the mid-1930s. Four generations of her family now live in Iowa. Family members have worked as migrant workers, truck drivers, service station attendants, and restaurant and clerical workers. Participation in the Catholic Church and community involvement are continuing family traditions. Mary came to Iowa at the age of five and has grown up within the Anglo and Latino communities. Her family has maintained its ethnic identity, with members involved in many aspects of Latino art, poetry, music, and literature. Mary feels strongly that if Latinos are to survive as a cohesive group, our children and grandchildren must have a knowledge of and appreciation for the traditions that surround them. This includes respecting elders, participating in fiestas, eating traditional foods, and listening to traditional music. She also feels strongly that the Spanish language is the most important common thread for Latinos in the state and that bilingual people are essential links for Latino participation in society.

* * * *

Thom was born and raised in California. His grandparents on both sides were from Mexico but immigrated to California and New Mexico after the turn of the century. Thom, the only person of any generation in his family to have lived in Iowa, came here seven years ago and is employed by the State of Iowa. Family traditions that he maintains include large Christmas celebrations, Mexican dinners shared with friends and, when possible, family, and "connecting" through hugs and kisses. When he moved to Iowa, he did not observe any ways that people treated him differently because of his ethnicity. He expects people to respect him for his abilities, accomplishments, and personality, not for or despite his ethnicity. His Latino heritage is valuable to him, but he is more than a Latino: he is a contributing member of American society, which is a medley of ethnicities. He maintains cultural ties through his appreciation of Latino authors, traditional music, and primitive Mexican art and crafts. He and his siblings were encouraged to be proud of their past and to practice a strong work ethic. They were trained to keep their Mexican traditions and values while acclimating to the English-speaking world. Thom mostly operates in this English-speaking world, except for when he plays his Mexican music, gets into Christmas, or cooks Mexican-style dinners for friends and family. He believes that our heritage and culture are the common threads among Latinos. Thom loves living in Iowa. The people are warm, friendly, helpful, honest, and trusting. His family's values are very similar to those of the Anglo Iowan: faith, family, and hard work.

The biggest challenge that Thom feels Latinos face is increasing prejudice, especially against Latinos with little or no education. He feels that we need to continue to impress upon Latino parents that education is the most important gift they can give their children.

Thom also expects that as more Iowans experience Latino culture, values, and traditions, they will accept and welcome this diversity. At the same time, Latinos need to learn to appreciate and accept the culture, values, and traditions of the many other ethnic groups that have lived in Iowa over the years.

* * * *

Sylvia has lived in Iowa for almost two years and is presently employed as an administrator for the State of Iowa. Family traditions that continue to be present in her life include language, foods, music, care for the elderly, Mexican holiday practices, and parental ties. Her ties to the Catholic Church remain strong, but there are variations among family members regarding adherence to church practices. The changes she observed coming to Iowa revolve around separation from family and a sense of loss but also personal and professional growth. She has found living in Iowa to be similar to her upbringing in her native Texas. Family get-togethers are cause for decorating the home, playing guitars and singing, and reading poetry.

Sylvia feels that she lives a bicultural, bilingual life. She operates comfortably in both Latino and Anglo worlds, but sometimes she feels as if she has two lives. She says that she even speaks differently in each life. She does not believe that the Spanish language is the common thread for Latinos in Iowa. Sylvia lives in Iowa because her work is here, but she would like to bring her family to Iowa because it is safer and is a better place for raising children.

Sylvia feels that Latinos face the challenge of further segmentation within the group—especially from those who are often illiterate and may also be here illegally. This is causing rifts within the Latino population, and as the state becomes more diversified, we will see not only more hate crimes but also legal attempts to keep certain people disenfranchised. She is concerned that if we do not continue in our efforts to find a "balance" among those who live in this state, we will see more poverty, discontent, crime, and violence. This could lead to ethnic minorities becoming scapegoats for many of these problems.

* * * *

As the three Latino portraits above help show, the Latino population in Iowa, like other ethnic minorities, has its "newcomers" and its generational families. Within the Latino population, there is strong church participation and community involvement. There is a continuation of Latino music, art, and literature, which are important to the individual's cultural identity. There is knowledge of and appreciation for cultural traditions and histories. There is comfort in living within an identifiable bicultural and multicultural framework. There is diversity in the comprehension and use of Spanish. And, there is commonality, expressing itself through faith, family, and hard work.

All humans are, in the end, basically the same. Do we not prefer success to failure, praise and recognition to rejection and condemnation? It would be foolish for me to permit the reader to think it is possible to portray Latinos as being painted with the same brush. Likewise, it would be dangerous to interpret behavior from a single, culturally determined point of view. It is in these overgeneralizations that we risk misleading people into believing that knowledge of Latinos as a group is sufficient to understanding an individual Latino or his or her family. I would rather that the reader view each Latino as a unique human being, who may or may not exhibit certain attitudes, habits, and beliefs.

I would suggest that all of us have a responsibility to become more culturally literate and that our growth in understanding comes from sitting down with one another, one-on-one, so that we can learn about our values, beliefs, hopes, and dreams as *individuals* who have made conscious decisions to become who we are today.

As for me, I am enjoying spending time learning more about my state. It has been a sincere pleasure to meet people who share a common love for family, who enjoy a more relaxed pace of living, who have a deep commitment to their faith, and who, like myself, desire to succeed and work toward a better tomorrow. Let us not forget that it is the simplicity of a sunset that makes us glad we are home ... in Iowa.

IN THE 1960s, freshmen students at Graceland College had two ways to satisfy their English composition requirement. They could take eight hours in a two-semester sequence, or they could take Barbara Higdon's six-hour Honors Communication class in the fall semester. I chose the latter, and my life changed suddenly and dramatically. I know memory plays funny tricks, but it seems to me now that she required a seven- to ten-page paper about every forty-five minutes for the next four months. But I learned to write papers! Meanwhile, she was writing books and is the author of *Good News for Today* and *Committed to Peace*.

Before teaching at Graceland, Higdon was one of the first white instructors at the predominantly black Texas Southern University from 1957 to 1963, during the tensions of the early civil rights movement. After teaching at Graceland for twelve years, she was named Vice President for Academic Affairs at Park College near Kansas City. In 1984, she returned to Graceland as the first woman to serve as president, a post she held with distinction for almost eight years. During her administration, the college developed exchange programs with several Eastern European countries, a remarkable accomplishment because the region was still under communist domination. She is a six-year member of the executive committee of the St. Cyril and St. Methodius International Foundation (Bulgaria). She also served as chair of the Iowa Peace Institute and is currently director of the Peace Center for the Reorganized Church of Jesus Christ of Latter Day Saints. She resigned her presidency in 1991 to pursue her interests in peace work.

CAN WE IMAGINE A WORLD FULL OF PEACE? TRANSFORMATIVE VISION IN THE WORLD AND IOWA

Barbara Higdon

THAT GRINDING SOUND you have been hearing lately may very well be the shifting of some familiar paradigms. Thomas Kuhn defines a paradigm as an accepted model or pattern from which springs a particular coherent tradition. In his book *The Structure of Scientific Revolutions,* he cited some major scientific paradigm shifts: evolution, the germ theory of disease, relativity, the uncertainty principle (University of Chicago Press, 1970). We all know what paradigms are in our daily lives: those comfortable assumptions, attitudes, and beliefs that we hang our behavior, even our lives, on. And just when our society gets really, really comfortable and settled and we are sure we have figured out how things are and how they must always be, along comes somebody or something that simply does not fit the cherished and familiar frame, and down it comes. We celebrate some of those shifts, such as Magna Carta, the Enlightenment, the civil rights movement; but some of us experience discomfort with others, such as feminism and gay rights.

When cherished paradigms come crashing down around us, then not only will the future be a great deal different from the present, but the process of change will be spectacular. To anticipate the arrival of new ideas, to watch them emerge and change and grow, to glimpse the power of our own new ideas—these are the uniquely human characteristics that give our lives interest and meaning. Also uniquely human, however, is the opposite attitude. We are driven by fear of change and dread of insecurity. Many of us need a view of the world that explains the mysteries and that helps us cope with the terrifying behavior of nature and society. To complicate our lives even further, because the present moment is so radically different from the past, so unstable and unpredictable, we cannot always rely on the past for guidance ("A Proposal for a Research Program in the History of Peace," *Peace and Change* 14 [October 1989], pp. 461–69).

A common theme runs through the following events that makes them, I believe, evidence of paradigm shifts and, as such, predictive of an alternative future that is possible. These developments suggest that the future is being invented. They differ significantly from the past experience of human beings. They grow out of the realization that we simply cannot afford to continue doing the business of living together as usual. Furthermore, they share what Richard Falk describes as a "transformative vision" of the future:

> *solidarity*—the sense of vital concern about the human species as a focus of emergent loyalty; *unity*—the shared and unified destiny of the planet; *space*—the non-territorial circumference of human concerns; *time*—the extension of human concerns in time to the ancient past and to the most distant future; *nature*—the experience of nature as encompassing, inspiring, and sustaining; *peace*—the renunciation of violence as the collective basis of security and innovation; *progress*—the gradual realization of human potentialities for joy and creativity in all dimensions of individual and collective existence; *humility*—the awareness of limits applicable to human endeavor; ... *spirituality*—the understanding that awe and mystery are as integral to human experience as bread and reason." (Richard Falk, "Satisfying Human Need in a World of Sovereign States," in *World Faiths and the New World Order,* edited by Joseph L. Gremillion and William Ryan, [Interreligious Peace Colloquium, Washington D.C.: 1978], pp. 135–36)

Here are a few of these paradigm-changing events; the list grows daily.

• On July 4, 1994, at Independence Hall in Philadelphia, Czech President Vaclav Havel delivered a "Declaration of Interdependence." He declared that the old ideas on which the United States was founded, ideas that proclaimed individual rights, have not nourished an awareness of human solidarity and social responsibility, without which our human future will probably be very bleak. Havel, who is attempting to establish an environment of meaning and moral values in his new nation, believes that without a sacred dimension, which he defines as a sense of "the miracle of Being, the miracle of the universe and the miracle of our own existence," a new world order based on a *universal respect for human rights* will not take root (*Newsweek,* July 18, 1994, p. 66).

• During his presidential administration, Jimmy Carter created the position of an assistant secretary of state for human rights and humanitarian affairs, a first step toward embedding in international diplomacy and in the minds of individuals an awareness of human rights issues and a sensitivity to their violation (Mary Gray, "A Human Rights Renaissance?" *The Stanley Foundation Courier* 12 [Winter 1993], p. 2). In his last address as president, Carter reminded us: "America did not invent human rights. Human rights invented America."

• At the 27th International Geographical Congress, held in 1992, leading geographers noted that the political map of the world is being redrawn. The powerful forces of ethnicity, democracy, and self-determination are creating a proliferation of nation states. One expert predicted that "the notion of boundaries as we've known them, in terms of absolute sovereignty and legalities, will in time dwindle" (Robin Wright, "Radically Redrawing the World Map," *Des Moines Register,* September 27, 1992, reprinted from the *Los Angeles Times*).

• On October 4, 1993, the German Parliament approved the Maastricht Treaty, the last of the nations of the European Community to do so. This action completed the process by which twelve European countries with a long history of animosity have voluntarily given up significant national powers to a supranational entity. Common passports, currency, trade agreements, legislative and judicial bodies, flag, and national anthem create a new era in the history of European civilization. Additional nations are requesting admission.

• A group of distinguished scientists issued the Seville Statement on Violence in 1986 as a contribution to the United Nations International Year of Peace. They affirmed that human beings have not inherited from primitive forebears a tendency to make war, that violent behavior is not genetically programmed into our nature, that war is not caused by "instinct" or any other single motivation. The statement concludes, "biology does not condemn humanity to war. ... Just as wars begin in the 'minds of men' peace must also begin in our minds. The same species who invented war is capable of inventing peace."

• In 1990 a new organization, the Unrepresented Nations and Peoples Organization, came into being to represent the less powerful and dispossessed peoples of the world. At its Second General Assembly in The Hague, it launched an effort to achieve nonviolent resolution of conflicts faced by ethnic and minority groups around the world. Its aim is to identify actions that could be taken to deter the use of governmental force against peoples who do not have a recognized state (Iowa Peace Institute, *Newsletter* 16 [August 1991], p. 1).

• Meeting in 1994 at the Wingspread Conference Center, the National Alliance for Non-violent Programming discussed how to reduce the negative effect of TV violence on children. Central to the discussion was the question "What kind of culture do we want our children to grow up in?" A broad group of experts—sociologists, public health officials, representatives from the TV and movie industries, and women's organizations—agreed to "collaboratively and comprehensively without censorship and without any invasion of First Amendment rights" develop strategies to reduce the violent quality of American culture (*Wingspread, The Journal* 16, no. 1, [Winter 1994]).

• Recent scientific investigation has led to the development of an exciting ecological theory. It holds that both ecosystems and individual organisms are self-regulated by harmonious cooperation among their infinite variety of parts. Rather than viewing the physical world as a collection of fragmented and independently operating systems, this hypothesis describes a collaborative wholeness of function in nature. Eugene Odum observes that the energy and material of ecosystems compose complicated information systems that communicate by means of physical and chemical networks which serve to regulate the system as a whole, responding not only to fluctuations in external environment but to internal changes as well (Eugene P. Odum, *The Way: An Ecological World-view* [Saunders College Publishing, 1983]). This intriguing line of thought leads some people to hypothesize the creation of a similar ecosystem composed of human beings through the use of modern technology. For example, the establishment of the great knowledge databases for law, medicine, and education may be a very rudimentary beginning for organizing and making available all of human knowledge.

These events are representative of many others that mark significant paradigm changes.

This same "transformative vision" is at work in Iowa increasing our capacity to better comprehend the world beyond our borders and raising our awareness of the peace and justice issues that cry out for response at home. Several recent examples reveal once again the basic generosity and vision of many Iowans and illustrate a process of inventing the future that is already at work.

• The Iowa Sister States effort began with compassionate concern for a tragedy half a world away from Iowa. In response to the destruction of crops and livestock in Yamanishi, Japan, in 1960, a hog and grain airlift from Iowa replaced lost resources and gave hope to devastated communities. The friendship has since included trade, cultural, and educational exchanges. Even before the end of the Cold War, the Sister

States initiative had established formal relationships with the Stavropol area in the former Soviet Union. For many years now, Iowa Sister States has identified common interests between international groups and Iowans in agriculture, education, science, culture, media, sports, and government (Iowa Sister States *Casebook,* 1992–93).

• In the late 1970s, Iowans responded to another international tragedy in a creative and compassionate way. Under the leadership of Governor Robert Ray, Iowa churches sponsored Laotian and Vietnamese refugee families to resettle in Iowa. Most had been living in refugee camps, driven from their homes in the cross fire of the jungle warfare. A central organization matched families that wanted to come with local sponsors. These sponsors found housing for the refugees, set up language classes, collected clothing, and found them jobs. In some smaller towns, the newcomers were often the only nonwhites. Some of the refugees stayed only long enough to learn the language and then headed to California to escape the harsh winters or to settle among larger Southeast Asian communities. But many stayed. With their strong family ties, work ethic, and thrift, most became self-supporting very quickly and added a new flavor to Iowa life. In the Des Moines telephone book, there are now seventy-five listings for Nguyen alone.

• In its final report issued in 1993, the Iowa K-12 Education Reform Study Committee wrote: "By the year 2000, the structure of schools will be substantially different. The change in how schools operate will be an effective response to the evolving needs of a new generation of students. Schools in Iowa will function as a logical whole due to a collaboration of involvement between administrators, teachers, parents, students and local stakeholders. ... Because of shared decision making, there will be widespread involvement from the stakeholders" (*Blueprint for School Transformation,* January 1993, Final Report, prepared by the Legislative Service Bureau, Des Moines, Iowa). This massive undertaking is being pursued by many different initiatives, including efforts of individual schools and communities and by organizations such as First in the Nation in Education Foundation (FINE) and the New Iowa Schools Development Corporation (NISDC).

• Founded in 1990 by the governor, the Iowa International Development Foundation focuses Iowa's resources on supporting the development of democracy and free enterprise abroad as well as on developing new markets for Iowa products. The Foundation has concentrated on four general activities: "1) building commercial and trade relations between Iowa manufacturing and agricultural companies and their foreign counterparts; 2) conducting educational programs in conjunction with commercial and trade activities, as well as facilitating educational exchanges between institutes of higher education; 3) creating relations with government to assist in building democracy with a focus on legislative exchanges and internships; 4) increasing ties between health care providers by encouraging the establishment of sister hospitals and donations of medical supplies" (Iowa International Development Foundation, *Annual Report,* FY 1992).

• The Iowa Mediation Service exists "to develop, promote and implement conflict resolution through mediation, negotiation, arbitration, facilitation and training services on a statewide basis." It came into being to help resolve farmer-creditor disagreements at the height of the farm crisis of the 1980s. It continues to offer assistance in that area, and its success has created a demand for its involvement with disputes over environmental issues, consolidation of schools and services, competition for economic development, and health care. The Service's successful record has demonstrated a powerful ability to "resolve, reconcile or restructure limited resource disputes." It also offers training for people who want to develop conflict resolution skills. Its efforts reflect its belief in the right of individuals to take control of how the disputes in which they are involved are settled and in the ability of people to discover win/win solutions to their problems (Iowa Mediation Service publication).

• The Iowa Peace Institute was founded in 1986 with funds provided by individuals, corporations, the educational community, and the Iowa legislature. Its efforts have focused on both local and international problems. Projects in Ukraine and Bulgaria have included agricultural extension–type educational programs, promotion of democratic principles and collaborative problem solving, and training in conflict resolution as well as English language instruction and the creation of English language libraries. In 1990 the Iowa Peace Institute and Business for Peace cosponsored an International Conference of Peace Institutes that brought together in Des Moines leaders from twenty countries. Recognizing the presence of significant international resources within Iowa, the Institute has for several years conducted an International Fellows Program that involves travel and community building for international students studying in Iowa. The Partners in Development program administers a fund to help international students studying in Iowa initiate and manage small-scale development projects in their home countries. Giving attention to Iowa problems as well, the Institute has developed global educational materials for the public schools, addressed the problems of gang violence within the state, and trained hundreds of public school children and teachers to resolve conflicts within their schools. Recently, the Institute has begun to offer leadership toward a new vision for dealing with crime. Called restorative justice, its goals are to elevate the importance of the victim and to hold the offender directly accountable to the victim. In contrast to the present philosophy of our criminal justice system, which has been described as "trail 'em, nail 'em, jail 'em," crime is viewed as a community conflict that should stimulate a dialogue in the service of a balanced solution (Iowa Peace Institute, *Newsletter* 24 [Summer 1994]).

• Although not without its opponents, the concept of global education is slowly taking root in the public schools of Iowa. Global education is an opportunity, through the creation of classroom resources and heightened awareness among teachers and parents, for students to learn about the diversity and become aware of the needs of the peoples of the planet. It also teaches young people to learn to care for the earth and safeguard the environment. It teaches a respect for human diversity, balances a cultural imperialism, and practices what

Stephen Covey calls an "abundance mentality," in which the recognition of the value of alternative beliefs and practices does not diminish the importance of cherished personal affirmations. It assists young people in preparing for the inevitable changes that will occur during their lifetimes as human beings and to become more fully aware of their interdependence.

What a remarkable record of international outreach and creative local problem solving. Does our concern for our neighbors near and far grow out of our profound sense of community because we have a such a strong identity with our hometowns? Because we have experienced authentic community on a small scale, do we have the spiritual resources to understand it internationally? As people everywhere struggle to define and create more satisfying and nurturing human communities, we Iowans are equipped to find new ways to establish that delicate balance between the freedom of individuals to pursue their own personal objectives and the demands of interdependence.

Finally, the task of peacemaking for Iowans, as for all citizens of our global community, must include an unprecedented effort of the human imagination. We must exert tremendous energy to overcome the tyranny that the past exercises over our vision of the future because the contemporary exponential explosion of knowledge has rendered even our immediate past of little use to us in envisioning the future. What is required for our time is the ability "to create compelling alternative visions of possible futures, to recognize and develop alternative conceptions of rationality, to create rich and imaginative alternative voices—diverse voices whose conversations with each other will invent those futures" (Carol Cohn, "Sex and Death and the Rational World of Defense Intellectuals," in *Women on War: Essential Voices for the Nuclear Age,* edited by Daniela Gioseffi [Simon & Schuster, 1988], p. 99). A creative response to what is certainly an unstable present will require us to enlarge exponentially those uniquely human characteristics—loyalty, respect, affection, and love. Their power will destroy the old, traditional ways in which we have lived together and bring into being a wonderful new world that we can now only dimly imagine.

The sounds that we hear today, in Iowa and throughout the world, may be the grinding of brakes attempting to slow the speed of desperately needed change, or they may be the sounds of old and useless paradigms shifting to make room for new patterns that will empower human communities in Iowa and in the larger world.

DAVE YEPSEN AND I are both alums of Jefferson Community High School, but since I was a senior the year that Dave was a lowly freshman, I would at the time never have acknowledged his existence. His ninth-grade picture in the pages of my 1965 *Jeffersonian* gives no clue that he would some day become the chief political editor of the *Des Moines Register*—a journalist to whom presidential hopefuls for Iowa caucus support come on bended knee begging for an encouraging word in his weekly column "On Capitol Hill." OK, let's be honest. For most of us, if you look at our freshman pictures, you wouldn't bet that we could figure out how a paper clip works. But somehow it happened, to the surprise of his classmates and the astonishment of his teachers. And on the way, he was elected governor of Boys' State in 1968, graduated from the University of Iowa, and earned a master's degree in public administration from Drake. In 1989, he was invited to become a fellow at the press-politics center at the Kennedy School of Government at Harvard, and in 1994, the American Political Hotline named Yepsen one of "America's best political reporters outside the beltway." In addition to his assignments for the *Register,* Yepsen provides a weekly radio commentary on WOI public radio and serves as a regular panelist on Iowa Public Television's "Iowa Press" program.

SURVEYING THE POLITICAL LANDSCAPE

David Yepsen

SURVEYING the Iowa political landscape for a sesquicentennial project is a daunting task for a reporter. We do well to figure out what happened yesterday, let alone look back over 150 years and analyze what it means for the next fifteen decades. And without a doubt, someone at the 300th birthday party will dig this book out of some attic and write one of those "look how far off base he was" essays.

But the 150-year landmark is an occasion to look back—and ahead—to see how Iowa's political culture has changed and what might be in store for us in the years ahead. We may be spending too much time looking back at the last 150 years and not enough time preparing for the future.

Political Forces in Iowa

The political culture is the sum of all the factors and forces that shape our politics. During the nineteenth and twentieth centuries, Iowa's politics was shaped largely by forces outside the state. That trend will only accelerate as the world becomes smaller and more interdependent in the future. Forces shaping Iowa's politics during the first 150 years include the following:

The Land. The rich prairie land was what enticed white settlers to come to Iowa and begin pushing native American tribes off it. Large numbers of white Iowans can trace their ancestry to immigrants who came to Iowa either to farm the land or work as part of the agricultural infrastructure that supported farming.

Farmers brought with them a Jeffersonian notion that, as tillers of the soil, they were somehow different from people in the cities. Some felt superior, seeing themselves as doing something more worthwhile than city dwellers. Others felt inferior, as urbanites looked down upon them as "hicks." This created urban-rural tensions and regional disputes that remain part of life in Iowa today.

Economic Adversity. Many of those original settlers were prompted to make the move by economic or political calamity in the Eastern states or Europe. The immigrant waves of white settlers are the first example of how Iowa was shaped by outside forces.

Accommodating those immigrants were the railroads, which encouraged people to come into the state and also enabled goods to be shipped out. The railroads helped create the beef cattle industry and the mechanization of agriculture. The refrigerator car allowed meatpacking plants in Sioux City and Waterloo to ship their products to the cities of the Eastern seaboard. Farmers turned their labor into raw materials that were then exchanged for urban-made goods. Construction of the railroads also brought construction workers. Many Iowans of African American, Irish, and Italian ancestries find that their Iowa roots begin with a railroad worker.

Depressions and panics helped create the populist movement of the late 1800s. In the 1930s, the Depression changed the way Americans and Iowans viewed government. Government became a place where all problems were taken for resolution. The Depression fostered the development of huge farm subsidy programs and the Social Security system. Today, Social Security and farm subsidy payments are the two largest types of payments the federal government makes into Iowa.

But Americans have been unwilling to pay for all the government services they want, which has led to a burgeoning federal budget deficit and debt. Deficit and debt issues are expected to dominate political debate in the United States for another generation. Younger Americans will have to pay more in taxes and get fewer government services. The crush of the debt burden has led some to predict an economic collapse or soaring inflation. If either happens, it will have an effect on Iowa the same way calamities like the Great Depression did.

The crush of federal debt is now leading many U.S. policymakers to talk of cutting back farm programs and limiting Social Security benefits. If this happens, it would mean Iowans are sending more money to Washington than they are receiving back in direct benefits. In the 1990s, it is about a dollar-for-dollar return. The federal government targeting scarce dollars at the nation's problems is likely to mean less money for Iowa because Iowa's drug, crime, welfare, and health care problems are not as bad as those of other regions.

Such is the joy of being part of a federal system.

The Iowa economy has often run in a counter-cyclical pattern to national trends. Anecdotal evidence suggests that rural economies take longer to slide into recession and are slower coming out. This pattern may change as Iowa's economy becomes less dependent on agriculture. In 1994, Iowa State University officials said that only 20 percent of the state's $55 billion gross state product is tied to agriculture. While that is the largest sector, it is also true that four-fifths of the state's economy is tied to other forces.

Regardless, economic cycles affect politics. If the economy is counter-cyclical, then politics here will run counter to national trends. For example, the farm crisis of the 1980s helped Democrats fare well in elections in Iowa, while nationally they were hurt by the booming economy that helped Republicans.

Values. Those early settlers brought with them certain values that have been passed along and still can cause conflict today, particularly over morality issues involving gambling, liquor, and abortion. At the same time, Northern European political mores call for activist, ethical, service-minded—sometimes even socialist—government, and traces of those influences are still seen in Iowa politics, as they are throughout the Upper Midwest. So, for example, in the early 1990s, Iowa became the first to construct a fiber-optic telecommunications network that quickly became one of the largest telephone companies in the state. Supporters justified it as necessary to help rural Iowa, but private companies objected to the government's intrusion on their business.

Iowans insist on honest, frugal government. Politics is seen more as a way to serve, not a way to do business or part of doing business, as it is in other political cultures in America. Ethical government is seen as efficient government, since issues are decided on their merits and not on money.

War. Volumes have been written about the Civil War and the two World Wars and the effect they had on the country. In Iowa, the Civil War gave rise to the Republican party, which, with a few interruptions, dominated politics for nearly one hundred years. The treaties ending World War I contributed to the Great Depression, which in turn led to a substantial expansion of government. That war also led to an increased mechanization of agriculture, which accelerated the decline of population in rural Iowa. World War II opened the eyes of many GIs to the fact there was a world outside the state. The GI Bill educated them and prompted the expansion of Iowa's college and university system. Another important ramification of World War II was how it spurred construction of the interstate highway system, making transportation faster. It also made it easier for people to leave rural Iowa and live elsewhere, turning many Iowa communities into bedroom communities. Studies show that growing numbers of Iowans use the interstates for long commutes to jobs in larger cities.

Religion. Organized religion has been a key factor in the development of Iowa and its politics. In early years, churches played a central role in the community and social activities. Many church officials and religious activists have been eager to weigh in on the great political debates in the state—from abolition and liquor to gambling and abortion. Often those values have conflicted with another ethic: the desire to be left alone. At the core of the conflicts over liquor, gambling, and abortion is an argument over whether government ought to protect people or leave them alone. Those issues have played a decisive role in many elections. Beginning in the late 1970s, Iowa saw a rebirth of religious political activism as religious conservatives started leaving the Democratic party and began exercising more influence in the state Republican party.

Demographics. Iowa's population is aging, and since 1880, the rural population has been declining. The mechanization of agriculture, combined with more economic opportunities outside the state, has prompted an exodus of the state's population. More than half of Iowa's voters in the 1992 election were older than fifty.

The population is 95 percent white. For many years, the state's homogeneous population has been considered an asset. But at the close of the twentieth century, the rest of the country grew more diverse. Local development officials reported that some businesses did not want to locate in Iowa because of monocultural traits. Attracting diverse cultures to Iowa and equipping Iowans to deal with an increasingly diverse world is a significant issue confronting policy-makers and educators.

Television. In the late twentieth century, the most important force in our culture became television. As with war, television altered our culture in a variety of ways. The effect of television in Iowa is no different from anywhere else: Iowans spend many hours watching television, which can lead to changes in schools and the demise of some community and social activities.

The high cost of television commercials has increased the cost of statewide political campaigns, which in turn has given more influence to special-interest groups that bankroll those campaigns. For example, in 1958, Neal Smith spent less than $10,000 to win a congressional seat and became one of the first

Iowa politicians to make extensive use of television when he purchased half-hour blocks of time to talk to voters. In 1994, he spent nearly $1 million in losing a seat, most of it spent for 30-second commercials to counter ads sponsored by his opponent. In the late 1800s, railroads gave politicians free tickets; today, special-interest groups give politicians large campaign contributions.

Television has also altered issues in Iowa politics. For example, in 1994, surveys revealed crime to be the most-frequently mentioned concern of voters. Yet statistics show Iowa has one of the lowest crime rates in the nation. One explanation is that as television pours stories of crime and violence into Iowa homes, it encourages Iowans to think that their problem is larger than it is.

Weather. Iowans enjoy—and endure—four distinct seasons. For many, this is one of the state's most attractive assets. Yet hard Midwestern winters have shaped the state and the people. Not only does the weather dictate what sorts of crops can and can't be grown, but it also has had an effect on the kinds of people who settled here and in other regions of the Upper Midwest. Immigrants from Northern Europe found the climate here to be similar to the one they left. Immigrants from more tropical parts of the world settled in other regions of the country. In the 1970s, Governor Robert Ray led an effort to help Southeast Asians displaced by war settle in Iowa. Many remain, but others said they found the climate too uncomfortable.

Weather continues to affect Iowa. It directly influences the profitability of agriculture, the state's largest industry. Cold winters are one reason why some retirees opt for warmer climates. That demographic trend may accelerate in the future as well-to-do baby boomers and future generations choose to spend their retirement years in warmer regions.

The weather also increases economic costs. In the mid-1980s, it was estimated that we Iowans spend about $5 billion a year on energy costs to warm ourselves in winter, cool ourselves in the summer, and process crops and industrial goods. This is a noticeable drain on the state's $55 billion gross state product. Reducing that expense through conservation, alternative energy sources, and more innovative farming and industrial methods will improve the standard of living in Iowa by keeping more money in the state and making the state's economy less vulnerable to outside sources of energy.

Meaning for the Future

What does this political culture mean for the future of Iowa politics?

As we enter the twenty-first century, it is fair to say that those same outside forces will continue to be the dominant forces in Iowa. War and economic problems elsewhere continue to prompt some people to settle in Iowa. In the early 1980s, the state saw the arrival of refugees from the war in Vietnam. In 1994, Des Moines residents helped resettle families displaced by the war in Bosnia. The state's meatpacking industry is heavily staffed by Mexican immigrants in search of better-paying jobs than they can find south of the border. While these new arrivals are sometimes met with consternation by longer-term residents, they are of the pattern of settlement in Iowa. The Native Americans didn't appreciate the arrival of white settlers; Germans disliked the Irish; and Northern Europeans resented Italians.

Still, Iowa's population continues to lack racial diversity. Many African Americans, with a slave-based aversion to agriculture, sought to avoid farming. Most racial minorities complain that Iowa's predominantly European origins have created a culture that makes it difficult for them to feel at home. Some feel that the state lacks a critical mass of minorities to develop communities, neighborhoods, and social structures. Iowa may be in a Catch-22 situation: Iowa leaders understand the world is becoming more diverse, and they say they want to expose Iowans to that diversity, yet they are frustrated in their ability to attract minorities because the state has so few.

Also, the state's demographics may change, thanks to difficulties elsewhere. Many people believe that the problems of crime and sprawl in the nation's larger cities have diminished the quality of life there. That, combined with the telecommunications revolution and the world's growing population, should prompt more people to come to Iowa in search of a little breathing room and a calmer lifestyle. Iowa may never become the "melting pot" seen in the nation's metropolitan areas, but it is likely to become more diverse. For example, 1993 saw a Thai couple open a travel agency in Des Moines to serve via telephone and computer the nation's burgeoning Asian community.

Iowa is also seeing demographic change that will pose challenges for policy-makers. An aging population means greater demands for government services to care for seniors. Yet an aging population does not earn as much as a younger population and is therefore less able to provide the tax revenues necessary to provide those services. Sometimes, well-to-do elders leave Iowa for warmer climes in retirement, taking with them their income tax payments and leaving behind the lower-income seniors who pay little in taxes but who require more government services.

Most population growth in the state has occurred in the larger counties. The population in the smaller counties continues to stagnate or even drop as populations get older. This has created what Iowa State University demographer Willis Goudy has described as "a tale of two Iowas," one relatively well-off and the other growing older and poorer.

The aging population may also mean a more traditional electorate less willing to take risks. Demographers have noted that as people age, most become less adventuresome and less inclined to push for change as they become more "settled in their ways." As a consequence, candidates advocating change must always combat "it was good enough for me" arguments. While many in Iowa see holding fast to traditions and proven ways of doing things as a strength, it is arguably also a weakness when it inhibits positive risk taking.

One of the challenges for future policy-makers will be managing generational tensions. Older Iowans, who vote, will insist upon government services they need. Younger Iowans, who don't vote in such great numbers, will also require government services for things such as schools and universities.

In 1994, spending on education comprised 60 percent of the state budget, and educators are asking for more. Iowa policy-makers in the coming years will have to try to balance these conflicting generational needs.

Urban-rural tensions will continue. (Many visitors to Iowa chuckle at how Iowans think they have "urban-rural" tensions when the largest city in the state is populated with fewer than 200,000 residents. But, politics is always a matter of perspective. When you come from a town of fewer than 2,000, well, a place with 200,000 people is a "city.") As rural areas have lost population to the larger and more dynamic communities, many rural leaders feel cheated. It is not hard to find people in rural areas who feel that too much of their tax revenues goes to larger communities to support things such as government bureaucracies or universities that have little direct economic benefit in their smaller towns.

Iowa's "suburban" population will add to the mix of problems and issues. In the 1990s, Iowa's largest counties have school districts growing in size while many rural districts or inner-city schools are getting smaller. There are arguments over sharing municipal services.

Policy-makers in the mid-1990s hope the construction of a fiber-optic telecommunications network will better tie Iowa together and enable rural residents to enjoy the same government services as urban residents, without having to assemble a large mass of people. They also hope the network can reduce the cost of government or enable some government agencies to be moved to smaller communities. Many Iowa policy-makers say they cannot forecast all the ramifications of the telecommunications revolution. Just as no one saw how interstate highways would enable more people to leave rural Iowa or commute to far-away jobs, no one can pinpoint all the effects of fiber-optic technologies.

The Future

Urban-rural tensions at the federal level will also affect Iowa politics. The election of 1994 created a conservative Republican Congress that promises to put an end to much of the government activism spawned by the New Deal of the 1930s and the Great Society of the 1960s. Iowa can expect to see fewer direct benefits. Farm subsidies will be reduced to help curb the deficit. Loss of farm voting power in Congress assures this. For example, the new House Minority Leader, Richard Armey of Texas, is openly hostile toward farm subsidies. The Rural Electrification Administration is openly criticized as no longer necessary because rural America is electrified. The rural-dominated U.S. Senate can protect some farm programs, but even there sentiment is strong to reduce subsidies because of the deficit and because of new trade treaties that require countries to drop such impediments to free trade.

Also, federal dollars tend to go where there are problems. So, for example, the Clinton Administration once proposed redirecting dollars for elementary and secondary reading programs. Why? Because most kids in Iowa can read, whereas many in urban ghettos cannot. This offends Iowans, who fear a loss of federal money, but it is a rational choice for federal policy-makers trying to find the best use of scarce national resources.

It is a pattern likely to be repeated on other issues in the future as the nation tries to solve problems and manage a debt at the same time. The fact that membership in the U.S. Senate is based on area and not population will mitigate some of this trend.

There will be increased regionalization. Anyone looking at a map of the United States can see that if you were laying out state boundaries today, you wouldn't draw them in the same places. The rivers and border disputes that fixed the boundaries when Iowa became a state are often of little relevance now. Instead, marketing areas for businesses, transportation, and telecommunications linkages are meaningful. One out of three Iowans lives in the tier of counties along the borders. That makes it easy to cross state lines to do things such as shop or recreate, if those amenities can't be found here. In the future, these regional realities will be increasingly important to commerce.

Community college boundary lines will become more and more important, often replacing county lines as significant government borders. Why? These community college boundaries often form a rough division of the state's natural marketing areas. County lines were chosen to allow everyone a "day's ride on horseback" to the county seat and back; community college boundaries are drawn to make every Iowan within commuting distance of an educational center. They are logical marketing areas for retailers and media organizations seeking advertisers. Also, post–high school education and adult educational programs will be tied to community college attendance centers. Job-creation programs will follow job-training programs that are based at community colleges.

People living in Des Moines will find their economic futures more tied to the Des Moines Area Community College than anything going on in Dubuque. In the future we will think less of ourselves as Iowans and more of ourselves as residents of our neighborhoods, hometowns, or regions. Bureaucracies in Washington or Des Moines will find themselves less relevant than local school boards, city councils, and neighborhood associations. Political boundaries will mean less and, in fact, may become a hindrance to many Iowans. In central Iowa, for example, overlapping urban and suburban government jurisdictions are seen as costly and inefficient for delivering government services.

Regarding schools, a 1984 study found that children attending the very smallest and the very largest schools had some of the worst test scores. While pressures have forced consolidation of many small schools in recent decades, no similar effort is underway to break up big, often impersonal school districts in the state's largest communities. It may come, however, as parents find that "smaller is beautiful" and force decentralization of school districts around high school attendance areas.

Economic activity will change. The ability to communicate and to transport communications and goods and services will shrink distances and make it easier for newcomers to prosper. Agribusiness, Iowa's largest industry, accounts for only 20 percent of the state's total economy. A wet 1993 flooded much of Iowa agriculture but barely dented state tax revenues. In the mid-1990s, there are signs that large portions of the hog and cattle industries are moving to southern climes and consolidating into larger operations. This will put further pressure on small producers. Also, the growth of the financial services and insurance industries in Iowa signals a growing diversity in the economy.

The telecommunications industry will make it easier for people to live in Iowa in the future, but it will work two ways: It will also make it easier for them to leave. People who process information for a living can easily live anywhere and do their jobs where they or their employer choose. The exodus from rural portions of the state may be nearing a peak in some areas close to larger population centers. While the numbers of farmers continue to shrink, an increase in small businesses, commuters, and information processors will enable some rural communities to grow, even if there are fewer farmers. Post-suburban growth in the United States offers hope for population growth in rural areas within a few hours' drive of urban centers.

The 1990 census and 1991 reapportionment produced the most compact congressional district in eastern Iowa where Iowa City, Cedar Rapids, and Davenport were put into one, thanks to population growth in the corridors linking those communities. Development in Dallas and Madison counties also illustrated this trend. As more highways are constructed, other counties near larger areas will be opened for potential use as bedroom counties.

Planners see two core "islands" of development in the state—in the Ames–Des Moines and Iowa City–Cedar Rapids corridors. Even today, many Iowans commute several hours to jobs in larger communities while living in a rural area where housing is available and less costly. But this trend has a downside. As more Iowans commute, larger communities in the state are seeing the collapse of their inner cities and erosion of their tax base. Several large communities are rapidly becoming economic doughnuts—sweet on the outside with nothing in the middle. Finding ways to help downtowns and nearby neighborhoods remain economically viable is one of the biggest challenges facing largely rural states in the future.

In the 1990s, policy-makers believe one way to improve Iowa's economy is to learn how to add value to the raw commodities produced here. Instead of selling corn, they want to sell cereal. Instead of selling cattle, they want to sell packages of meat. Some small meat processors in Iowa now find it profitable to grow meat for the Japanese market and ship the finished produce via air. Some soybean processors now grow special soybeans for use in producing soy flakes that are shipped to Japan and processed into tofu.

The 1994 passage of the General Agreement on Tariffs and Trade is an example of how sales to foreign customers have helped to "internationalize" Iowa politics and make the state less isolationist. Every member of the Iowa delegation voted for GATT and for the North American Free Trade Agreement that preceded it—despite objections from trade protectionists and isolationists. Senator Tom Harkin, a Democrat who enjoys strong support from opponents in organized labor, had reservations but eventually voted for both.

Using Iowa agriculture to produce for world consumers, as opposed to just U.S. consumers, is expected to be a factor in Iowa politics in the future as policy-makers argue over the best ways to spark "value added" industries. The increased mechanization and monopolization of the meat-processing industry threatens to displace many smaller producers.

Much of Iowa's economy and politics will be fashioned elsewhere. In addition to a farm and interest rate policy made in Washington, rural policy of the future will also depend on the activities of world trade organizations and treaties. Iowans like to be left alone—our ancestors came here to get away from problems "over there"—but we also like to make money, which is why the "free traders" are winning most of the political arguments in Iowa.

Electoral politics will change as well. Donald Avenson, speaker of the Iowa House from 1983 to 1990, has said there is a "Washingtonization" of Iowa politics occurring. The advent of annual sessions of the Legislature means that serving in the Legislature, which once required a few months every two years, now requires five months every year. Annual sessions are defended with the argument that government and issues are more complex and that policy-makers must spend more time tending to business. But lawmakers' salaries have not substantially increased. The average lawmaker earns less than $23,000 in salary and expenses. Many middle-class Iowans cannot afford to raise families on that wage, so they leave public service or do not enter it. As a result, Iowa winds up with full-time lawmakers earning part-time pay.

This has several ramifications. It can lead to ethics scandals, as members find outside employment that might conflict with their duties as lawmakers. It also means that the Legislature ends up with a number of relatively young members who lack career experiences outside of politics. It also includes a number who are well-off financially or retired. Many middle-class merchants or middle-aged Iowans say they cannot afford to serve in the Legislature, which leads to the question of whether we are getting the best of Iowa to serve in public office.

Low pay isn't the only reason people decide not to get involved in politics. Public life has always meant a surrender of privacy. America in the post-Vietnam, post-Watergate era has grown cynical about public officials. Issues of personal character, less rigorously covered in the 1960s, make front-page news in the 1990s. Many potential candidates say they are unwilling to subject themselves and their families to such scrutiny or the negativism of campaigns.

In addition, the cost of campaigns has exploded, largely to finance television commercials. A competitive seat in the Iowa state senate will cost as much as $100,000. In 1992, an estimated $4 million was spent on state legislative campaigns. The costly trend is expected to rise as candidates are forced to pay for increasingly expensive and diverse communications technologies to get their messages to voters. Expensive campaigns also breed a dependence on special-interest groups that provide the money.

These factors—low pay, lack of respect and privacy, and

the high cost of campaigns—mean many Iowans don't come forward to serve. They have also contributed to the lack of diversity in the Legislature. In 1992, only 22 of the 150 members of the Legislature were women, despite the fact that Iowa's population is more than 50 percent female. In 1994, there were still only 27 women in the Legislature. Political experts say this is because women still do much of the nurturing of children in society. Many potential women candidates say they are unwilling to leave their families to serve in the Legislature. Sometimes potential women candidates opt for elective office at the county level, where the pay is higher and they can remain at home. Recent years have seen a growth in the numbers of women serving in county governments.

In summary, I believe that Iowa's policy-makers will face at least fifteen major issues and challenges in the future. They are:

1. Balancing the expensive needs of an aging population with the expensive needs of younger Iowans at a time when middle-income voters demand tax cuts. Most public services are demanded by the very old and the very young and are paid by those in the middle.

2. Managing a more ethnically diverse population.

3. Making Iowa businesses and educational systems competitive with global adversaries. Nowhere is this more obvious than in the debates over the future of farming. Policy-makers will continue to be asked to help farmers in order to preserve the ways of life farming and small towns have brought to our society. At the same time, these small producers and communities may no longer be the most economically efficient ways to produce goods and services. Also, the process of replacing farm labor with technology, a process that began in the late 1800s, will continue to be a factor policy-makers will have to manage in the next 150 years.

4. Encouraging more risk taking and entrepreneurship in a tradition-bound state.

5. Managing a state that will get less money from the federal government.

6. Protecting the land and water. Iowa will not be exempt

from the growing national conflicts between private property rights and public rights. The 1990s debate over construction of large livestock confinement facilities and the environmental provisions of the 1995 farm bill are examples. New technologies can help Iowa do this. Reforestation, restoration of agricultural lands through sustainable agricultural techniques, recycling, and development of wetlands will help. So will the development of municipal sanitation systems that use natural, bio-friendly treatment systems instead of chemical-based ones.

7. Creating more recreational opportunities. Iowa has one of the lowest levels of public ownership of land. Good land is farmed, not made into parks. Buying up low-grade farmland and woodlands for future recreational use will improve Iowa's quality of life.

8. Managing a state economy in time of global economic booms and downturns. Since much of Iowa's economy is based on forces outside the state's control—interest rates, trade policy, the value of the dollar, federal farm legislation—Iowa's policy-makers in the future will face the same challenge they do today: trying to second-guess these trends and position the state accordingly.

9. Finding ways to reduce Iowa's $5 billion energy bill to conserve resources and keep dollars at home.

10. Replacing the infrastructure of public facilities to foster economic growth in the future.

11. Rebuilding Iowa's aging housing stock at a time when it often costs more to build a new home in a small Iowa town than the home will sell for in the market place.

12. Reducing the cost of campaigns and restoring confidence in the ethics of public officials.

13. Balancing the state's tax laws to raise public dollars fairly and equitably and spending them where the greatest needs are. Providing a tax policy that sparks economic growth yet provides for public amenities that make Iowa a desirable place to live is a never-ending balancing act for policy-makers as they try to be competitive in a world economy. For example, Iowa is one of the few states that taxes the interest earned on

the municipal bonds sold by local governments. Exempting that income from taxation would keep Iowa dollars in Iowa and provide revenues needed for infrastructure repair. Also, Iowa's population and area are about mid-range among all fifty states, yet our income and property taxes are relatively high, suggesting that steps be taken to lower them to remain competitive. Phrases like "cost-benefit" and "cost-effective" and "bigger bang for the buck" will be heard more often in the halls of government as officials have to do better with less.

14. Managing rural, urban, and suburban tensions and rivalries. Such regionalism saps cooperative efforts needed to solve all other problems.

15. Preparing for growth. Recession-shocked Iowans of the 1980s need to be careful what they wish for: they may get it in the future. Colorado, Oregon, and Florida are all states where growth management is a problem. As urban problems multiply, some Iowa communities will face similar problems.

As Iowa celebrates its 150th birthday, one hears a lot about the good things in life here. If you ask an Iowan in 1994 what makes our state great, you are likely to hear "tradition," "family," "clean," "caring," "hard work," "good schools," "stability," or "conservative." A birthday is a celebration, which means a focus on the good things and memories. But our strengths can also be our weaknesses. At what point does maintaining "tradition" become "hidebound"? At what point does "conservative" become "unwilling to take risks"? At what point does our "compassion" make us reluctant to make "tough choices"?

Iowans have a strong sense of history, largely a function of the fact that more than 70 percent of Iowans are born in the state. Iowa means hometowns, high school reunions, and memories of the rhythms of life growing up. But in that celebration of the past, are we forgetting the future? Iowa has lots of museums that celebrate the last 150 years, but no think tanks are looking at the next 150 years.

Also, there is some evidence that the positive factors we are touting this birthday year may be overblown. Other states and countries can boast of good schools and strong work ethics. Iowa has no corner on the market for being "a nice place to raise a family." And Iowa has its share of warts too, from racist incidents to gang violence to teen pregnancies. Problems like these, played against the backdrop of our political culture, will form the political battles of the future.

Celebration of the 150th birthday is good. But just as much time and effort needs to be spent looking at the future as has been spent remembering the past.

STEVEN FINK is the rabbi of the largest Jewish congregation in Iowa and the oldest one in Des Moines, Congregation B'nai Jeshurun. Born and raised in New Jersey, Fink moved to Des Moines in 1983 and has made it his home. He claims that the friendliness, warmth, graciousness, and hospitality of Iowa remind him of the small town in which he grew up. He, his wife Sally, and their three children, Nathaniel, Miriam, and Benjamin, are confirmed Iowans.

Fink was educated at Franklin and Marshall College in Pennsylvania and the University of Lancaster in England before entering the Hebrew Union College to become a rabbi. He studied at the Jerusalem, Los Angeles, and New York campuses of the College and was ordained at the latter in 1979. His first position was as assistant and then associate rabbi of Congregation Keneseth Israel in Elkins Park, Pennsylvania.

Fink has served on the boards of the Iowa Civil Liberties Union and Planned Parenthood of Greater Iowa and has been chairman of the Iowa affiliate of the Religious Coalition for Reproductive Choice. He has been, since 1984, a lecturer in the Religion Department at Drake University and a Des Moines Police Force chaplain. He is also a frequent contributor to the *Des Moines Register*.

In 1994, two teenagers sprayed anti-Jewish graffiti on Fink's synagogue. When they were apprehended, they were sentenced to do community service at the Temple—one hundred hours of physical labor and one hundred hours studying Judaism with Fink. What happened next? The two became friends with Fink and his custodian, Jack Huff. When the miscreants married each other a few months later, they invited Fink and Huff to the wedding.

CAN YOU GET DELI IN DES MOINES? IOWA JEWS AND JEWISH IOWANS

Steven Fink

EARLY IN THE MORNING of Thursday, March 4, 1994, while taking their usual route to Merrill Middle School in Des Moines, several students discovered that the synagogue they passed each day was covered with swastikas and Nazi-type graffiti. The students immediately reported their discovery to their principal, who called the administrator of Temple B'nai Jeshurun. Once the police were called and the incident was reported, the media began broadcasting information about what would become the most publicized anti-Semitic event in Iowa's history. Public response was instantaneous. People were outraged. Calls, letters, donations, flowers, and offers of help flowed in. The Des Moines police assigned six detectives full-time to the case. On Sunday, March 7, the Des Moines Area Religious Council sponsored a rally at the Temple that was attended by more than one thousand people. Speakers included Governor Branstad, Lt. Governor Corning (who chairs the Governor's Council on Diversity), and representatives from the major Protestant denominations, the Catholic Diocese, the Muslims, the NAACP, and the National Conference of Christians and Jews. Later that same afternoon, the mayor of Des Moines, John "Pat" Dorrian, sponsored a rally against bigotry at City Hall attended by Senator

Harkin, Governor Branstad, the U.S. Attorney, and other civic leaders. This outpouring of support and instant condemnation by authority figures led the public to participate in the search for the perpetrators. Aided by a phone tip, police apprehended the alleged offenders just a week later. The two, an eighteen-year-old man, a self-proclaimed Nazi and skinhead, and his seventeen-year-old girlfriend, whom the police described as "losers," unhesitatingly confessed to the crime.

The show of support for Temple B'nai Jeshurun and the Jewish community was more than symbolic: It was indicative of the fact that the Jews of Iowa are part and parcel of mainstream Iowa society, that they are part of majority culture, that an attack against Iowa Jews is perceived as an attack against the fabric of society itself. The Jews are not outsiders or strangers. They are not stigmatized by their minority status. They are fully accepted and perceived to be as "Iowan" as the Methodists and Lutherans who live down the street. This is a status that the Jews of Iowa have long coveted, for the story of Iowa's Jews is the story of progression from marginality to accepted minority status.

Who Are the Jews?

The Jews are members of a worldwide family that traces its common ancestry back almost four thousand years to the patriarch Abraham of the Bible. The ancestral homeland of the Jews is the land of Israel, which Jews believe was given to them by God as part of a covenantal relationship. The Jews are both a people and members of a faith community. Until relatively recent times, this combination of faith and nationality was unique. In this respect, only the Sikhs can be compared with the Jews. One is born into the people or can become a part of the Jewish nation through conversion to Judaism, the religious system of the Jews. While Jews differ a great deal among themselves, they are united by ties of kinship and family loyalty.

These ethnic ties, in and of themselves, would not have sufficiently bound the Jewish people together for four millennia. It is Judaism, the religious civilization of the Jewish people, that has sustained the Jews throughout the ages. It is the Jews' devotion to God and His teachings that has enabled the Jewish people to survive. Stubborn loyalty to God and their ancestral faith permitted the Jewish people to persevere and prosper from ancient times to this day.

The Jewish people are descended from the tribes of Judah and Benjamin, which, in ancient times, comprised the population of the Kingdom of Judah. The name "Jew" is itself derived from the Hebrew word *Yehudi,* one who is an inhabitant of Judah. Following the destruction of the Temple in Jerusalem by the Babylonians in the year 586 B.C.E., much of the population was exiled to Babylonia (modern Iraq). Thousands of other Jews made their way to Egypt, where they established the largest Jewish community of antiquity. Thus began the Diaspora, the dispersion of the Jews around the world. Since that time, more Jews have lived outside the land of Israel than within it. During Roman hegemony, Jews spread from the Middle East throughout the Mediterranean world. Jewish communities existed in such far-flung parts of the Roman Empire as England and Germany. After the Muslim conquests, the locus of the Jewish world shifted once again to Mesopotamia and then later, to Spain. Small Jewish communities in Western Europe generally prospered until the commencement of the First Crusade in 1096, which ushered in a long and dark period of persecution and wandering.

As a result of one such instance of oppression, Jews first made their way to what would eventually become the United States. In 1654, twenty-three Dutch Jews of the former Dutch colony of Recife in Brazil fled from the Inquisition recently introduced into their home by the Portuguese conquerors. Their ship took them to New Amsterdam, where they were coolly greeted by the governor, Peter Stuyvesant. After many trials and tribulations, they were eventually allowed to remain, thus creating the first American Jewish community.

Jews Come to Iowa

Alexander Levi has the honor of being the first Jew known to have settled in Iowa. Born in France in 1809, Levi landed in Dubuque in August of 1833 and soon opened a grocery store. He had the distinction of being the first foreign-born Iowan to become a naturalized American citizen. He became a prominent and charitable resident of Dubuque, making his living through retailing and mining. His daughter, Eliza, was the first Jewish child born in Iowa (Jack Wolfe, *A Century with Iowa Jewry, 1833–1940* [Iowa Printing and Supply Company, 1941], p. 29). Other Jews followed and were found at first in the river towns along the Mississippi. Before the Civil War, Keokuk probably had the largest number of Jewish settlers. Jews soon settled in Davenport and then moved inland along with other pioneers, taking advantage of economic opportunities as they came along. William and Minnie Kraus were among the first settlers in Des Moines, arriving in 1845, where they set up a dry goods shop in a log cabin erected by the soldiers at Fort Des Moines.

Most of the Jews who came to Iowa were single men of German background who had much in common with the other immigrants flocking to Iowa in the fourth and fifth decades of the nineteenth century. They were looking for economic opportunities and freedom, both personal and religious. Jews in the various German states suffered at this time from severe restrictions. Only the oldest son was allowed to marry. Schools and many occupations remained closed to Jews. They were forbidden to own land. Liberal political reforms that would have extended citizenship to Jews were rejected with a violent conservative backlash. Younger sons, in particular, unable to marry and unlikely to receive much in the way of inheritance, joined the great exodus of Germans of all faiths to the promised land called America. Along with the thousands of German Catholics and Protestants who journeyed to Iowa was a handful of these German Jews. Rather than settle on farms, as did most of the Germans, these Jewish men began their life in Iowa as peddlers. Unfamiliar with farming and urban by experience and inclination, they earned their living as middlemen between the manufacturer and consumer. They landed at Keokuk, Burlington, or Davenport, sometimes with just their clothes and a pack full of wares on their backs.

The peddler performed an important function for the

farmers of rural Iowa, distributing merchandise and information. The peddler would buy a horse and cart and transport to market the farm goods that he received in trade. As he learned the language and saved his money, he would eventually open a store. He would sometimes branch out into dry goods, clothes, jewelry, or general merchandise. If he was successful, his store would expand to become a five-and-dime or even one of the department stores that so changed the nature of American retailing in the late nineteenth century.

At the beginning of the Civil War, fewer than 500 Jews lived in Iowa in thirty-five different communities in all parts of the state. Most worked in merchandising. About 100 Jews made their living as peddlers, and an additional 125 owned retail establishments. There was also a Jewish physician in Keokuk, a dentist in Rochester, a surveyor in Jefferson, a saloon keeper in St. Claire, a watch maker in Davenport, and a miner in Dubuque. According to military records, 35 men known to be Jews served in Iowa regiments during the Civil War. Four died in the fighting (Wolfe, *A Century with Iowa Jewry,* p. 43).

It was, and is, exceedingly difficult to be a Jew alone, without being part of a Jewish community. A lone peddler would find it almost impossible to observe the Sabbath and holidays away from home and family. It was equally as burdensome to obtain kosher food. Many found that their Jewish observances, and their Jewish identity, evaporated in the Iowa air. They fell in love, married non-Jewish women, and settled in towns where their former Jewish identity was not an impediment to their acceptance and assimilation. Many non-Jewish Iowans find Jewish names in their family trees as a result of this process, which was repeated countless times across the Iowa landscape.

Jewish continuity fared much better in towns. A *minyan,* a quorum of ten Jewish males over the age of thirteen, is required to hold a service and to establish a synagogue (in Reform and Conservative synagogues, women are counted in the *minyan).* Iowa's first, called B'nai Israel (the Children of Israel), was organized in Keokuk in 1855. In 1861, the Jews of Davenport organized what was to become the oldest continuous Jewish congregation in the state when they, too, created a Congregation B'nai Israel, whose building was later named Temple Emanuel in honor of a benefactor. The Jews of Des Moines purchased land and formed the Emanuel Burial Association in 1870. Three years later they created Congregation B'nai Jeshurun (Children of Righteousness), rented a hall at Second and Court Avenues, and worshiped together for the High Holy Days. This pattern was repeated within the next few decades in Council Bluffs, Dubuque, Sioux City, Cedar Rapids, Iowa City, Ottumwa, Mason City, Marshalltown, Fort Dodge, Waterloo, Oskaloosa, Centerville, Burlington, and Muscatine.

These synagogues were not just houses of worship but educational, social, and community centers as well. If the non-Jewish Iowan's life revolved around his or her church, the Jew's life revolved even more intensely around the synagogue. Jews were generally accepted throughout all strata of Iowa society, but although some Jews were quite prominent as business, civic, and political leaders, Jews overwhelmingly socialized with one another. Although anti-Semitism in Iowa never reached the levels it did in other parts of the country, Jews were not welcomed in certain clubs, residences, and public establishments. During the Gilded Age after the Civil War, exclusion became the rule rather than the exception. "Old money" in the United States desired to exclude from its social circles those who made fortunes in the wide-open post–Civil War economy. This exclusion was extended to all who were not of the proper "pedigree." Jews, by definition, did not have the "proper" antecedents to be accepted by the elite. Rejected by the socially prominent, Jews found comfort fraternizing with their coreligionists. After all, they did not have to explain themselves or their customs to one another. Sharing religious, cultural, business, social, and marriage ties, Iowa Jewry, to some extent, was a community unto itself.

The Community Grows

The majority of the Jews in Iowa before 1881 were of German extraction. Even if they had emigrated from Poland or from a part of the Russian Empire, they became "adopted members" of the German Jewish community as they acculturated in Iowa. The German Jews eagerly embraced American life and assimilated as quickly as possible into Iowa society. By the latter two decades of the nineteenth century, Iowa's first Jewish immigrants had "made it." They were proprietors of successful business establishments. Some had become respectable attorneys. A few owned factories. They were building homes in the finest parts of town and sending their children to Eastern schools. The German Jews had become middle class. In Des Moines, the forty members of Congregation B'nai Jeshurun were affluent enough by 1887 to build the first Temple at Eighth and Pleasant Streets. The *Saturday Times* reported on October 21 of that year, "It is with much pleasure that the *Times* gives its readers a picture of the new and beautiful Jewish synagogue just completed. ... No church in Des Moines has been more prosperous or made more rapid strides than has the Jewish. From its organization in 1872, when twenty five persons constituted its full membership, it has rapidly grown and today witnesses the brightest fruits of its devoted followers." The forty members who constituted the membership of the Temple in 1887 raised more than twenty-nine thousand dollars to erect this facility, a tribute to their dedication and a monument to their success.

Temple B'nai Jeshurun and the other congregations throughout Iowa were quick to join the burgeoning Reform movement (the Union of American Hebrew Congregations) founded in 1873 by Rabbi Isaac M. Wise in Cincinnati. The Reform movement came to America from Germany. It seemed to be the perfect synthesis between Judaism and American life. Mixed seating was allowed in the pews; sermons, organ music, and choirs were introduced; the use of English was encouraged; and the reading of Hebrew was vastly reduced, as was the time of the service. Many ritual requirements were eliminated, and distinctive clothing and head covering were abolished. Jewish peoplehood, one of the core elements of Judaism, was deemphasized. Jews became practitioners of Judaism, a faith group whose adherents were united only by belief. This theological revolution allowed the Jews of Iowa, like Jews in the rest of the country, to emphasize the American aspect of their identity. They were now Americans first and Jews second. Even the word "Jew" had pejorative connotations, so American Jews now became American Israelites or Americans of the Mosaic persuasion. In the Reform movement, Jews had finally found the vehicle that allowed them to be simultaneously middle class, Jewish, and Iowan. Major congregations in the state, in Des Moines, Cedar Rapids, and Davenport, adopted Reform practices and ideology.[1] Reform rabbis, graduates of the Hebrew Union College in Cincinnati, came to lead these congregations. Rabbis such as Eugene Mannheimer in Des Moines, Albert S. Goldstein in Sioux City, and William H. Fineshriber in Davenport were important leaders in both the Jewish and civic communities. The impact of these men cannot be overstated. They represented Iowa's Jews in an exemplary manner. They were erudite and educated, well spoken and well appointed, progressive, and ecumenically minded. Under their leadership, the Jewish community was ready to meet its next challenge.

The Russians Are Coming!

Czar Alexander II was assassinated in 1881 by a Russian anarchist, unleashing a torrent of reaction that especially affected the Jews of Russia. The Russian government created the one-third plan: one-third of the Jews would be forced to emigrate, one-third would be killed, and one-third would be converted to Christianity. Pogroms, government-inspired massacres, were inflicted on the Jews, spurring a massive exodus of Russian Jews to the Western Hemisphere. Between 1881 and 1924 when Congress cut off immigration, one and a half

[1]Sioux City was an anomaly in this pattern. Its flourishing meatpacking and grain-marketing industries attracted large numbers of Russian Jews, who brought their Orthodox practices and synagogues with them to their new homes. The Orthodox, who comprised twelve hundred of Sioux City's fifteen hundred Jewish inhabitants in 1912, dominated Jewish communal life until recent decades. See Michael Bell, "True Israelites of America, the Story of the Jews of Iowa," *Annals of Iowa* 53 (Spring 1994).

million Eastern European Jews emigrated to the United States. The vast majority stayed on the Eastern seaboard near the ports where they disembarked, but hundreds of Russian Jews eventually made their way to Iowa, changing forever the make up of the Jewish community.

These Russian Jews were "ethnic." Judaism for them was not just a religious faith; it was their culture and their way of life. They spoke and read Yiddish, ate kosher foods, dressed in distinctive garments, observed religious rituals, and were, in general, quite impoverished. The Russian Jews established Orthodox synagogues to meet their religious and social needs. These *shuls* were as foreign to the German Jews as they were to non-Jewish Iowans. A report from the August 10, 1902, edition of the *Des Moines Register* gives us insight into how they were viewed:

> The Russian Jewish tabernacle, a plain little church on the corner of East Second and Des Moines streets, gives no indication from the outside of what a quaint foreign world is to be found within. ... On entering, a confusion of meaningless sounds struck the ear, for a lively talk in either the Hebrew or Russian tongue was going on. ... For the most part ... the atmosphere was of the market place rather than of a house of worship, the keen, eager look on the faces of the long-coated little Hebrews and the gestures so universal an accomplishment to a Jewish bargain suggesting that matters material rather than spiritual were being discussed ... parts of the service were intoned by different speakers, quaint, bearded figures, their coats reaching near their ankles and derby hats giving almost a grotesque touch to what was doubtless a service.

The German Jews were shocked by their strange-looking, Yiddish-speaking Eastern brethren. These newcomers represented all that the German Jews had escaped and left behind in Europe. Now these modern, assimilated Iowa Jews had to help resettle these "landsmen" from afar. The appearance of the Russian Jews embarrassed the German Jews. Their manners, customs, and religion were Old World and decidedly non-American. The Russians reminded the Germans that they were only one generation beyond assimilation and poverty. The Germans believed that the blatant Jewishness of the Russians would precipitate a wave of virulent anti-Semitism, from which they had so far been spared. While they would not socialize with them nor invite them to worship in their Temples, the German Jews did extend a helping hand. A keenly felt sense of kinship and a desire to Americanize the Russians as soon as possible caused the Germans to create settlement houses, find housing and employment for new families, provide health care, and try their best to integrate the Russians into this society. The two communities, the Reformed and Orthodox as they were called, existed side by side. In Des Moines, the Reformed Jews lived on the west side of town in the recently developing residential areas and hence were known as the Westsiders. The Orthodox lived east of the Des Moines River and therefore were called the Eastsiders. By 1888, there were more Eastsiders in Des Moines than Westsiders. By 1895, there were 150 Jewish families living on the east side while only 100 lived on the west side. But for many years, the social gulf between them was much wider and deeper than the river that separated them. This situation was duplicated in every other Jewish community in Iowa.

The Americanization of the Eastsiders continued over the next few decades. Many advanced from peddling and pushcarts to their own small businesses or grocery stores. Some became scrap dealers, and others went into manufacturing. It did not take more than a generation for this hard-working group of Jews to advance economically to the point at which many moved to the more affluent west side of Des Moines.

The younger, American-born generation was not content with the Old World Judaism and synagogues of their parents yet, with few exceptions, could not embrace Reform, with its lack of familiar rituals and melodies. This led to the creation of Conservative synagogues in Des Moines (Tifereth Israel, 1907), Sioux City (Shaare Zion, 1925), and Iowa City (Agudas Achim, 1916). In future decades, Orthodox synagogues in Fort Dodge, Waterloo, and Ottumwa would affiliate with the Conservative movement. The Conservative movement retained many of the traditional practices with which the older generation was familiar while developing an English-speaking, modern American ambiance.

The growing number of agencies established to help resettle the Russian Jews inspired a move to coordinate their activities and fund-raising. In 1908, representatives of the Ladies' Benevolent Society, Hebrew Ladies Aid Society, and the Hebrew Ladies Relief formed the Federated Jewish Charities. Rabbi Eugene Mannheimer served as the president of this organization for more than thirty years. This agency was the precursor of the Jewish Federation of Greater Des Moines, which serves as the fund-raising and organizational arm of Des Moines Jewry. Similar organizations were formed in Sioux City and Davenport (1937). In the latter decades of the twentieth century, the Federation, in partnership with the synagogues, became the leading institutions within the Jewish community.

In the years after World War II, the differences between the German and Russian Jews dissipated for many reasons. (1) In Des Moines, the Eastsiders literally moved to the west side. Most of Iowa's Jews became middle to upper middle class and moved to the burgeoning suburbs surrounding the major cities. (2) American Jews realized that, in light of the Holocaust, the distinctions that separated them were petty. It had made no difference to Hitler whether a Jew originated in Germany or Eastern Europe; they were all doomed to die. So, too, the Jews themselves needed to ignore differences in order to live. (3) The struggle for the creation of the State of Israel caused Jews to unite in support of Israel, irrespective of their backgrounds. (4) Some second-generation Eastern European Jews were attracted to the ideology of the Reform movement. Their influence, as well as the renewed emphasis on Jewish peoplehood caused by the Holocaust and the creation of Israel, precipitated Reform's turn toward tradition, reducing the ideological and ritual differences separating it from Conservatism. This made Reform more attractive to all Jews. By the 1960s, the issue of one's origins became meaningless within the Jewish community.

The Jewish population of Iowa reached 15,000 in 1923 and peaked at 18,000 in 1937. It began to decline as early as 1939, when it was recorded at 17,000. The population stabilized during the war years, with a great decline in Iowa's Jewish population beginning after the war. The baby boomers left Iowa for good as they went off to Eastern schools which had, after World War II, shed their Jewish quotas. By the sixties, most of Iowa's Jews became part of the mobile middle to upper middle class. They (or their children) moved to areas of greater economic growth. Jews followed the jobs that left Sioux City, Cedar Rapids, and Davenport. Many of the smaller Jewish communities, such as Marshalltown, Oskaloosa, and Centerville, were forced, because of declining numbers, to close their synagogues. Others, in Fort Dodge, Waterloo, Mason City, and Burlington, are still clinging to life. In Sioux City, the Conservative and Reform synagogues merged in 1993 because of substantial population loss. However, the Jewish communities in Des Moines and Iowa City are experiencing slow, sustained growth, as are both of these metropolitan areas. A Jewish community of fifty to sixty families has emerged in Ames within the last quarter of this century. The fastest growing Jewish community in the state happens to be in Fairfield. Attracted by the Maharishi International University and its emphasis on Transcendental Meditation, approximately two hundred Jews have formed their own congregation and religious school. In 1994, the Jewish population of Iowa stands at between 5,000 and 6,000. Half the population lives in Greater Des Moines, with the rest in Sioux City, Cedar Rapids, Iowa City, Davenport, Ames, Fairfield, Grinnell, and several smaller towns previously mentioned.

From Marginality to Minority

Until the early 1960s, Jews stood on the margins of Iowa society. They desperately wanted to be accepted as social equals. Although some individual Jews had become prominent business, political, or civic leaders, Jews were rarely accepted as social peers. Business and social relationships were cemented in churches and private clubs from which Jews were excluded.

The secularization of American society in the middle of the twentieth century played a major role in opening the door to a greater equality for Iowa Jews. Suburbanization, greater mobility, the loosening of family ties, increasing access to education because of the GI Bill, and the acceptance of Judaism, along with Protestantism and Catholicism, as one of the three major religions to which Americans belonged, helped to create an environment in which Americans of different faiths and ethnic communities could participate as equals in American life. The American Jewish historian Arthur Hertzberg has written:

> Though the Jews who were moving into suburbia were often invading restricted enclaves, the cult of "Americans All" dictated to the churches that they had to exercise neighborliness. Whatever the theological differences, they were now expected to behave, in practice, as if they accepted each other as equals. President Dwight David Eisenhower drove home this point. Just before coming into office, Eisenhower had joined a church. ... The President had pronounced all religion to be good, provided that the sects did not squabble with one another, and that they joined in teaching their believers to take pride in the United States. Eisenhower himself provided the best definition of this ideology: "Our government makes no sense, unless it is founded in a deeply felt religious faith—and I don't care what it is." Jews were now part of this "civil religion" that had been fashioned during the Second World War and was now the "official" religion of American society. (Arthur Hertzberg, *The Jews in America* [Simon and Schuster, 1989], p. 322.)

The secularization of American society did not foreshadow the disappearance of the Jews, as eighteenth-century Christian advocates of Jewish emancipation had hoped, nor did it eliminate the prejudice that still manifested itself in the professions, business, and trades. Secularization did not guarantee a place at the table—only entrance into the room. Placed in the role of supplicants in a Christian-dominated society and eager for social acceptance, Jews in Iowa, as elsewhere, eagerly embraced the new secularism. Secularism became the "religion" of many Jews who tried their best to become more Iowan than the mainstream, more cultured than the elite, and more mannerly and dignified than the local patricians.

This began to change in the sixties when America was forced to become more inclusive and pluralistic. A watershed was reached in 1964 when, under pressure from its membership, the board of directors of Wakonda Country Club in Des Moines opened its membership to Jews. Over the next thirty years, barriers fell and some Jews became part of Iowa's power structure. Their Jewishness has not been an impediment to their acceptance in any facet of Iowa life. The presence of Jews in Iowa's political, business, civic, medical, academic, and arts communities has became an established fact. Today, Jews are present and active in various parts of Iowa life and culture far out of proportion to their meager numbers.

Most of Iowa's Jews live in the state's urban areas. Jews have virtually disappeared from the small towns. As in the rest of the country, Jews are overwhelmingly college-educated. More than 90 percent of Jews go to college, and more than half have graduate degrees. Very few family businesses are left among Iowa's Jews. Most, like Younkers, have been sold to large corporations or were dissolved when the children left the state. Jews tend to become professionals and are well represented in the medical, legal, and academic communities.

Judaism instructs its adherents, in the strongest terms, to give *tsedakah* (to be charitable) and to engage in *Talmud Torah* (the study of Torah and holy texts). In secular America, these practices were transformed into philanthropy and education. Studies have shown that Jews are more philanthropic than other groups and are among the most highly educated of Americans. Perhaps as a result of their education or because of their history of oppression, Jews also tend to be politically more liberal than the population as a whole. It has been said that because Jews have, on average, incomes that exceed those of Episcopalians, they should, according to political theorists, become conservatives. Yet Jews continue to vote as if they were impoverished immigrants. This is as true in Iowa as it is in the rest of the United States.

Jews also tend to be on the cutting edge of economic change. Iowa Jews have established computer software companies as well as firms dealing in genetic engineering and environmental preservation. Yet despite this general economic and social success, Iowa's Jews are a tiny minority, comprising less than one-quarter of 1 percent of the state's population. There are many non-Jewish adults in Iowa who have never met a Jew. Jews often have to explain themselves and Judaism to non-Jewish Iowans. Jewish children are often the only non-Christians in their schools. Living in a Christian-oriented culture causes discomfort, especially during Christmas and Easter, because Jews are, by definition, excluded from participation in these holidays and their festivities.

This minority status, however, also helps to create stronger Jewish communities, as Jews cling to one another for understanding and support. In the larger cities, an individual Jew can disappear into the crowd. In Iowa, every single Jew becomes an important member of the synagogue and Jewish community.

Iowa Jews and Jewish Iowans

Iowa Jews are to Iowa what New York Jews are to New York. If it is true that Iowans in general are more open, relaxed, polite, and friendly than New Yorkers, so, too, are Iowa Jews. If Iowans are less sophisticated, aggressive, confrontational, and frenetic than New Yorkers, so, too, are Iowa Jews. The essential difference between Iowa Jews and New York Jews is that Iowa Jews have undergone a true transmutation in their identity. Iowa Jews assimilated to the overwhelmingly Northern European Christian culture in a way that was not possible for Jews in the polyglot, ethnic environment of America's big cities. For Jews to survive in Iowa as Jews, they had to assimilate. Rabbi Jeffrey Portman of Iowa City has said that Iowa Jews have used assimilation as a strategy for survival. They are less visibly Old World Jewish than Jews on either coast. Michael Bell has written:

> Their prosperity, security, and liberty derive in large measure from their assimilation to the midwestern American culture that encircled them. From their first days in the state, Jewish Iowans adapted their religion, their customs, and themselves to the Iowa way. In every city, town, and neighborhood where they lived, they surrendered their language, transformed their faith, and adapted their customs to the rhythms of the daily life that surrounded them. Again and again, when offered the choice to keep the public identity they brought with them from Europe, Iowa's Jews chose to change themselves to be more like their neighbors and to adopt the values of American life. (Bell, "True Israelites," p. 124.)

Iowa Jews are less distinctively ethnic than Jews in large cities because Iowans, in general, exhibit less ethnicity. There are no Jewish neighborhoods, delis, restaurants, magazines, musical groups, community centers, country clubs, or other manifestations of Jewish culture that are evident in metropolitan areas with large concentrations of Jews. To identify as a Jew in Iowa requires an active personal commitment. Jews choose to be Jewish through their participation in organized Jewish life. To be a Jew in Iowa, one must become part of the Jewish community through membership in a synagogue and by contributing to and becoming involved in a Jewish Federation. Today, Jewish identification and cohesiveness are primarily through Judaism, or religious observance, rather than through Jewishness, or ethnicity. Most Jews are indistinguishable from other Iowans with the exception of their religious affiliation. The only possible relative differences are those that stem from the observance of religious precepts. Michael Bell adds:

> Jews ... learned that any decision to be made was personal. Slowly at first, but inevitably and inexorably, the conditions of community membership shifted from external to internal and from inherent to discretionary. In a sense, then, the

> story of the Jews of Iowa is one in which the possibility of choice replaced the necessities of tradition: in Iowa not only might Jews choose whether or not to remain Jewish, they were able to choose the kind and quality of Jewish life they would have. (Bell, "True Israelites," p. 126.)

Can Jews Survive in Iowa?

Iowa has been among the most hospitable and welcoming places the Jews have ever lived. Never before in history have Jews been so accepted. In no other place have Jews been so much at home. Nonobservant, secular Jews fit right into Iowa society. They are no different from other Iowans of similar income and educational levels. That is both the problem and the challenge. Because there are few differences among Iowans other than religious ones, nonreligious Iowa Jews have no compunction in marrying non-Jewish Iowans. In many cases, their blended families identify with a Christian denomination, and the children are not raised as Jews. The intermarriage rate nationally is 52 percent. Although there are no firm figures for Iowa, it is possibly as high as 70 to 75 percent. It is obvious that the Jewish community in Iowa cannot sustain itself unless it makes Jewish survival a priority. Unless there is a major influx into Iowa of Jews from the coasts, Iowa Jews must try to save themselves. The Jewish community can do this through the promotion and encouragement of Jewish religiosity and observance, Jewish education, and outreach to non-Jews and the non-Jewish spouses of Jews. It has already been demonstrated that Judaism is a viable religious alternative for many Iowans who were not born as Jews. It is possible that Iowans in larger numbers will voluntarily become part of the Jewish community in Iowa.

There are three Jewish denominations, ranging from Reform on the left to Orthodoxy on the right, with Conservatism trying to cling to the middle. While possessing differing ideologies and relationships to Jewish law, rabbis of all three major Jewish movements are striving to bring their assimilated and secularized congregants, most of whom are equally nonobservant regardless of their synagogue affiliation, to a more serious and sustained level of Jewish observance and knowledge. Jews who study Jewish texts, live by Jewish values, order their days and years by the Jewish liturgical calendar, and make a determined effort to keep the dietary laws will be able to maintain their identities in a form that Iowa and American culture can understand and accept. The author of Iowa's bicentennial history will be able to reflect on whether or not Iowa's Jews were successful in ensuring their community's survival.

FOLLOWING FAMILY TRADITION, Robert Morris became a journalist. He began that career by working at the *Iowa Bystander* for his grandfather, James B. Morris, Sr., who published the paper for half a century from 1922 to 1972. The *Bystander* had the largest circulation of any African American newspaper in the state and was considered by many people to be the most influential. Morris wrote for the paper under his grandfather's tutelage and decided he liked the profession. He took a leave of absence for a few years to pick up a bachelor's degree at the University of Iowa, where he founded the Iowa City chapter of the NAACP and served as its first president in 1979. In 1982, he presided over the Iowa/Nebraska NAACP State Conference. In both instances, he was the youngest president ever to serve.

Morris is currently CEO and president of the Morris Communications Group, which produces video and film programs. His documentary "Tradition and Valor" for Iowa Public Television recounts the history of African Americans in Iowa and has received critical acclaim for its content and production. Other assignments have taken him all over North America in the past ten years. He was named Iowa Minority Contractor of the Year in 1993 by the U.S. Small Business Administration and has been active in several civic organizations in the Des Moines area.

In 1994, Morris published an Anniversary Edition to celebrate the centennial of the first edition of the *Bystander* in 1894. Included below is a brief personal history of the *Bystander* by Morris and two excerpts originally published in the Anniversary Edition, by Robert Boldridge and Simon O. Roberts, about the African American experience in Iowa.

MORE THAN A NEWSPAPER

Robert Morris

"FEAR GOD, TELL THE TRUTH, AND MAKE MONEY," was the motto of Iowa's first black-oriented weekly newspaper published one hundred years ago last year. On June 8, 1894, the *Iowa State Bystander* began a publishing tradition that would cover two world wars and a civil and human rights movement that forever changed the way Americans live. More than a newspaper, the *Iowa Bystander* documented the struggle of this state's nonwhite citizens and articulated issues of direct concern to the black community. It also served as a tool to educate the white majority about their own prejudices and how racial discrimination works to the detriment of society as a whole.

Like hundreds of Iowa's black men and women, the *Bystander* provided me my first job. I learned how to work in a production operation while acquiring a love for reading and an interest in journalism. The small fee I received for hand folding and bundling newspapers was big money to an eight-year-old. Our publisher was also my grandfather, attorney James B. Morris, Sr. Every Thursday night the back room at 221 Locust Street became a school for life preparation for the ten to twenty young black men working there. Numerous young black women provided administrative, clerical, and journalistic support during the day.

A strict disciplinarian, J. B. Morris did not tolerate tardiness, sloppiness, or profanity in his shop. Instead, he stressed responsibility, proper grammar, education, and a working knowledge of black history. J.B.'s vision was a better future for young black men and women, an ambition he backed up with jobs, training, and guidance. Many of the young black men and women who worked at the *Bystander* during J.B.'s fifty-year tenure as publisher became some of Iowa's leading citizens.

More than a newspaper, the *Bystander* held cooking schools for young wives and mothers and fostered community pride with best-kept lawn and talent contests. J.B.'s predecessor, attorney John Lay Thompson, sponsored many of the same "pride building" initiatives during his two decades of publishing from 1900 to 1922. The *Bystander*'s first editor, Charles S. Ruff, had also espoused racial pride and achievement during his 1894–1900 tenure.

In 1903, the *Bystander* welcomed the first black troops to the newly built Fort Des Moines. Expecting white cavalry, local whites were shocked at the arrival of the ebony soldiers of the 25th Infantry instead. In 1917, the newspaper greeted the first black officer candidates at Fort Des Moines, while scolding local black residents who sought to ban Southern newcomers following the enlisted black troops to Camp Dodge. Following World War I, many of the black officers returned to Des Moines and became some of our most prominent community leaders. During the 1920s, the *Bystander* battled the powerful Iowa Ku Klux Klan, whose membership reached one hundred thousand members in 1924. The newspaper constantly called for anti-lynching legislation to save the hundreds of blacks being murdered in the Jim Crow South and in the urban North. In the midst of the 1930s Depression, the *Bystander* rallied community pride and pressed for human rights. In the next decade, World War II news followed Iowa's black soldiers' comings and goings as well as war news on the black contributions overseas and on the home front.

The 1950s and 1960s provided constant news of the struggle for civil and human rights, and the *Bystander* played a major role in articulating issues of concern to black and white

Iowans. I recall working at the newspaper in 1968 when the news of the assassination of the Rev. Martin Luther King, Jr., came in. The *Bystander* called for peace at a time when racial violence was a ticking bomb.

Though it has been out of print since the mid-1980s, the long legacy of the *Bystander* provides the best source of black Iowa history available. Fortunately, most of its issues have been preserved on microfilm by the State Historical Society from which future generations can see and learn. Publishing the 100th Anniversary Edition as a full-color magazine was a real thrill for me as J.B.'s grandson. Only my "Tradition and Valor" documentary for Iowa Public Television, also highlighting my family, provided a greater thrill for this writer who is big on history and legacy.

It seems ironic that after one hundred years of struggle the problems facing Iowa's black citizens are larger than ever. Poverty, drugs, crime, and illegal gang activity are rampant in urban Des Moines where homes once owned by proud families are deserted and nightly gunfire is a common occurrence. What happened to the community pride once promoted on the pages of the *Bystander*? Though we have more rhetoric than ever, who is backing their commitment to black youth with jobs, training, and guidance?

When Iowa lost the *Bystander,* it lost more than a newspaper. It lost an institution that cared about the status and future of Iowa, its communities, and its youth, backing its editorial content with jobs and career guidance for several generations of black youth locked out of the mainstream job market. We should remember the *Iowa Bystander* for its important contributions to the growth of this state and its people of all colors.

* * * *

The two essays that follow are reprinted from the *Bystander* Anniversary Issue.

A LOOK BACK:
BLACK FARM LIFE IN IOWA

Robert Boldridge

TODAY AS I LOOK BACK at growing up as an African American on a family farm in a predominantly white small farm community, the thing most people would find to be quite astonishing, and some downright unbelievable, is just how insignificant the racial aspects of it were.

I was the third of five children born to William and Dorothy Boldridge. We were raised on a 210-acre farm, seven miles south of Algona, from the World War II period through the 1950s. Our family, which included my three sisters and younger brother and my paternal grandparents who lived about three miles away in nearby Irvington, were the only black people in Kossuth County at that time.

Our story, which some might actually find refreshing, is just one unique situation that happened in one time and place and has nothing to do with the racial problems around the world today. The stark reality of it all is that we weren't much different from any of the other families who farmed in the area during that period. We knew them as our neighbors; they knew us as the Boldridges.

I have always been somewhat reticent about talking about our farming experiences and how well we got along with our neighbors because a lot of times such talk is greeted with skepticism and even cynicism, especially by those people who consider themselves to be experts on race relations. The last thing these experts want to hear is something new that might mean conceding that, just maybe, they didn't know everything there is to know about the racial situation. Perhaps I should have made something up about how the white farmers drove by on their tractors and threw pitchforks at us or that the cows wouldn't let us milk them because we were black (except that everybody knows that cows are colorblind).

We were the third generation of our family to live there. I was born there. We didn't just move there from the streets of

Detroit or Chicago or from somewhere down south. Most of our neighborhood farmers were men that my dad had been pitching hay with since he was about twelve years old. Most of their parents had known my grandparents before that. Everybody knew, or knew about, us. They knew who we were, a farm family trying to make a living. You had to be tough just to survive on a 200-acre farm back then, so that pretty much eliminated any stereotyping.

All the clichés about country farm life—the character-building virtues of watching things grow, the solitude, nearness to God, splendor of nature—were true for us. They probably had the same affect on us that they did on our neighbors. My dad didn't waste any time thinking about that. He believed farming was an honest living and something he enjoyed doing.

Another aspect of our lives was that we represented 100 percent of the live exposure that our neighbors had to black people. Some of them had never seen a black person in the flesh before, so we got to make the first impression, and that was kind of neat. Since we were so isolated, we had no choice but to handle the situation as a black family. That "us vs. them" collective group mentality was out of the question. Besides, we had no self-appointed black spokesperson to come in and represent us. It's a wonder we were able to survive.

It would seem that after my grandparents moved to northwest Iowa everything seemed to fall into place. The big decision for them was deciding to move up there to begin with. In 1902, William Boldridge, Sr. (Grandpa Boldridge) and his new wife, the former Fannie Rose Riding, who had been a school teacher at a little black country school, moved from near Lexington, Missouri, to the Britt area. Grandpa's uncle had preceded them about fifteen years before. They eventually rented a farm near Woden, a little town located at the very eastern edge of Hancock County about fifteen miles northwest of Britt. According to Grandpa, his Uncle Will, who had settled there earlier, sent word back that the people were friendly, open-minded, and willing to accept others on the basis of hard work rather than color. ...

As a tenant farmer and horse team trainer, my grandfather became acquainted with many farmers throughout the community. My grandparents were God-fearing, righteous people with impeccable reputations, and since they were alone, there was no reason for anyone to feel threatened by them so they made many friends. They raised my dad and his three sisters and eventually migrated to the area south of Algona where they rented several farms over the years, including the one which my dad eventually bought back in 1948. When they retired from farming in 1940, they settled in Irvington, a typical small town whistle-stop where grandma served as Sunday School superintendent for many years. Even back then I was in awe of how comfortably they lived for an elderly retired couple. They led such a simple peaceful life. Grandma had her church activities and flower garden, and Grandpa had his chickens, pigs, and a large vegetable garden in the backyard.

My dad was born in Woden in 1907. He grew up in what would have to be considered an almost Amish-like farming environment. As a young man he spent much of his time plowing the fields with a team of horses, which some farmers claimed is one of the most peaceful and satisfying things in the world. The only time my dad ever did anything close to being illegal was when he would occasionally skirt the fish and game laws, and then only on our property and for the food. We weren't able to get food stamps so we had to make do when times were hard. Since we had a river right over the hill from our house, we used a fish trap, which may not have been legal. I used to empty it out every night during the summer and anything that we didn't plan to eat went back into the river. In the wintertime my dad carried a 4.10 shotgun under the car seat which he used to shoot rabbits and pheasants that he sometimes spotted while driving the gravel roads bordering our property. That was his version of a "drive-by shooting."

One of our neighbors was an older farmer who would always come around and sometimes tell these off-color racial jokes. The guy was really harmless. He was just trying to be cute. My mother thought he was a jerk, but my dad overlooked his personality flaws because this neighbor was the person who combined our oats and soybeans and his wife was our babysitter. I remember her as a sweet old lady with granny glasses who wore her silver hair in a bun and read to us until we fell asleep.

As far as hardships, our biggest obstacles were the weather and the economics of farming. Of course, we had no control over the weather. We didn't really have any control over the economics either but it was always a concern. My dad's complaints of "us vs. them" would actually mean small vs. large farmers. ...

I was about four years old when one of the last threshing rings came to our farm. Prior to the combine, some of the neighborhood farmers would have to join forces to harvest the oats. The plan was simple. You would get about six other farmers to help you do your oats and when you were finished with yours, you helped them do theirs. By working together, you spared each other the expense of having to pay an outside crew to come in. ...

There was the time my dad got the mumps. Several white farmers came in and did the chores for about a week. They milked the cows, ran the separator, slopped the hogs, fed the chickens ... everything. Of course, my dad was always the first to help them when they needed it, too.

I always liked it when we sowed oats in the spring. I was about eight years old when I got to stay home from school to help get the oats in. I rode in the back of the oats trailer and made sure the grass seed dispenser never got empty. When I returned to school the next day, I couldn't wait for the city kids to ask if I had been sick so I could tell them that I had stayed home because "*my dad*" needed me to help with the spring planting. ...

During the fall we would get carloads of black men who would come up from Des Moines for squirrel and pheasant hunting. Our farm included forty acres of timber so there were many good hunting spots. They were all doctors, lawyers, and businessmen, a kind of "who's who" of Des Moines' black aristocracy. ... It was nice to have company. We didn't care what color. If they had kids my age, that only made it much better. Our neighbors felt the same way about us. Since we were poor, we were one of the last families in the neighborhood to get TV, which wasn't so bad because it meant that whenever one of our neighbors got a new TV set, they would invite us over to watch theirs.

When we finally quit farming in 1958 and moved into Algona, it was quite an adjustment for the whole family, especially for my dad who had been farming all his life. But he scraped around and did whatever he could to make ends meet. Mother was a very stabilizing force in the family at the same time. Her steadying influence kept us all on the beam in what were some pretty hectic times. Eventually my dad took a job with the city park commission. Among other things, he was caretaker of the Algona Rose Garden, which is now known as the Boldridge Rose Garden.

Our parents always taught us to take pride in ourselves, and I will forever value the experience of growing up on an Iowa farm.

* * * *

DAVENPORT

Simon O. Roberts

THE CITY OF DAVENPORT was a major industrial point around the turn of the century. From 1895 to 1925, the city grew rapidly, moving from an economy based on lumber, woodworking, metal and iron works to the beginning of the farm implement industry. During that time, a number of social and political movements and events shook and shaped the development of the city. The predominant German American population was a vital social and political force. Davenport was a city of neighborhoods, separated by natural and cultural barriers, with northwest Davenport reserved for German immigrants, Cork Hill in east central Davenport for the Irish, and with 125–200 Negroes scattered throughout the central and north central area of the city. ...

The primary migration of African Americans to the Quad City area and Davenport occurred in the early 1900s as a direct result of recruitment of laborers to work in the fast-growing farm implement factories of John Deere. Additional economic opportunities on the railroads, primarily as dining car waiters and porters, provided many blacks with the opportunity to settle in this area. Much of the population increase also occurred again in the early 1940s as a part of the World War II buildup and production of weapons and munitions at the Rock Island Arsenal.

In 1850, the Negro population in Iowa was estimated to be 333. In 1890, the population count in Davenport was 752, two percent of the city's inhabitants. ... From 1900 to 1925, the population of the city doubled. New housing sprinkled across the city, including the exclusively white neighborhoods of Central Park and Oak Land and the affluent McClelland Heights. New parks, a swimming pool in downtown Davenport called the Natatorium, skyscrapers like the Putnam, Kahl, and MacManus buildings, and two new bridges at the beginning of this period contributed to Davenport's reputation as an industrial transportation center in the Midwest.

But little of this advancement translated into benefits for the black citizens of Davenport. Here are a few facts regarding blacks in the Davenport area during the 1900–1945 period:

(1) There were no black clerks or retail sales people in any downtown stores or establishments (unless they were "passing").

(2) Residential housing segregation became a visible reality, and most blacks lived in two areas of the city: in central Davenport ... or on the east side of town.

(3) Discrimination even existed in the school athletic programs. The first black basketball player allowed to participate

at Davenport High School was Phillip Ashby in 1931. The second was Gene Backer in 1940 who became a standout baseball player in the 1950s and 1960s with the Chicago Cubs and Pittsburgh Pirates. ...

(4) Public accommodations for blacks is a post–World War II phenomenon indeed. Discrimination in hotels and restaurants existed in Davenport well into the 1950s. Most long-time residents remember the lawsuit filed by Nat "King" Cole when he was refused accommodations at the Fort Armstrong Hotel. Such famous performers as Louis Armstrong and Cab Calloway received the same treatment and could only stay at the homes of prominent black residents.

(5) Open housing only became a reality in Davenport in 1968 when the first such law in Iowa was passed by the Davenport City Council. The vestiges of housing discrimination continued well into the 1970s. Today, although plagued with similar housing problems in comparison with similar cities, Davenport has several programs in place to make affordable housing a reality for many of its citizens.

(6) The efforts to bring Davenport and the Quad Cities into the struggle for equality and human rights has always involved the total community. Early pioneers like Fathers John and Ed O'Connor, Jack Smith, Father Marv Mottet, Reverend Rims Barber, Jack Schneider, Sister Concetta, Jack Real, and Jesse and Henry Vargus made a real contribution. Long-time NAACP members Harriet Gordon, Josh Roberts, Powell "Sonny" Owens, Bernice Jones, Julius Collins, Charles Toney, Charles Berry, and Rev. Nathaniel Butler were black pioneers of the '40s, '50s, and '60s.

With the decline of the prominence of the farm implement industry, the local economy has been in transition from an emphasis on manufacturing to one rooted in tourism and service. Increased jobs in those areas have been beneficial, but the lower wages have created a variety of problems for the general population. African Americans have suffered disproportionately from this change. Unemployment, lack of medical insurance coverage, dysfunctional families, domestic violence, and crime are decimating the African American communities in Davenport and the Quad Cities. The existing system of employment opportunities continues to be closed to many African Americans. Although some attempts have been made through our local school systems, the access continues to be difficult for African Americans. The "underground" economy continues to draw more and more of our young into lives of crime, violence, and drugs.

Several local organizations have taken on a responsibility to help change these problems. Chief among these are the Metro Youth Group, the Metro Comm Branch of the NAACP, United Neighbors, Neighborhood Place, and the SCLC. The area has many black Greek Alumni Chapters and service clubs committed to providing real change and opportunity for our black youth.

So much of the future progress made in Davenport will depend on the commitment of many in both the black and white communities. Today, that integrated effort continues through many individuals and groups. Davenport and the Quad Cities area continue to possess the potential to become a modern, diverse model in the true sense of the American Dream.

I RECEIVED A LETTER one day from Mary Swander asking if I'd be willing to consider an essay from a friend of hers, Connie Mutel. Mutel had written *Fragile Giants: A Natural History of the Loess Hills* and had coedited with Swander a collection of essays on the same subject. Swander recommended her highly. OK with me, I responded. Shortly there arrived this poignant tribute to a neighbor. I didn't have to threaten or wheedle or whine or promise to feed her to get it. It just arrived. In a perfect world, that's how all collections would get put together.

Mutel grew up in Madison, Wisconsin, took a bachelor's degree at Oberlin College and then a master's in plant ecology from the University of Colorado. An Iowa resident since 1976, she is presently employed as a scientific historian at the University of Iowa's Institute of Hydraulic Research; she is also working on a biography and is involved with the Center for Global and Regional Environmental Change. In addition to her publications on the Loess Hills, she has written several books on nature themes, including the Colorado Rockies and the tropical rain forests, and is working on a handbook on prairie restoration. She has also published a study of the Einstein family.

You will meet the rest of the Mutel family (and several neighbors) in her essay.

ELEGY FOR MILVER

Cornelia Mutel

MILVER DIED on Sunday afternoon. I was standing at the kitchen sink peeling carrots when I heard the first sirens. My boys ran from the basement to join me as I watched first the sheriff's car, then the rescue vehicle, turn down Milver's lane. By the time I heard the ambulance from the city, the boys were on their dirt bikes racing down the road to where they could leap the ditch into the pasture, chase aside the cows, and peer down on the valley and farmhouse where Milver had lived for forty-two years. I came more slowly. I knew it must be another heart attack. I entered the pasture through the gate, nodded to an unseeing gun-clad deputy, and climbed through the stubble to tell my boys to go with me down to the farmyard where white-uniformed medics raced in seemingly meaningless circles, as if their frantic, diffuse energy could bring back the dead. The boys descended in a flurry, spewing gravel with their tires, their games of mission for once meeting reality.

Milver's daughter had driven out from town that afternoon, where she and her sisters live now, still present but always distant. She came out of the farmhouse to stand with me in the mud of the yard, where puddles in the tractor grooves were just beginning to ice over. Winter was setting in. The breath of the cattle smoked white. We cried and clutched our arms to our chest to keep warm while the medics finished loading their bags and climbed into the four-wheel-drive rescue vehicle, threw back a look of self-importance to the boys, and drove through the cattle lot and up the hill toward the timber. Milver had gone there with his son—the only child of six to stay and farm—to pull a tractor out of the mud before it froze in for the winter. "That's how I knowed it was meant to be," his wife Mary Ann told me later. "He was leaning over to attach a chain to the hitch, and he just keeled over. It would of happened no matter where he was." We watched the rescue vehicle disappear over the crest of the hill, and then we waited for them to bring out the body.

We wait for forty minutes. The bevy of boys jig to keep warm, and they box one another, but none of them asks to go home. By the time they bring Milver out, the night has set. The lights on the slowly descending rescue vehicle light a sliver of the hill, beckoning the rest of the household to come outside and see. All six of Milver's children have gotten here by now, and his city-bred grandchildren too. "He looked so bad, he didn't have his teeth in and his face was white," one of them whispers. (She had gone up to the timber before they summoned the ambulance.) The boys cluster around the rescue vehicle, shoving to be the first to peer into the opening doors while staying respectfully clear of the family. We see the soles of his brown rubber boots first. They form a floppy vee at the end of the stretcher as his legs jostle back and forth. Then his patched blue-striped overalls, pulled down to his waist. His chest covered with monitors, a cup over his mouth and nose, a heavy medic pumping on his breast. "I don't think Milver would of wanted all this," Mary Ann says, but too softly for them to hear. Milver's son steps up and tells them to turn it all off, "He's dead ain't he?", then cusses them out as they refuse to stop. "We'll tell you if he's dead when we get him to the hospital." But Mary Ann knows, we all know. The doors slam shut on Milver once again and he is borne up his lane away over his hills for the last time, with the red blinking light above his head beckoning the angels to come and attend their duty.

* * * *

My boys were born with their dancing shoes on. Their baby feet danced in the air to the crooning of their coos. They toddled through flurries of falling leaves and drifts of snowflakes. They galloped in the garden, and fell laughing on summer-heated sands, soaking the earth's warmth into their swim-chilled bodies, feeling her spirit of life pulse and breath beneath their own tiny hearts and lungs. They laughed as they danced, at the antics of the birds, at the slowness of the snail. And they sang as they laughed, sang to the forests and the owls and themselves, sang the song of the earth reincarnated in their own growing bodies. My boys danced to the stars and back, fully believing that where their minds traveled their bodies would follow, that they could grasp and hold forever the miracle of everlasting life.

Where are you dancing now, Milver? Are your feet jigging from one star to another? Does the movement warm your chilled, bloodless body? Or are your legs itching to polka but mired in the mud of the grave? Can you visit Mary Ann through her dreams, as when you courted her fifty years ago, and can you hold her once again in a slow waltz? Will you come and visit me here, Milver? Will you hoe your potatoes as I weed my carrots? Will your farm be big enough for you once your flesh is gone and only your spirit remains? Where are you dancing now, Milver?

* * * *

When I first moved to the country, the sky lay bottomless above me, black and silent. Now cities have grown up on both sides, Cedar Rapids to the north, Iowa City to the south. In the winter, black trees form silhouettes against the dull pinkish glare that reflects off of low-lying clouds. And to the east, a radio tower blinks red at four levels, off-on, off-on, to passing planes. From the west, I can hear the interstate seven miles distant. On all sides the misshapen fingers of scattered subdivisions reach toward me. I shudder at the thought of their touch.

Milver's farmstead lies in a black hollow, the core of a cluster of farms homesteaded by Bohemian Catholics over a century ago. Whenever he left his house, he had to climb up: up to the mailbox, up to the road, up to the timber or pasture or cropland. Up to town and people and city-bred pleasures. But usually he stayed down. He puttered with his tractor, and wired together his combine, and hoed his vegetables, and chopped firewood to sell cheap to anyone who would come and pick it up, and swung his grandchildren on the tire swing under the broad oak when they drove out from town. Lately he had been growing flowers to sell, and iris bulbs.

Milver had a yard light, but he rarely turned it on. At night, only a few lights beamed from his windows. Milver seemed comfortable with the dark and its mysteries. Surprisingly, Milver did not seem to mind the arc of mercury-vapor yard lights that grew ever brighter around his hollow. At least he never complained about them to me, but then I never heard him complain about anything. In a sense he even promoted them because most of the mercury-vapor lights illuminate homes built on snippets of land he had cut from his cornfields to sell to city people who wanted to return to the land. Now those lights crown his dark hollow with a yellow halo. Mary Ann turns on the yard light sometimes, but usually she leaves it off, as if making her lonely house a black bull's-eye that each night beckons Milver's soaring spirit home.

* * * *

What do children see in the still, silent specter of a dead body? How do they shed the frightening drag of its weight?

The night that Milver died, my oldest son decided to practice his trombone outside. He climbed the fence into Milver's pasture and blasted jazz to the stars. I think he danced as he played. And then the tone changed, and I heard a wailing taps drift and cry and flow through the hollows, for a moment only, until the boogie grabbed that horn and spun it to the sky once again. He returned home announcing that he would repeat his performance the following night, in the nude.

My middle son chose to sweat away his stunned silence. He visited a friend to practice wrestling techniques for the next meet.

Only my littlest was young enough to babble out his fears and lay them flat on the table. Looking through the window at the night sky, his questions began: "What does it feel like when you have a heart attack? Does it hurt? Do you know you are dying? Do you see other dead people when you are dying? How long does it take until you rot away? Do your clothes last longer than your skin? Are you buried with your shoes on? Will Milver be buried on his farm? Why can't he be, if that's where he lived? Where do you want to be buried? When I die, can I be buried with you? I think I just saw a shooting star. Is that Milver going to heaven?" And then, "Mom, look, LOOK, I just saw a meteor, a big meteor and it hit the ground! I know it hit the ground right over there and I was the only one to see it! I'm going to have to tell Dad about this!"

* * * *

I first saw Milver's land on a windswept stormy day in the late fall. Having just moved to Iowa City from Colorado, where I had roamed the mountains and lost myself in their mysteries, I was depressed by the straight lines that ordered Iowa's endless cornfields and city streets according to efficient human use. Thus a few weeks after arriving I took off along the river, intending to wander its forested meanders for the entire day. I climbed through brambles and over logs for six hours until a cold rain chilled me and I yearned once again for warmth and shelter. Then I turned away from the river and entered the surrounding agricultural land, hoping to find a road that would provide a shortcut home.

I walked with my eyes down, trying to keep out the rain, my numb legs unaware that they were climbing a steep hill until I arrived at its top and my eyes were called upward by the shrill screams of a pair of soaring and plunging hawks. I was skirting a woodland bordered by a rickety fence that encircled a hilltop field where twenty or so Black Angus huddled with their back ends to the wind, which crashed through the trees and surrounded me like storm waves on an ocean's shore. Far below me in a narrow valley nestled the white house and red outbuildings of a farmstead. Around me, relentlessly driven strings of cloud shot eastward like arrows. Above, the two hawks climbed the thermals—but no, not two, now I saw more, many more: far above, an endless chain of migrating broad-winged hawks streaked southward on the wind's wings, pulling along with them all the threads of wildness and home that I had ever found in the mountains.

Those hawks and the cold wildness of that day once again soared through my mind on the afternoon that Milver died. How could I have known, that day long ago, that we would buy the woodland a year later and with our own hands build a small house there, like the old miner's cabin we had left in Colorado, and that this solid stretch of green-clad earthy mud and rich humus would become home not just to me and to him but to our three babies, each fastening his sparkling eyes on the birds that soared and plunged there ever after. And that Milver, his lanky body wrinkled and greying, his toothless mouth perpetually smiling, would climb up from the house in the valley to plant his garden just across the road from where I planted my own, and that we would exchange sweet potato slips and strawberry roots, and that he would teach me how to sow oats as ground cover, and chide me for mulching rather than hoeing my potatoes. "I did that one year," he'd yell across the road each spring, "and the potatoes tasted jest like dirt. You'll be sorry."

Not that I always agreed with Milver or his approach to the land. Just when the bobolinks had succeeded in seducing their mates and were ready to lay eggs in his alfalfa field, he would go ahead and mow. When rare orchids bloomed in his timber, he'd pick them for a table bouquet. Once he shyly led me behind his barn to a great-horned owl that he had shot illegally the night before because it had been bothering his chickens. "Now don't tell no one," he warned, "and you can take whatever you want from it. The wings, the feathers, the head, the whole thing." When I told Milver that I was planning to turn half my garden into a small prairie, he warned me against planting "them tall reddish grasses. Once they get going, you'll never get rid of 'em." Questioning him further, I learned that just thirty years earlier, he had labored to rid parts of his own land of these deep-rooted natives—becoming one of Iowa's last farmers to plow under native prairie healthy enough to throw the plow broken back into his face.

Yet the earth seemed to love Milver. He knew just how hard to push without breaking it. No matter what he did, his farm continued to spill out new life. Piglets, chicks, calves were born in abundance there. Corn flowed from his bins and vegetables erupted from his garden. Potatoes especially. He loved to plant potatoes. Thirty, forty pounds of seed potatoes, secretly multiplying under the ground into hundreds of pounds more, all hoed and dug by hand. He took them to the farmer's market three times a week along with his other vegetables, and in between times he took them to his friends. Once, as we were pulling out of the driveway for a two-week vacation, Milver appeared with two feed sacks full of sweet corn. "For your freezer," he announced with a smile. Once when snowflakes sifted through the bitter cold, he appeared at the door with a bucket of brilliantly red frozen strawberries. "For your Christmas dinner." Just this last summer I found a string-bound bundle of muddy iris bulbs in my mailbox with a note stuck between the dried leaves. "No charge. Milver." He collected nuts, hickory nuts, black walnuts, whatever he could find. He snipped bittersweet and grapevines from his fencelines to weave into wreaths that his daughter sold at her flower store.

The last time I saw Milver, his thin cracked fingers were prying his garden's soil for sweet potatoes. I was pulling turnips. He waved a bare bunch of roots in the air and yelled across the road, "Some years they grow and some years they don't. This year was no good. Got to just keep trying and see what you get." I took him over a fat bunch of turnips. "These look sweet. Mine was no good this year. Cracked and hollow. Thanks."

Milver never moved out of the township where he had

been born. His funeral mass was held in the same church where he had been baptized seventy-nine years earlier. We buried him in the churchyard, under a wreath decorated with nuts and bittersweet and Indian corn he had picked just the week before, and then we returned to the church basement to eat ham and potatoes, potatoes from Milver's garden, potatoes peeled and cooked by Milver's children the day before.

* * * *

My boys walk with me back up the lane. The sky is black now, the stars an icy cold crown above our frosted breath. Ahead of us, the ambulance moves slowly along frozen ruts, its red light blinking but its siren muted. There is no need for speed now. Mary Ann's car follows. She yells back to us as we near the hilltop. "Say would you be sure the gate is shut tight when everyone is gone? It wouldn't do for the cattle to get out tonight."

Cows, calves, hogs squirming through the fence, babies born kicking and bawling, beheaded chickens hanging by their feet from the clothesline to bleed, squealing life, bitter death—the context of Mary Ann's life has stood her well. But then these are tough farm neighbors I have here in the country. Bohemian Catholics all, whose grandparents homesteaded these hills and bore their babies at home and raised them on turnips and potatoes. Our neighbor to the west is ninety-two, with legs swollen like an elephant's. His wife hung herself in the old farmhouse twenty years ago and he has lived alone on Milky Ways and Pepsi ever since. He has trouble cleaning himself now with his swollen, stiff hands. His overalls hang open in the crotch and he smells. That scares my boys. But look in his face I tell them, and you will see the smile of the angels. And there it is, hidden among flaps of creased skin and smeared chocolate, fronting a mind as sharp as any of theirs. He still gardens with a fervor, watering his beans and pickles at 5:00 A.M., picking before the sun gets too hot. Too stiff to stoop, he crawls through the rows, dragging behind him buckets of tomatoes and peppers, cucumbers and cabbages. Whenever our phone rings before we are awake, I know he is offering us his excesses.

The widow to the north lives on the old family farmstead with her daughter. They come one evening to collect money to help Mary Ann pay for the burial. I invite them in and they enter smiling. "Remember our neighbors, boys?" I say. "The ones who love to burn?" And they beam and say "Yes, YES, why we was burning just today. Leaves from the old schoolhouse yard." And dried grasses in the summer, and old dirtied straw in the winter and spring. They burn whatever they can to create warmth and light and excitement in their farmyard. The mother tells me that she doesn't know what she will do without Milver. "He was always doing kind things for us neighbors. He used to put up my storm windows for me in the winter. I can't handle them ladders too good any more." She is eighty-nine. And then, as an afterthought, she adds, "There was all boys in my husband's family, and only one girl, and she died when she was a baby. She froze to death in the bedroom. Houses was different back then." When she leaves, she lifts high her index finger, which is strangely crooked and somehow stretched an inch longer than all her others. Shaking it at my teenage son who towers more than a foot above her, she commands him, "You be a good boy. You study hard and like your schoolwork, and you'll do okay." And then she smiles approvingly and whispers to me, "He looks like a nice boy."

These are the guardians of my neighborhood. They have watched the mini-vans and carbon-fiber bicycles take over their farm lanes and greeted the new with grace. While we built houses with multiple commodes and double garages, they turned the corner of their kitchen into a bathroom and painted their wooden siding white yet one more time. Smiling silent sentinels, they blessed our children and heralded us from their tractors as they watched us leave the land to drive off to our city jobs for the day. Milver was one of them. He stood among his potatoes grinning at the commuters, offering any bicyclist who stopped a taste of his raspberries. His arms waved hello to the world while his feet curled into the soil and held him firm. He tended the land and beckoned us home.

WHEN JOHN CHRYSTAL ran for governor in 1990, he was sometimes identified as "Des Moines banker John Chrystal." That was true, of course, because at the time he was chairman and CEO of Bankers Trust, one of the largest banks in the state. But such a title did little to describe his long record of public service and unique accomplishments. A nephew of hybrid corn promoter Roswell Garst, who hosted Nikita Khrushchev's historic visit to Iowa in 1959, Chrystal has played a quiet but critical role in promoting better relations between the world's Super Powers, making many trips to Moscow to offer suggestions on improving Russian agriculture and trade relations. In 1981, Chrystal was the first American to visit Mikhail Gorbachev, who was then just an officer in the Soviet Communist Party. He has served on the Iowa Board of Regents and on the boards of the Iowa Peace Institute, the Iowa Civil Liberties Union, Grinnell College, and the Iowa Bankers Association. A graduate of the University of Iowa, Chrystal holds honorary degrees from Clarke, Grand View, Simpson, and Iowa Wesleyan colleges.

Chrystal is a man of vision who is as at home in a small-town coffee shop or an international conference. And in John, the two worlds become one. He can start telling a joke he heard in Coon Rapids and blend it effortlessly into what effect the disintegration of the Soviet Union will have on Iowa farmers. There is no one better to take a look at Iowa's future.

THE FUTURE OF IOWA: CAN WE BE A PLACE TO GROW?

John Chrystal

I HAVE BEEN ASKED to predict what Iowa will be like thirty years from now. If asked that question thirty years ago, I suppose that my answer would have been more optimistic than today's reality of a shrinking, aging Iowa less economically viable than its neighbors. But since 1960 I have had a varied life experience and the opportunity to see economic data develop. I have been active in both small-town and city economies. I have been a participant in large industry. So, based on my own experiences and observations, I foolishly accept the obligation of forecasting. If nothing else, I have seen something of where Iowa has been.

My earliest memories are as a farm kid in the early 1930s. My dad was an average- to above-sized farmer. Our family had other assets besides the farm, making us a part of the "400" in Coon Rapids, a town of twelve hundred. In this case, the "400" was the upper economic one third, not the upper one third of 1 percent. My father wasn't lazy, but farming wasn't his greatest interest. He served a term and a half as a state senator, idolized Franklin Delano Roosevelt, and disliked "vested interests."

My maternal grandfather and then his heirs owned parts of the main local dry goods store and bank. The community golf course and swimming pool are now located on part of his otherwise fairly worthless farm. My uncle, Roswell Garst, started a seed corn business locally. He was a contributor to the planning of the New Deal farm program and knew its architects. People came from across the Western Corn Belt to visit him and observe the production and processing of the new hybrid corn. Uncle Bob and I were close when I was a child, so I got to meet many of these people and listen to conversations about agriculture's bright future. Those times were difficult, but almost every American believed things would be better in the future. Occasionally, I would get to travel with Uncle Bob in Nebraska or Missouri or Kansas as he sought salesmen and spread the gospel of his cornucopia. The seed company was our town's largest employer, but the owners did not have much money because of the business' needs for cash. Vision was a substitute for greenbacks.

After college and farming for ten years, I became (I think) a successful, respected banker dabbling in liberal politics and agricultural relations with the Soviet Union and then its dismembered parts. My Uncle Bob had started me down the Eastern European road after Khrushchev's visit to his farm in 1959, and I followed.

During my early childhood, middle-American farming didn't have the three classes of rich, middle, and poor—only two: middle class and poor. People had household help only when the work was too much; luxuries were not admired. The poor were very poor, materially poorer than the rural poor today. Nobody crossed the Atlantic or Pacific oceans except for war. A few farm children went to college, but just a few. Electricity and tractors were just starting to come to farms. The Iowa State Fair was a major family trip. Sickness could be a financial disaster. Ordinary clothing and sometimes even food could be problems for some respectable but poor rural families. Welfare was a shameful solution to difficulties. Fortunately, the rural population's standard of living since World War II has increased a good deal.

Today, I am still socially and economically middle class; however, I do belong to an elite group that has had a front-row seat and even taken part in Iowa changes of the last sixty years. That gives me the ability to look forward, unless, like too many Iowans, I am too satisfied with the present. Often, Iowans are as afraid of success as failure. We are afraid of change.

My observation is that even though we Iowans present ourselves as average Americans, we privately enjoy an above-average self-appraisal of our way of life, education, peacefulness, and the productivity of our land and people. We think of ourselves as our own dream come true. But are we? I was disappointed recently at our state government's willingness to pay any price, do anything, to retain "well-paid" jobs with Lennox Industries, an industry born in Marshalltown, Iowa, and to acquire four hundred new jobs in the same firm. Those new jobs would pay seven dollars an hour. We "won" and were ecstatic, hailing the defense as a great victory. Labor unions joined in the effort and celebration, but seven dollars an hour for two thousand hours is just above the poverty level. What a victory!

If such effort and wages and results are considered wonderful, then maybe Iowa should give serious thought to self-reappraisal. In Iowa the average family income in 1980 was $20,100 and in 1990 it was $26,229. The U.S. consumer price index (CPI) in that same period rose 60 percent. Considering that, Iowa families were relatively worse off in 1990 than in 1980. A comparison of ourselves with our fellow Americans indicates that our financial progress is below average.

- Our state's total population shrank 5 percent in the 1980s, but the Golden Circle and the Johnson-Linn County corridor grew enough to make their local leaders proud. The Golden Circle grew 30 percent and Johnson-Linn, 15 percent. Most of that growth was a shift away from rural Iowa.
- Manufacturing jobs in Iowa grew not at all, and the hourly wage in that ten years grew one-half the increase in the CPI. Nonsupervisory job wages grew less than 15 percent while the CPI was increasing 60 percent. Nonmanufacturing job wages grew slightly more than 30 percent. Very large farms and small moonlighter farm numbers grew in Iowa

while the number of medium-sized family farms shrank appreciably.

It seems obvious that Iowa's economic development efforts are less successful than those of our competing neighboring states, all of whose population grew during the 1980s.

Most jobs Iowa has attracted or created in past decades do not pay well. They are too close to poverty level and are not nationally competitive. Poor wages attract more poor-wage jobs. Population figures indicate we don't even win many contests attracting low-paying companies, so we should get out of the day-to-day contest for jobs. Our efforts for economic growth should be longer term: We should make Iowa a more attractive place to work and live. We obviously have not been adequately attractive to blue-ribbon companies.

Continuing our same failed efforts for improvement seems foolish to me. For sixty years the rural population of Iowa has been shrinking for two interlocked reasons: Low income compared with comparable urban areas, and the ability and necessity to farm more ground. The rural standard of living earned by equity and labor in my youth was not as high as in the city; there was a great desire for improvement. One way to correct this imbalance was to increase the yield per acre or daily rate of gain and thus profit through genetics or chemistry. Another was to improve farm machinery, which increased the numbers of units that one worker could handle, thus cutting costs. Hybrid corn is a perfect example. Breeding made yield per acre greater, and the new strength of stalks made the mechanical corn pickers feasible. The addition of fertilizers and chemicals to other scientific advancements has in sixty years increased yield per acre by 400 percent while equally increasing the acres one family can work. Therefore, such advances in production were population retardants.

Likewise, in recent decades much livestock production in America has been industrialized, creating a more uniform, efficiently produced product while cutting labor needs. I don't know a single Iowa farmer that has a flock of chickens today—not one. All chickens are produced in buildings housing tens or hundreds of thousands of birds. Hog production is racing in the same direction. I think another decade will see the end of traditional farmer-raised hogs. Cattle fattening is not as far down the trail of industrialization as hogs and chickens, but half of America's fat cattle are fed in large feed lots. All these efforts toward bigness shrink numbers of necessary farm labor and do not increase slaughterhouse or feed mill labor numbers. Not affecting farm worker numbers a great deal but also an important change is the elimination of smaller, less-efficient undercapitalized gatherers and processors of farm produce, that is, slaughterhouses and elevators, among others. Currently we need only 2 percent of our U.S. population on the farm.

Sixty years in the span of time is an instant. The United States has been the champion of improvement; even more changes will come more quickly in the future. Today's farm subsidy program is thought by many to be obsolete. But America should never forget the value of production control and price support plans during the middle decades of this century. Minimum prices or farm income guaranties made agricultural research and investment possible; subsidies made banks willing to loan for progress. Iowa's own Henry Wallace built a base for farm progress for all of American agriculture and planted the seeds for a smaller farm population.

Let me use statistics from Greene County where I lived as a farmer in the 1950s. Greene has been a "showcase" county, having wonderful people, high-quality soil, excellent education and transportation, and social stability. But compare the discouraging figures from the 1980 and 1990 censuses shown in the table.

Not only has our farm population shrunk drastically, so have the size and composition of small towns. Rural America's average age has increased, with the small town aging most. Proof lies in the necessity for school merging, the lack of new rural housing or commercial construction, and the disappearance of numerous retail and service outlets. The relative value of small-town land, buildings, and business has plummeted to a fraction of that a few decades ago. This shocking change has

Greene County statistics from the 1980 and 1990 census

	1980	1990	Variance
Population	12,119	10,045	–17.1%
Average age (1978–1987)	48.8	49.7	+1.8%
Number of K-12 students	2,329	1,905	–18.2%
Average farm size	327	377	+15.3%
Number of farms	1,090	940	–13.7%
Number of cattle, fed	23,000	11,000	–50.0%
Number of cattle, cows	18,000	8,400	–54.0%
Number of hogs marketed	230,000	163,000	–30.0%
Population receiving welfare	5.4%	5.9%	+8.8%

occurred not only because of declining farm numbers and thus farm population, but because of improved transportation—roads, cars, and trucks. Hard-surfaced roads are everywhere, allowing small-town buyers to drive quickly and easily to larger towns where there is specialization and a greater variety of goods and services. Thus, non-farm jobs not only have shrunk overall, but many have moved to regionally centered locations.

New kinds of merchandising are greatly affecting small-town rural America. Convenience stores keep a low overhead of frequently purchased items, leaving items of diversity for the inventory of regional shopping centers. Even regionally centered merchandising is often served by warehouse retail chains. These no-service, cash-sale, volume outlets allow low prices that are difficult for traditional retailers to match. The weakest or most directly competitive of previously successful rural merchants are going out of business.

Part of the rural population demanded and has achieved a standard of living comparable to that of their city cousins who have like net worths. The desire for improvement often requires off-farm jobs for one or both family adults. The lack of nonfarm employment and the increased difficulty in raising their standard of living make the choice of staying in rural Iowa or migrating less difficult for young Iowans.

Iowa has not been an economic self-starter. Investment banking is almost nonexistent in the state. Although quite a few insurance companies' home offices are in Iowa, not one bank of national stature is headquartered here. Iowa's leading newspaper is owned by a holding company whose home office is elsewhere, as are the main TV stations. Agricultural companies recognized nationally and headquartered in Iowa are limited to Pioneer International and a very few others. Pioneer is followed by small manufacturers such as Kinsey farm equipment and a small (by IBP standards) slaughterhouse, Iowa Packing Co. We have one national household appliance manufacturer headquartered in Iowa, Maytag. Winnebago and Ruan are involved in different aspects of national transportation (service and manufacturing). This is not a large number of Iowa-headquartered national companies, is it? One theme common to these few companies has been strong founders. They were not started by groups aided with investment banking capital. Iowa is so rich in renewable resources we think too often we can afford to be economically conservative.

As a result of economic pushes and pulls in Iowa, the population of most Iowa areas has shrunk. As farm population has gotten smaller, people have moved past nearby towns to cities or other states where more job opportunities exist. Schools, churches, hospitals, and county governments are among those public institutions whose shrinking clientele offers the opportunity of merging or sharing of employees. Television and videocassettes as well as shrinking population numbers have injured the economic health of fraternal lodges, movie houses, and social and entertainment organizations.

I believe there will be an accelerated rate of advancement in agricultural science in the decades ahead, creating even higher yields and a smaller farm population. With this development will come lower unit prices for farm products as we compete with lower-cost Third World or nearly Third World farm producers. Income subsidies for the large-in-size, capital-heavy, and high-volume U.S. farmers will surely decline as the public sees their assets necessarily increase.

Some people say that one way of maintaining Iowa's population is by economically protecting the family farm. There is little doubt that more family farms mean a greater farm population that might buy products and services in small towns. A larger population very simply means more commerce. I have heard two suggestions for the enhancement of family farms. First is progressive property taxes on agricultural assets. At some level of tax, this idea would make large farms or agricultural complexes unattractive to investors. Second would be a stop on any government payments, loans, or rents to farm operations that hold assets exceeding some level of value. Neither will be politically successful.

However, I think not to have some kind of government production or "nonproduction" subsidies for all farmers in an unfettered world market with U.S. agricultural input costs as high as they are today would bring financial ruin to agriculture, especially large farmers. Small farmers, with lower overhead and a higher percentage of gross income from off-farm employment, would have a better chance of survival without government aid, and their success would be a comparative cinch with it. Passage of these two ideas into law would require a political magician to defend against the charge of social engineering. But in fact, they are no more social engineering than Social Security, the G.I. Bill, or quite a few existing governmental programs considered ordinary today. The problem is that programs of selective restriction or denial have a history of failure. The farm size tide is rising; changes caused by technology, education, and communication are inevitable and generally beneficial to the public. We need to recognize that certainty of change and try to manage it. To look ahead and plan, we must look around us and then ahead with a positive attitude for a bright Iowa future.

If American numbers of farm workers and suppliers and gatherers of produce fell by half tomorrow, the overall effect on the United States would be modest—from 2 percent of the population to 1 percent. The big emigration has already happened. Traditional farming does not have much to do with the demographic or economic future. The pain of change would be great for those few immediately involved, including Iowa, but for the consumer the price and quality of food and fiber may improve.

It seems to me there are two kinds of economic development structures needed for Iowa: regionalism and education.

We have nine hundred towns in this state with populations less than five thousand. Most of these towns have a dubious future. Some, more than twenty of the larger towns outside the Des Moines–Ames and Iowa City–Cedar Rapids areas, will be regional industrial centers and thus job centers for themselves and smaller towns within commuting distance. I do not mean at all that the small towns should waste away, but their expectations must be different. Development money spent locally should have new goals, and those small towns should be willing to participate in the economic development of the area's regional center.

Without good jobs in a region, new housing won't be built, retailers will disappear, and population loss in the young-adult age group will accelerate. If what I suggest is true, municipal solutions will be quite different according to size: the smaller will seek to maintain, and the other will emphasize growth. Smaller places must realize and agree that unequal development expenditures may well be necessary for everybody's success. Many towns and their governments, including county governments, must recognize that they are neighborhoods in a larger community. Those pleasant, pretty places to live can have a healthy, amiable survival—maybe even growth—if enough jobs are available at their regional center. Those centers are where investment must be made. To not be a participant in change will mean small-town money will be spent to no avail, with a dismal future as a result of not trying to realistically create opportunity.

Jobs will not just happen in Iowa, and I don't believe jobs can be bought at prudent prices. New companies must be born and grown in Iowa. Existing companies must be drawn here for reasons other than low taxes, anti-union laws, or bribes. We need leadership to create a better-educated citizenry and an even more pleasant place to live, as well as to attract risk investment money in amounts capable of funding business development and growth.

There is no question in my mind that educational needs will expand and be more specialized and complex as we move further into a scientific future. We must take the chance that we can capitalize on new discoveries before others profit from our research. Ideas don't know geographic boundaries. Our children must be participants in the exploding sciences of biotechnology, digital communications, metallurgy, lasers, mathematics, and chemistry, among others, and such learning must continue on the job for adult workers. Mostly, however, we must stop arguing about football teams and spend more money on education, from kindergarten through doctoral degrees. Education is floundering in the swamp of our self-satisfaction. We gloat over the literacy rate of Iowans, but we forget that our nation's children compare poorly with students from the schools of our international competitors in important fields. We do not move actively enough to regain our position of being first. It is not just a matter of money but of desire and leadership.

Our universities must change somewhat in their goals. To compete or stay ahead, we must have basic sciences lead the world in cooperation between business and academia and leave applied science where the big money is: Industry. Academicians must aim more directly at creating new or improving existing industries. Business and academia must continue to have carefully protected independence, but also carefully agreed upon goals. Other states have done it; we must follow, no matter if late.

Academicians should advise leaders but must be braver in suggesting public economic investment outside of education, planning for governmental aid, or changes in organization for the common good. They should promote regionalization. Such advice may mean financial denial by some—tough politics.

All of this must be done without damaging the traditional post–high school course schedule. Such change in our educational structure will cause another round of school mergers and cost a lot of money. I doubt that a shrinking state with 2.8 million citizens of modest income can afford three state universities, each striving to be first class in too many things, plus sixteen area vocational schools and more than twenty private colleges.

Ambiance is a word that can mean the pleasant atmosphere of an environment or setting. As life in the big cities and on the coasts becomes less attractive to some, Iowa ought to be sure that its lush and beautiful productivity is combined with recreational facilities such as parks, lakes, bike trails, forests, theaters, museums, and other attractions for children and working-age people as well as older people. New recreational offerings will have to be subsidized in the early days, probably forever, but such investment is necessary to attract new jobs.

Bootstrap business starts will be harder in America as research becomes more important. By far, most of the nonbasic research for American industry is done by big private players, not universities. Mergers and acquisitions make market entry very difficult for companies that are not in the big leagues. Even the new area of biogenetics has few miraculous company start-ups—the big boys have won. But, wonders can and will happen if capital is available.

Investment capital. Iowans might create the most wonderful technical ideas in the world, but implementation of those ideas into jobs cannot occur without risk money. Successful risk capital pays good returns because the failure rate of new ventures far exceeds that of ordinary investment. I have long thought that Iowa needs a large risk capital fund—a combination of public and private money, with the public funds suffering a high percentage of first losses. Such an arrangement would make private funds easier to attract in large amounts.

As mentioned above, leadership is the most important needed ingredient for progress. Without leadership, government cannot hope to make public investment unequally. But Iowa cannot afford to make investments unless economic potential exists. Most towns in Iowa can never attract the jobs they dream about. Without explanation from strong leaders, the public simply will not stand such unequal public investment.

Economic regionalization requires identifying those regions and their centers. I know how to identify regional centers cheaply: Let's use the survey money companies have already spent to identify where to build their McDonald's, Colonel Sanders, Hy-Vee, and Wal-Mart and K-Mart.

The good life—expanding educational and recreational efforts—is necessary for progress, and yet they are expensive. Are Iowans willing to pay up front for long-term profit? I don't know, but I do know they should be given the opportunity. The presenter of the options, I hope, will be prejudiced in favor of change and in favor of spending for profit.

Our neighbors Missouri, Illinois, and Minnesota are all union-supportive states, all have higher taxes than Iowa, and all are more prosperous than Iowa. We have too often seen programs that are the result of defensiveness. Defensiveness doesn't win many games. The best thing Iowa has done since the days of Harold Hughes and "one person/one vote" has been Governor Branstad and the Legislature building a fiber-optic network. Both showed leadership. Such moves can pull us ahead of the crowd. It is the stuff of leadership and the stuff of economic development.

What will happen to Iowa if leadership does not make the moves I suggest? Nothing much. We will only continue to drift down. In fact, undirected regionalization will occur with or without good public management. School and government mergers will happen anyway because money needs will leave no choice. State population growth either won't occur or will be at a much lower rate than it could be. The university system will not be able to halt the erosion of standards by spending smaller amounts of taxes paid by a smaller population. The bad will come naturally; success will elude us.

Without jobs that pay well to keep young citizens here and without new industry, the relative decline of Iowa will be a self-fulfilling prophecy. Building prisons for young criminals treats symptoms instead of causes. Unless we are willing to spend money in new ways, Iowa will not succeed in the relative national economic development contest. All our troubles might be over if oil or gold or diamonds could be discovered here, but dreams are no substitute for reality.

In my opinion, the chance of Iowa being at either extreme of opportunity is remote. We will do some good things, though not enough, even without leadership to urge us on. Thus far, while using "a place to grow" as our slogan, Iowa has shrunk. We need Iowa's population wanting Iowa to be a place to grow, willing to sacrifice to make that slogan come true.

I make my following predictions for the next thirty years based on the last thirty:

1. The farm-operating population will shrink a good deal because of animal industrialization as well as larger farm size. Rural small towns will shrink even more.

2. Farm income will decline per unit of production, but larger farm units will mean higher income per farmer. Sustainable agriculture will grow in popularity for economic reasons as well as the fear of environmental damage.

3. The situation of towns smaller than five thousand people will worsen in most ways, including recreation, services available, employment, education, and population.

4. Twenty or more regional population centers will be promoted by government or will develop by default without governmental help.

5. Certainly the Des Moines–Ames and Cedar Rapids–Iowa City regions will remain vibrant, vital areas. They may approach, but not equal, the economic health of sister locations around the nation.

6. There will be a larger number of "haves" in our state and a larger percentage of relative "have-nots." Income disparities will continue to widen as the percentage of blue collar workers is smaller than the national average.

7. We will become even more a kind of a national economic colony as we continue to sell Iowa-based companies without offsetting acquisitions or creation.

8. Environmental difficulties will increase and require important solutions so change can occur. Animal industrialization creates large amounts of concentrated manure and the attendant odor and possible pollution. A solution to this serious

environmental trouble must be found by technology and/or science, as with other such problems of new methods and their effect on nature.

Please do not curse me as a pessimistic defeatist. I would love to be wrong in my forecast. We Iowans cheer when young folks from crowded cities and earthquake-broken coasts come back here to live. But we cannot passively rely on young people growing dissatisfied with other areas for our growth. And, my friends, young people in any kind of effective numbers will not move here to no jobs or low-paying jobs.

One economic opportunity Iowa has is the possibility of value-added agricultural processing, industries we have let pass us by. There can be new chances with new products created by an investment banking industry working together with government and university and private research. Since the world's most productive farmers are in Iowa, why not build on that excellence? We have John Ruan's prestigious World Food Prize. Why not use his idea of making Iowa the agriculture capital of the world? Making an Ag Capital building a working symbol could add a new dimension to Iowa State University's offering the world the latest farm information, education, and communication while conducting a continuous international exposition. Iowa could have a new attractive face. We are the best, so why not invest in ways that call the world to our doorstep? President Clinton has led us toward a necessary world market with the North American Free Trade Agreement (NAFTA) and the General Agreement on Tariffs and Trade (GATT). U.S. government endorsement of food irradiation will make international transportation of Iowa's products better, improving quality and taste. The whole planet can be our customer.

Iowa is a fine place to live. I am proud to have been raised and to have spent my life here. Iowa was a lovely place when I was a kid, and life on farms is even better now because of better genetics, transportation, fertilizer, and chemistry, among other things. I don't measure only money, but things such as beauty, freedom from disease, bountifulness, and privacy without lonesomeness. We have changed but kept our rural values. We must change even more quickly now but guard and save our way of life. No place holds a candle to Iowa. Its natural production jumps at you, and its lushness is overpowering. The air is pure, the people wonderful, and integrity and honesty a way of life. The towns are clean and neat—good places to live. Why don't more people join us to live and work in such a pleasant place? They will, if we help them find us and make our state more attractive economically, educationally, and physically.

Leadership may be lacking, but for leadership to be effective, the public must want change, be willing to sacrifice for future benefit, and be willing to be led.

What will Iowa be like in thirty years? It will be a wonderful place for those who choose to live here and can earn a decent income. Will it be more? Will it be a vital, vibrant state with bustle, with young folks confidently reaching out to find prosperity? That depends on us. We must do more than "go along to get along." I hope we do so.